The Gospel in the Age of the Judges

The Gospel in the Age of the Judges

P. J. Hoedemaker

Translated by Ruben Alvarado

PANTOCRATOR PRESS

PANTOCRATOR PRESS
An imprint of WordBridge Publishing
Aalten, the Netherlands
www.wordbridge.net
info@wordbridge.net

Dutch original: Dr. Ph. J. Hoedemaker, *Zonde en Genade: De Tijd der Richteren* (Amsterdam: Höveker en Zoon, 1887).

ISBN 978–90–76660–79–0

COVER ILLUSTRATION: "Jael and Sisera" (c. 1620) by Artemisia Gentileschi, Museum of Fine Arts, Budapest. Courtesy of Wikimedia Commons. This photographic reproduction is in the public domain.

TITLE PAGE: Ark of the Covenant, image by Gustave Doré (1832–1883) from the book *La Sagrada Biblia* T.4, Felix Torres Amat 1884, p. 167. Courtesy of Wikimedia Commons. This photographic reproduction is in the public domain.

TABLE OF CONTENTS

PREFACE

This commentary on the book of Judges and the first part of 1 Samuel gives a fine example of Hoedemaker's Reformed covenant theology, of which he was a pioneer practitioner. He wrote it when he was a professor at the Free University in Amsterdam, for the purpose of acquainting his students with modernist Bible criticism. The treatment is therefore peppered with scholastic interactions, adding a scientific dimension to the more popular elements of the discussion. This makes for a document that is both readable and scholarly.

The basis of Hoedemaker's approach is a high view of Scripture, indeed one which makes it the cornerstone of human knowledge and science. "The Old Testament is for us not only the *witness* of revelation, the story of what God has done to prepare and bring about redemption, but the *record of revelation itself* which encompasses every sphere of thought and ability and every area of life. In Holy Scripture we learn to know not only God and man, not only sin and grace, but also *life in all its circles and forms;* popular life, not according to the abstract concept embodied in the modern state, in which no account has been taken either of the origin, the history, or the vocation of the people, and in which its inner unity, which in our Christian, Protestant nations finds its highest expression in religion, is utterly overlooked – but popular life as it *really* is" (p. 123 below).

This being so, Hoedemaker had no truck with the Bible critics who argued that Judges was the first historically sound book in the Bible. He agreed with the critics on there being a discontinuity between the first five books of Moses and the book of Joshua, on the one hand, and the book of Judges on the other. But that is not because these other books were products of fancy while the latter was based in historical fact; rather, it is because in the former books, God took a leading role in events, while in the latter He stepped back and allowed Israel to take the lead. This emergence of the human element is what makes Judges seem realistic, but it is not realism which it displays, but human sinfulness. In the Age of the Judges, Israel is called to respond in gratitude to the salvation that God has accomplished for it; instead, it shirks its duty, fails to eliminate the Canaanites, and reverts back to idolatry.

The task God gave to the Israelites, precisely to eliminate the Canaanites, is not something lower in the ethical scale, pertaining to the "bloodthirsty" period of Israel's history, but instead the pinnacle of closeness to God. For God is holy and cannot abide sinfulness, and only those who are holy can carry out His will with regard to sinfulness.

Moralist human beings tend to think themselves above the sort of vengefulness here displayed in Scripture. "*They* spare the generation of those whom God had ordained to destruction. The children, the powerless, those who were found without weapons in hand, men and women from whom they hoped to derive some sort of benefit, it matters not: we discern here the *arbitrariness* that nullifies obedience, because an obedience that does not go beyond that which is consistent with one's own interest or understanding is simply not obedience; we see here the *carnal mind* that does not submit to the law of God; the *loftiness of heart* that corrupts God's judgment, the enmity that wishes to be more merciful than God and implicitly accuses Him of arbitrariness and cruelty, and we find in it a revelation of man's condition before God" (p. 29). And Christians find it far more amenable to imitate the gentle Christ than the Christ to whom authority has been given to execute judgment (cf. John 5: 27). "Natural sympathy enables us to imitate Christ the Consoler, that is, the Savior in the gentle aspect of His revelation, at least as far as outward acts are concerned. But something entirely different is required for *judgment*. Sin must then have revealed itself to us in its true form, as the abominable, the desecrating, the doom-worthy thing that must be expunged from before His holy face" (p. 27).

Israel shirks this duty, but this does not catch God by surprise – another of Hoedemaker's themes. It is entirely in line with God's plan. It is His will that the Canaanites remain, in order to test the Israelites: "I will no longer drive out before them any of the nations Joshua left when he died. In this way I will test whether Israel will keep the way of the LORD by walking in it as their fathers did" (Judges 2: 22). Likewise in order to teach them warfare: "These are the nations that the LORD left to test all the Israelites who had not known any of the wars in Canaan, if only to teach warfare to the subsequent generations of Israel, especially to those who had not known it formerly" (Judges 3: 1–2).

Furthermore, he notes that God had given the Canaanites ample time to repent, but they had refused.

> In the light of this word, then, the entire history of Canaan falls under the viewpoint of the forbearance of God. That the Patriarchs dwelt in this land, that Abraham, Isaac and Jacob called on "the name of the Lord" here, that the king of Sodom was not allowed to say, "I have made Abraham rich," it all has to do with the Lord's intention to give time and certainly many an exhortation to repentance to the nations over whom judgment would be brought. That they were not ignorant of the purpose of Israel's coming is evident, among other things, from the song of Moses and Miriam: "The nations will hear and tremble; anguish will grip the dwellers of Philistia," and again, "those who dwell in Canaan will melt away" (Ex. 15: 14–15). It is also evident from the history of Rahab, and stamps her act, which from any other viewpoint would be considered a reprehensible act of faithless and cowardly betrayal, as an act of faith (p. 24).

The pattern of temptation – affliction – need – redemption repeats itself throughout the history of this period. That does not mean that nothing is accomplished, that no progress is made. God works through this process to prepare Israel for the coming of the kingship and eventually of the Messiah. To this end, prophecy is transformed. God returns to Israel, in His Word. "*From Samuel onward Jehovah dwells again among Israel, in the word of prophecy*" (p. 165).

A few highlights along the way:

1. Deborah was *not* a warrior princess, despite the common portrayal of her among contemporary Christians who wish to enlist her in the cause of female officeholding in the church. Rather, she is one who steps up when the men shirk responsibility. "When religious life has sunk to the lowest level, God honors woman by putting her in man's place" (p. 65). And she keeps her place, enabling Barak to take charge: "Here is a woman who cannot place herself at the head of the army, a woman who herself honors the orderings of God when she commands Barak to bring

about the redemption of his people; not a heroine of freedom, not a Joan of Arc or a Kenau Simons Hasselaar, but one who prophesies, judges, and places herself in the background when the moment arrives in which the redemption Jehovah already initially wrought among his people will become visible" (p. 65).

2. Jephthah does *not* offer up his daughter as a human sacrifice. Hoedemaker's detailed refutation of this viewpoint is in itself worth the price of admission.

3. Samson is a Nazirite, and thus a throwback to the original condition of the Israelites under the Sinaitic covenant as a royal priesthood. After the golden calf incident, Israel had to relinquish this universal priesthood to the Levites, but the institution of Naziriteship kept the memory of the original condition alive. And this was the source of Samson's strength.

4. Samson paved the way for Samuel, who like Samson was dedicated to the priesthood from childhood, while also filling the function of a judge.

The capture of the ark of the covenant by the Philistines was the ultimate judgment on faithless Israel. The tabernacle service had been neglected for centuries; the priesthood was mired in formalistic ritual while engaging in dismally unethical practices. Despite this, the people attempted to use the ark as a shibboleth with magical powers to defeat the enemy. Instead, they themselves are defeated. This sordid incident brought down the curtain on the tabernacle service.

But God used all of it to prepare the way for His further revelation, whereby the gospel in the Old Covenant finds its further expression in kingship and temple, before its ultimate fulfillment in the New.

AUTHOR'S INTRODUCTION

Where sin abounded, grace did much more abound.

Romans 5: 20, KJV

The Bible is for us the foundation of our faith, the touchstone of truth, the guide for our path, the compass, the map, the light by which we sail. The Word of God is for us at the center of all knowledge. Not only is our Christian confession drawn from it, and do we consider ourselves called increasingly to conform to it, not only does it teach us to know God and man, ourselves and life, but it also contains the basic features, the outlines, the fundamental ideas and principles that are applicable to every field of science.

As Reformed churchmen we have gone from the pope back to the church fathers, from the church fathers to the church, from the church to Holy Scripture, in a word, from the word of man to the Word of God, and demand that the science which uses that Word, interprets it, teaches us to know and assess its components, starts by bowing to it unconditionally; in other words, that it not place itself over Scripture, but under.

Our faith is not bound to any particular theory of the inspiration of Scripture; we are bound, in the manner so simply, profoundly, and inimitably, beautifully described in our Belgic Confession, solely to the *fact* by which we must test every theory, the fact that in Scripture we possess *the Word of God,* and in such a way that we are incapable of distinguishing between form and content, between Scripture and something in Scripture that in a more real and complete sense may be called "God's Word." The historical as well as the moral, the dogmatic no less than the practical parts of either the Old or the New Testament are *God's Word* to us, and do not allow moral and religious feeling, the experience of the church, science and philosophy or anything else to stand in judgment over them.

Without judging how much freedom one may allow oneself in the historical-critical examination of Scripture without wrecking or even damaging one's faith, we consider indispensable, both for faith and for life and science, an unshakable trust in the fact that Scripture, the whole of Scripture, Scripture as it stands, i.e., as given by God through the intervention of men, in words derived from human language, is the *Word of God.*

There are Blondins in the field of the study of Holy Scripture who, with admirable tact, manage to keep their balance on the tightrope of the theories of the time; we do not accompany them on this, their tour de force.

There are those who have arrived, by the ladder of Scripture, at the height of faith on which they now stand, who look down without fear on the attempts made on the ground below to remove that ladder. For our part we are convinced that the ladder is also the fulcrum on which the whole building rests, and in this we are less at ease. But however this may be, if and as long as we adhere to the fact just indicated, we derive from it the *governing principle of our investigation of Scripture.*

If we have not examined everything, if we have not understood everything, if we have not yet discovered the connection between everything, if we have not yet found the solution of apparent contradictions, if we have not yet found the answer to important questions, we do not wish to give a lesser proof of confidence in the Scriptures than that which Alexander showed in his physician, when he in one gulp emptied the cup put before him at the very moment of being warned in an anonymous letter that the drink contained a fast-acting poison. We must not put less trust in God than we would put in a friend whose character we think we know but whose actions often have something of the mysterious, which if less trusted could arouse and apparently justify suspicion.

By this same example we could demonstrate, however, that our faith need not be unreasonable, not such a blind confidence that we would no longer be able to verify and appreciate the facts, to conduct an investigation, and to consider that investigation open until all the data had been properly taken into account. Confidence is an incentive to investigate even that which would otherwise have been overlooked, and a safeguard against hasty and untimely conclusions. As long as it is not clear to us that what we think we know is really confirmed, as long as the character of our friend is not splendidly vindicated, we await more light and look for more that is relevant.

Be that as it may, we do not wish to pursue this line of thought any further, and, in fact, cannot do so without being led further and further, finally to write a treatise rather than a preface.

This study of the Age of the Judges was prompted by a conversation with the publishers about a review of the newer criticism of Scripture, namely of the well-known theories of Kuenen, Wellhausen, and Robertson Smith, which I wished to make available for the press.

After the departure of my colleague at the Free University, Prof. F. W. J. Dilloo, I was assigned to teach the course on "Introduction to the Old Testament." Not without trepidation I took up by way of introduction the *History of Israel* by Wellhausen, compared it with what Kuenen had said and what was to be found in the various works of Robertson Smith on the subject, and tried, starting from the principle just developed, both negatively and positively, to give a representation of the genesis of the Israelite people.

My fears concerned not so much my own faith as that of my students, not the question whether Kuenen et al. were right, but rather the doubt as to whether I would succeed in discovering error wherever it occurred and exposing it as such. After all, it is one thing to know something about this subject and to have studied it in general, as every theologian is bound to do, and quite another to face the objections of astute and learned men such as those mentioned above.

What I found, however, had given me reason to be grateful for the opportunity to devote myself to the historical-critical research of the Old Testament, grateful also for the confirmation of my own faith obtained in this way and the new points of view opened up by it.

My intention was to publish an adapted version of what I had treated with my students. Much to my regret, however, the publishers informed me of the sales of similar works, which was calculated to discourage or at least not encourage the work required for a study of the subject with a view to its publication. They also suggested that the results of my research should be presented in a popular form, less refutational and more assertive, in a book the object of which was the explanation of a portion of the Holy Scriptures. Hence these essays, which differ from Bible readings only in that I have sought to examine the material from one point of view and to make that material serve one main idea.

I have chosen the Age of the Judges because Wellhausen's discussion recently drew my attention to it. Should it prove desirable, it is my intention to follow with a similar work on Israel's kings before the separation of the two kingdoms, and anything else that may fit into the same framework.

May this little work serve to stimulate the independent study of the Holy Scriptures of the Old Covenant and contribute something to the knowledge of that Word, of which, after every examination, one will have to testify: "I have seen a limit to all perfection, but Your commandment is without limit" (Ps. 119: 96).

Amsterdam
July 15th 1887

P. J. Hoedemaker

1. FROM GILGAL TO BOCHIM

Judges 1: 1–2: 5

If only My people would listen to Me, if Israel would follow My ways.
Ps. 81: 13[1]

If the first chapter of the book of Judges were our only source of knowledge of Israel and Israel's history, we should not get the idea that this people stood in any special relationship to the Lord.

Suppose for a moment that we had in this chapter a fragment of some ancient historical work concerning a people known to us only by name, taken from the annals and memorials of some other people. In that case we should not feel at all obliged to subscribe to the meaning which every believing reader of the Bible attaches to the message in v. 1, that "the Israelites inquired of the LORD, 'Who will be the first to go up and fight for us against the Canaanites?'" and in v. 4 that "when Judah attacked, the LORD delivered the Canaanites and Perizzites into their hands," whereby this special relationship is understood. For all ancient peoples used to fight their wars in the name of their gods, and to attribute every victory won by them to those gods. And yet, with the exception of Adoni-Bezek's striking confession in v. 7, that the humiliation which he suffered, and the suffering inflicted on him, was due him from the God of Israel as a punishment for the way in which he had treated others, there is nothing in this chapter of even a general religious character.

Judah, we read in v. 19, "could not drive out the inhabitants of the plains because they had chariots of iron," even though the first part of this verse states that "The LORD was with Judah."

"The Benjamites … failed to drive out the Jebusites living in Jerusalem" (v. 21).

"Manasseh failed to drive out the inhabitants of Beth-shean" (v. 27).

---

[1] Unless otherwise noted, Bible translations are taken from the Berean Study Bible. Other translations are chosen in accordance with their similitude to the Dutch translation used by Hoedemaker.

The same is said in almost the same words in v. 29 of "Ephraim," in v. 30 of "Zebulun," in v. 31 of "Asher," in v. 33 of "Naphtali," in v. 34 of "the Danites"; while of the latter tribe it is further recorded that the Amorites "did not allow them to come down into the plain."

Where is the God who caused the walls of Jericho to fall at the sound of Israel's trumpets, after the waters of the Jordan, in the midst of harvest time, had been cut off so as to provide him a passage through the land of his inheritance?

Where is the God of "Gibeon" (Joshua 10: 1ff.), of "Merom" (11: 5ff.), where Jabin and his allies were defeated?

The first chapter of the book of Judges informs us of nothing that could not have been done at any other time, by any other people, under any circumstances.

Therefore, if we could put ourselves in the position of the scholars who study the history of Israel not in the light of the Christian confession concerning God, Scripture, sin, redemption, but in that of their science, we would immediately acknowledge the assertions of Kuenen, Wellhausen and others, that it is to the book of Judges that we have to look for the first reliable reports concerning the genesis of the Israelite people. After all, what we have said of the first chapter applies to some extent to the entire book, indeed to all the later historical books of the Old Testament.

From this point, the continual activity of God – which made the history of the patriarchs as well as that of Moses and Joshua a revelation of His counsel and will concerning the lineage of Abraham, and in that lineage concerning the election, preservation, education, and redemption of a people whom He is not ashamed to call *His* people – gives way to *the continual activity of man,* activity which only here and there is interrupted by miracles, i.e., by divine intervention, as often as necessary to save that people, to preserve them from ruin, and to fix their hope in God and their expectation on the future.

Again, from the point of view of the above-mentioned scholars, it is perfectly true that in perusing Israel's history up to the death of Joshua, we meander about in a world of miracles, while after his death we are brought not only to different but also to lower ground. When we read the accounts of the exodus from Egypt, the journey through the desert, and the entry into Canaan, it is as if we are travelers moving on a highland, breathing the fresh mountain air and enjoying an unobstructed view, with the goal of the establishment of the kingdom of God, the fulfillment of the promise of Paradise, ahead of us.

But as soon as we have witnessed the solemn act at Ebal and Gerizim, where Israel accepts the promised inheritance, and have thereby reached the point from which we hoped to see the imminent fulfillment of all that was comprehended for faith in the covenant of God, we find ourselves unexpectedly shifted to entirely different ground, Joshua 8: 13ff. The horizon is limited to the history of a few tribes, sometimes just one. We are like a hiker in a mountainous region who, passing through densely overgrown passes, goes from one valley to another, while all round the eye encounters the surrounding mountains, while there is nothing to indicate that one is nearing the end of this journey, but on the contrary that the valleys are becoming narrower and more inaccessible, so that finally they might more accurately bear the name of gorges.

Even so, we can apply to the written Word what is said of the incarnate Word: "this Child is appointed to cause the rise and fall of many in Israel" (Luke 2: 34). That which human reason must resent when it does not allow itself to be informed by the Word of truth, is precisely that which, for those who believe, often contains the highest revelation of the wisdom of God, of His faithfulness and grace. Holy Scripture also contains many mysteries, much that we cannot readily comprehend. But in the end, the truth remains that everything it tells us *had* to happen this way. The facts it relates are not accidental but stand in a necessary connection with the course of revelation. They are the expression of one great idea of God.

Nevertheless, it is necessary for the great prophet Jesus, of whom this Scripture bears witness, to come to us as He did when He joined the Emmaus travelers and make us see that this enigma finds its explanation in His person and work, that is, in the whole plan of redemption.

It is undeniably true, for example, that the book of Judges places us at one of the great turning points in the history of Israel and of revelation; but it is just as true that this is consistent with all that we know of God and of man and can learn everywhere in Scripture. The way of the Lord traverses through the depths but leads to the heights from which we oversee everything, and where we must stand to be able to testify that this way was seemingly neither the shortest nor the best, but nevertheless was the appointed, and ultimately the only way.

The riddle which the first chapter of the book of Judges sets before us in connection with what precedes it is fully explained by what we may call the sure law of revelation, namely, that man is called to accept and appropriate the grace of God and consequently to take action, so as to be active on the basis of what God has wrought.

It also goes without saying that under this law the history of the people of God does not follow a normal course. Man is not normal; he is therefore unable to maintain himself at the height on which God initially placed him. But this also reveals the way in which God always works. Everything He promises, does and bestows is perfect, like His own being. Therefore, what is highest in the history of revelation is always at the beginning. But inasmuch as it appears that man, owing to his unbelief, is unable to take up the gift of God, to fulfill the calling of God, but sinks ever deeper and deeper from this – to the same degree the Lord changes, not in His purpose, not in His plan, but in His revelation. He allows Himself, as it were, to be determined in His actions by man's actions, descends deeper and deeper, keeps His distance and withdraws more and more, but in such a way that this withdrawal and this descent opens the way to a new and glorious revelation of His *grace*. The whole history of revelation is thus an ongoing elucidation of Paul's words: "where sin abounded, grace did much more abound" (Romans 5: 20, KJV).

It therefore goes without saying that, in line with the reports of the book of Judges, Israel – after God brought it into Canaan with a mighty arm – should no longer be passive but act; that it was called, as junior partner in the covenant, to maintain what God bestowed, to accept what He promised, and to use its sword in the service of the Lord.

It proceeds here according to what we have called a sure *law* of revelation. As long as redemption, the word taken this time in a narrow sense as redemption from sin, is not an accomplished fact, it proceeds entirely *outside man* as a secondary cause. It is God's work just as much as is the creation, the glory of which must go to Him and Him alone.

However, as soon as it is accomplished, as soon as man can be regarded as pardoned, as redeemed, the work of God for man passes over into a work through him and in him, and it is in *this* work, i.e., in redemption in the more general sense – which will not be completed until sin with its consequences has been done away with – that *man* also, as a second cause, has a *vocation to fulfill.*

After all, the grace of God must be accepted and processed. Otherwise it would be utterly useless. In other words, *gratitude* follows redemption.

Let us clarify this through an example. As long as Israel has not left the house of bondage, the work of God has not yet been accomplished; on the other hand, as soon as it is led out of Egypt with a strong arm, it stands in a different relation to God, even though the final goal of liberation has not yet been reached. Whoever has sung the song of liberation has to do the work of one who is liberated. At Baal-Zephon, for example, Israel was in great distress: Pharaoh behind it, the sea before it – doom seemed nigh. Its deliverance, however, is part of God's work for it; without this the work would not be complete. Hence, we hear Moses cry out to the frightened people: "Do not be afraid. Stand firm and you will see the LORD's salvation, which He will accomplish for you today; for the Egyptians you see today, you will never see again. The LORD will fight for you; you need only to be still" (Ex. 14: 13–14). Yet at Raphidim in the desert of Sinai, the need is no less great. Israel is not only menaced by a formidable foe but most treacherously assailed "when she was weak and weary, and would have died of thirst" had not the Lord God evidently intervened to cause a fountain to spring forth from the rock. However, this time Joshua receives the command: "Choose some of our men and go out to fight the Amalekites!" (Ex. 17: 9a). Israel must fight, though Moses has appended an assurance to the command by which it is most plainly evident that his expectation, even now as formerly with Baal-Zephon, is only from the Lord his God. "Tomorrow," he says, "I will stand on the top of the hill, and the rod of God will be in my hand" (Ex. 17: 9b), implying that without it, resistance would be useless. Therefore Joshua also must have knowledge of this purpose of Moses in order to appeal to the promise, the trustworthiness, the covenant of God. Through this, the command which he received is justified in his eyes.

Why draw the sword? we would be inclined to ask, in a battle which is settled neither by the sword, nor by the valor of the combatants, nor by the strategy of the commander, but – as the outcome showed – from moment to moment by Moses' intensity of faith?

The answer has already been given.

With both Raphidim and Baal-Zephon, Israel owes its salvation to Jehovah. The inscription of the altar erected after the defeat of Amalek speaks the same language as the song sung on the shore of the Red Sea. "The Lord is a man of war," sings Moses after the downfall of Pharaoh's army. "The Lord is my banner!" he exclaims when Amalek is wounded by the edge of the sword. Now, though, the life of gratitude has begun for Israel. God saves, but He does so indirectly, no longer directly.

In the same way we can now explain the difference between the book of Judges and the preceding books. After all, the entire period preceding the conquest of Canaan may be reckoned to some extent to the first stage of the work of redemption. For only when Israel was placed in possession of its inheritance, fulfilling the promise of God and completing His work of redemption, does the new age begin in which the privileged people, second party in the covenant, are called to show their gratitude; hence their faith, their obedience, is put to the test.

That from this point forward the human factor should manifest itself, that Israel itself should act, is therefore a matter of course. If we only keep in mind that, as has already been said above, its history cannot correspond to what has been presented to us, typically, in the battle against Amalek at Raphidim, because by means of its sin Israel breaks relations with Jehovah, then we hold in our hands the key to explaining that which is peculiar and puzzling in the course of that history.

The people who violate the covenant of their God must either be destroyed or left to their natural development. What in the eyes of the scholars mentioned above is a guarantee of the historical character of the book of Judges, namely, that the history it furnishes is a "purely human history," we must view as a direct result of its apostasy, which placed it on a par with all other nations. What they regard as strange elements in that history, namely, the miracles by which Jehovah intervenes to help and to save, prove to us that Israel's unfaithfulness does not nullify the faithfulness of God. As the people sink deeper, as they go further astray, the grace of God becomes more apparent, as does His justice. The Lord lets Israel walk in its ways, withdraws His presence, but does not for that reason let it go; on the contrary, He prepares the full redemption, which will not be completed until the new song is lifted up which gives Him and Him alone the glory of that wonderful thing, that such men, by such means, by such ways, are delivered from the bondage of sin to be led across the sea of tribulation to the true Canaan.

We still must call attention to what we may also regard as a continuous feature of revelation, namely, that Jehovah conforms to man's condition, descends to him, and therefore appears to arrive at a lower stage of development.

Two examples from the Old Testament and one from the New Testament may serve as clarification.

When Israel was called at Sinai to enter into the covenant on its own account, Jehovah said, "You shall be a priestly kingdom to Me." There is no mention here of a separate priesthood. God deals directly with His people. It is Israel itself who expresses the need for a Mediator: "we should die if we continued to hear this voice" runs the word by which, as it were, it abdicates the privilege of coming directly into relation to its God and King. Forty days later, as a result of its apostasy, the Levitical priesthood is instituted.

It is true, the calling and gifts of God cannot be revoked. In the days of the New Covenant, in the universal priesthood of believers, what was already seen under the Old Covenant is fulfilled. But for the time being the ideal is apparently abandoned. The redemption of the firstborn on the fortieth day, and the Naziriteship, i.e., the original priesthood by which Israel's original destiny was kept in remembrance, were intended to keep in remembrance, as the normal condition, what had been forfeited through its own fault. But for the time being, a definite decline is noticeable here.

The same decline is also to be noted – this is the second example – in Israel's former and later relationship with the Angel of the Lord who dwells in the midst of Israel. "Behold, I am sending an angel before you to protect you along the way and to bring you to the place I have prepared. Pay attention to him and listen to his voice; do not defy him, for he will not forgive rebellion, since My Name is in him" (Ex. 23: 20–21). According to this promise God Himself would be its guide. But then we hear, "Leave this place, you and the people you brought up out of the land of Egypt... to a land flowing with milk and honey. But I will not go with you, because you are a stiff-necked people" (Ex. 33: 1, 3); it is Jehovah speaking to Moses when the apostate people, after the breach of the covenant at Sinai, were spared but without being restored to God's favor.

The difference between the one promise and the other is so slight that it might perhaps have escaped our attention, had not the last word quoted caused deep perplexity among the tribes of Israel. "When the people," we read in Ex. 33: 4, "heard these bad tidings, they went into mourning, and no one put on any of his jewelry." Bad tidings! And the promise is renewed, that it shall inherit Canaan! The special help of God is even promised here.

If, as is often said, Israel's only desire, or at least its highest object, was to inherit the land of Canaan, to possess outward privileges, then it had nothing more to desire, and in one respect its condition was even improved. For from now on it had no longer to fear that "this Angel," as was said before the breach of covenant, would not spare it when it left the way of the Lord.

This new promise is not accompanied by any threat. And yet more apparently is desired. God *Himself* must remain at the forefront. "By this alone it would be known that they found favor in His sight" (Ex. 33: 16). It is on this ground that Moses speaks in v. 15: "If your countenance will not go with us, do not bring us up from here!" Though his prayer is granted this time, yet the possibility has been posited by Jehovah that He might withdraw His visible presence so that the revelation, so that Israel, so that the covenant would be placed on lower ground.

It is this possibility which we later see realized, namely, when the Angel appeared at Bochim to announce the judgment, not of complete rejection, but of widening distance from God. Something similar took place under the New Testament when the Lord Jesus, after the cleansing of the temple, went back to the work of John the Baptist in Ephraim, preaching, like him, the baptism of repentance, thereby suspending the work of redemption in order to continue that of preparation.

When He came into his Father's house to remove the leaven, as every householder in Israel was called to do at the Passover, to him a reminder of the deliverance from Egypt, and to the Savior a sign of the work which the Father had given Him to do, the word of Malachi was hereby fulfilled (Malachi 3: 1–2): "'Behold, I will send My messenger, who will prepare the way before Me. Then the Lord whom you seek will suddenly come to

His temple—the Messenger of the covenant, in whom you delight—see, He is coming,' says the LORD of Hosts. But who can endure the day of His coming? And who can stand when He appears? For He will be like a refiner's fire, like a launderer's soap." It was Israel's sin, now revealed only in the attitude of Israel's elders, in other words the initial rejection of the Messiah, which compelled Him to stop the work and prepare the way for Himself, prior to revealing Himself to them again as Savior.

In the same way now Jehovah deals with Israel when it made a covenant with the inhabitants of Canaan, breaking the covenant of its God. He withdraws His full revelation and henceforth no longer dwells among Israel in the full and proper sense of the word. The people are blessed, but the true blessing, the rule of God in its most complete and glorious manifestation, is withheld from them. This is what is declared by the Angel at Bochim: "I brought you up out of Egypt and led you into the land that I had promised to your fathers, and I said, 'I will never break My covenant with you, and you are not to make a covenant with the people of this land, but you shall tear down their altars.' Yet you have not obeyed My voice. What is this you have done? So now I tell you that I will not drive out these people before you; they will be thorns in your sides, and their gods will be a snare to you" (Judges 2: 1–3).

Nonetheless, the narrative itself must make clear the message of Judges 2: 1–5, in connection with the whole of this history. Here we have an Angel who does not *appear*, who is not *seen* in the direction of Gilgal, but *comes up* from there to Bochim. The people therefore knew that he came from there; what is more, the Angel seems not to have *descended* at Gilgal but to have tarried there until this very moment.

When an angel appears, he is, as it were, already invisibly present before the eye discovers him. Wherever, either in the Old or the New Testament, there is talk of the activity of these heavenly messengers among men, we have to think of such apparitions. So much the more striking is the expression "came up" used in this instance, and it is understandable that some interpreters have taken the word "angel" here in a figurative sense, as meaning a man, a prophet, or a priest, for example Phinehas, who as "messenger" of Jehovah and a messenger of repentance came into the midst of the assembly of the people to announce the judgment over their disobedience.

This "Messenger," however, does not act in the name of the Lord, but speaks as only he can speak who is with God, and is even God Himself, the Angel of the Covenant, Israel's Redeemer from ancient times.

This action of this Angel is fully explicable to us, therefore, only when we assume that the tabernacle still stood at Gilgal and that the visible sign of the presence of God came to Bochim to declare with an audible voice, not that the covenant has been suspended altogether, for this is out of the question, but that the great object of the covenant, the manifestation of a people in the midst of whom God dwells and reigns, from this point should remain unfulfilled.

Let us investigate whether this representation can be reconciled with the relevant data. If , as indicated by the positioning of the message in Judges 2, the revelation of the Angel of the Lord in Bochim took place after the death of Joshua and the events in Judges 1, the tabernacle was then set up at Shiloh.

In both these chapters, however, we find *an overview of Israel's history beginning with the division of the land among the tribes and their separate actions*. Much of what is stated in chapter 1 applies to a much earlier time, as becomes clear from a comparison of Judges 1: 10ff. with Josh. 15: 14ff., Judges 1:27 with Josh. 17: 11–12, Judges 1: 29 with Josh. 16: 10. Judges ch. 2 likewise belongs to this overview; it explains the significance of the events recorded in the first chapter, so that we have to assume that what we see reported in vv. 1–5 preceded in time that which is recorded in ch. 1 (cf. Josh. 18: 1). This is shown by Judges 2: 6, where we are removed to the time when "Joshua had let the people go, every man to his inheritance, to inherit the land."

Yet it also lies in the nature of the matter. For when Achan seized the spoil of Jericho, Israel was defeated at Ai. No more than thirty-six men fell under the enemy's sword on that occasion; but the significance of this defeat was felt by Joshua and all the people. God had forsaken His people. He would not suffer His covenant to be treacherously violated, even if only by a single Israelite. "Beware of his face," had spoken the Lord in reference to the Angel who guided Israel. "He will not forgive your transgressions, for my name is within him" (Ex. 23: 21). This threat was fully realized at Ai, when only one had transgressed against the command of the Lord.

But would not the disobedience of whole tribes have been punished in the same way? There was a ban among Israel from the moment that a covenant was made with the Canaanite. That this had already happened prior to the death of Joshua is evident from Josh. 13: 13; 15: 63; 16: 10; 17: 13ff. At this time, therefore, *after the first division of the country*, the Angel acts at Bochim. He came "up" from the plain, where Gilgal lay, to the high place where the children of Israel had probably withdrawn for fear of the Canaanites. For we read in Judges 1:19, that Judah "drove out the inhabitants of the hill country, but was not able to drive out the inhabitants of the valley, because they had chariots of iron."

This was not the normal state of a people whose God is the Lord, but a repetition in another form of what happened at Ai. Israel was henceforth left to itself. The covenant was broken. This took place at Gilgal, and although the fact itself is not stated in the book of Joshua, the consequences of the fact are also manifested in this, that the initial division in terms of the standard not of what Israel actually possessed but of what had been promised to it, was immediately discontinued. "I Myself will drive out [the Sidonians and the Philistines] before the Israelites," said the Lord, Josh. 13: 6. "Be sure to divide it by lot as an inheritance to Israel, as I have commanded you." This whole arrangement, however, expired due to Israel's unbelief and the withdrawal of the Lord. Not until much later do we find the tabernacle at Shiloh, where a *second division* is made according to an entirely different principle, 18: 2ff.

The Angel of the Lord therefore did not come to Bochim as a preacher of repentance to bring about conversion, but to announce the judgment which had already been threatened on so many prior occasions. Many interpreters have failed to notice this, altogether because they have not made a proper distinction between the commandment of the covenant and the prohibition of idolatry.

"You shall make no covenant with them or with their gods. They must not remain in your land, lest they cause you to sin against Me. For if you serve their gods, it will surely be a snare to you" (Ex. 23: 32–33).

"Be careful not to make a treaty with the inhabitants of the land you are entering, lest they become a snare in your midst. Rather, you must tear down their altars, smash their sacred stones, and chop down their Asherah poles" (Ex. 34: 12–13).

> When the Lord your God brings you into the land that you are entering to possess, and He drives out before you many nations – the Hittites, Girgashites, Amorites, Canaanites, Perizzites, Hivites, and Jebusites, seven nations larger and stronger than you – and when the Lord your God has delivered them over to you to defeat them, then you must devote them to complete destruction. Make no treaty with them and show them no mercy.... For you are a people holy to the Lord your God. The Lord your God has chosen you to be a people for His prized possession out of all peoples on the face of the earth.... You must destroy all the peoples the Lord your God will deliver to you. Do not look on them with pity. Do not worship their gods, for that will be a snare to you.... And you must not bring any detestable thing into your house, or you, like it, will be set apart for destruction. You are to utterly detest and abhor it, because it is set apart for destruction" (Deut. 7: 1–2, 6, 16, 26).

Such is the *condition* upon which God will be Israel's God and grant them the *full* blessing of the covenant. As soon as Israel disobeyed this command, it descended from the lofty position on which it was originally placed: the nearer, special relation to Jehovah into which God had brought it ceased henceforth. The prohibition against idolatry, on the other hand, must be counted among the general requirements of the moral law. The fact that the people are later also guilty of this idolatry is proof that they could sink even deeper. But this only came later.

At Bochim it sacrificed "to the LORD," Judges 2: 5. At Shechem Joshua sets before it the choice to serve either the Lord or idols, and chooses the service of Jehovah with determination, Josh. 24: 21. Of course, let it be said in passing, there would have been no question of a choice if the special relationship between it and Jehovah had not given way to a more generally human, religious relationship.

The punishment for worshiping idols is *complete rejection*. "If you transgress," says Joshua, "the covenant of the LORD your God, which He commanded you, and go and serve other gods and bow down to them, then the anger of the LORD will burn against you, and you will quickly perish from this good land He has given you," Josh. 23: 16.

Israel could be lowered without entirely forsaking Jehovah or being wholly forsaken by Him; but as soon as it fails to exterminate the Canaanites and thereby fulfill the condition of the covenant, the distinctive element which is inseparable from the indwelling of the Lord ceases. God does not dwell in the midst of the people "like a traveler who stays but a night," Jer. 14: 8. The indwelling of God would make Israel's history an ongoing miracle. It would have become the fulfillment of the promise in Paradise.

Let us elucidate. When God revealed Himself to Moses in Egypt after Pharaoh had refused to let the people go, He identified Himself as Jehovah, "He that is," but also "He that shall be," also "He that shall come." Then, as an introduction to the glorious promise "I will take you as My own people, and I will be your God," v. 7, He spoke this word from which so many illegitimate inferences are drawn: "I am the LORD. I appeared to Abraham, to Isaac, and to Jacob as God Almighty, but by My name the LORD I did not make Myself known to them," Ex. 6: 2–3. The *name* of Jehovah was not unknown, but under this name, that is, as the Redeemer promised of old, *God* had not made Himself known.

When the expectation that the promised Seed of the Woman would soon appear seemed thwarted by a series of sad experiences such as found expression in the names Abel ("vanity—disappointment"), Enosh ("weak and mortal man"), people began, we read in Gen. 4: 26, "to invoke the name of the *LORD*," i.e., Jehovah, i.e., Him who shall be or shall come. That is to say, not to institute the public worship of God, which is how it is usually understood – for this is inseparable from the exercise of religion in the family and in the race – but *to expect the promised salvation FROM ABOVE, and to intreat the coming of the Savior.*

That God Himself should be "He that shall come" was first revealed to Moses, and this initial revelation becomes more and more clear and complete. This name is "My memorial-name," Ex. 3: 15 (NASB 1977). The bearer of that name is the Angel who guides and captains Israel, Ex. 23: 21. Of the same name Moses desires and receives a further revelation, when in answer to the prayer, "Please show me Your glory," i.e., your hidden being, Ex. 33: 18, he beholds some of this, and hears the name of the Lord being called, Ex. 34: 5–6.

The Angel of the Lord is also the God *who dwells in the midst of His people;* He is also *the Redeemer* who was to come. He abides among Israel in the cloud which advances at the head of the army and soon descends into the sanctuary. *This,* however, *does not exhaust the mystery of this indwelling.* When we read that after the breach of covenant spoken of above, the pillar of cloud "would come down and remain at the entrance, and the LORD would speak with Moses," Ex. 33: 8–9, then we think of a revelation of God *in human form.* But the connection between that "cloud" by which the face of the Lord is covered, so that "no one can see Me and live," Ex. 33: 20, and "a body You prepared for Me [i.e., Christ]," Heb. 10: 5, becomes clearer to us, less open to doubt, when we see later that the revelation in the cloud is replaced by the appearance of the "Commander of the LORD's army" (Joshua 5: 14).

The first thing mentioned after the arrival at Gilgal, or rather after the act from which Gilgal takes its name, the rolling away of the reproach of Egypt, that is, renewal of the sign of the covenant and the observance of the memorial day of the exodus into Canaan territory in Josh. 5: 3ff., is the coming of the Angel of the Lord in the form of a man, that is, of a warrior, as proof that the conquest of Canaan is His work, and that He will henceforth lead His people as He has led the way to this point. "This is how you will know," said Joshua before the crossing of the Jordan, "that the living God is among you and that He will surely drive out before you the Canaanites" etc., Josh. 3: 10.

This is now to be fulfilled. The highest point in Israel's history has thus been reached. Now, in the shadows of the Old Covenant, is seen what John beheld on Patmos: *God dwelling with and walking in the midst of His people.* Nay, in those shadows is only seen, and can only be seen, what God's *purpose* was with Israel, the privilege of which it would have partaken had the terms of the covenant been fulfilled on its part. Now, though, the miraculous lies only in what God does for His people in the fall of Jericho and the defeats of the Canaanite kings. Now Joshua and Caleb, as forty years hence in the days of the spies, are the only ones in whom the people initially fulfill their destiny. The word of Joshua: "O sun, stand still over Gibeon, O moon, over the Valley of Aijalon!" Josh. 10: 12, and Caleb's demand that he be permitted to cut off the children of Anak, Josh. 14: 6ff., are examples of that to which *the whole nation* was called.

And so we return to our starting point. Israel will certainly have no cause to regret sacrificing to the Lord and choosing to serve God and not idols. This is the condition upon which it is permitted to remain in the land and to count on the help, nay, even on the special help of God. But more was required to attain that which was the actual purpose of its redemption: *the restoration of God's lordship in this world* which had fallen away from Him, the requisite for which was *perfect obedience.*

And yet, when we look at its history from this point of view, a fact strikes us which once again sheds a brilliant light on the course of revelation. Man's sin, unbelief, and unfaithfulness *seem* to thwart the purpose of the Lord, run counter to His holy will, make impossible the fulfillment of His promise. But in retrospect it becomes clear that this outcome does not surprise the Lord at all; in fact, it is included in the development of the plan of salvation and is finally made subservient to His own purpose with which it seemed to be in direct conflict.

We encounter this history in the mood of the disciples at Emmaus, who say to one another, "We hoped that the redemption was near," and who are then referred to Holy Scripture, from which we learn that the very thing which seemed to frustrate the expectation, fulfilled it.

Take for example this regression of Israel to the lower position from the covenant relation in its highest realization. This was already foretold at the second apostasy of the people. It refused to go to Canaan. Again the decision is announced to bring forth a new nation from Moses. The mediator now also pleads on the faithfulness of God, on the Name which was revealed to him at Sinai. "Pardon, I pray," we hear him exclaim, Num. 14: 19, "the iniquity of this people, in keeping with the greatness of Your loving devotion, just as You have forgiven them ever since they left Egypt!" The prayer is also answered this time, and the forgiveness is announced. But there is no mention of the renewal of the promise of Ex. 34: 10. Now we hear this: "I have pardoned according to thy word: But as truly as I live, *all the earth shall be filled with the glory of the LORD!"* (Num. 14: 20–21, KJV).

This one word would suffice to shatter all the theories of science falsely so called. That word, diametrically opposed to Israel's view of itself, the ages have not comprehended, but it comes to us from the word of Isaiah, "*all flesh* shall see the salvation of God," Luke 3: 6 (KJV)—and also in Paul's preaching, "the *Gentiles* are fellow heirs... and fellow partakers of the promise in Christ Jesus," Eph. 3: 6.

What the Angel of the Lord announces at Bochim is furthermore the fulfillment of what was threatened at the solemn transfer of office to Joshua.

> Then the LORD appeared at the tent in a pillar of cloud (it is the last mention of this) and the cloud stood over the entrance to the tent. And the LORD said to Moses, 'You will soon rest with your fathers, and these people will rise up and prostitute themselves with the foreign gods of the land they are entering. They will forsake Me and break the covenant I have made with them. On that day My anger will burn against them, and I will abandon them and hide My face from them, so that they will be consumed, and many troubles and afflictions will befall them. On that day they will say, Have not these disasters come upon us *because our God is no longer with us?* And on that day I will surely hide My face because of all the evil they have done by turning to other gods.... When I have brought them into the land that I swore to give their fathers, a land flowing with milk and honey, they will eat their fill and prosper. Then they will turn to other gods and worship them, and they will reject Me and break My covenant. And when many troubles and afflictions have come upon them, this song will testify against them, because it will not be forgotten from the lips of their descendants. For I know their inclination, even before I bring them into the land that I swore to give them' (Deut. 31: 15–18, 20–21).

Israel's history, understood according to the purport of the covenant, begins and ends at Gilgal, and the sorrow with which it sees the angel of the Lord depart from it is but an example of the great lamentation in the valley of Hadad-rimmon, when they shall see "the One they have pierced" (Zech. 12: 10). Israel's national existence is not yet abolished; there are other threats in abeyance in Deuteronomy, ready to be fulfilled. But *in its highest revelation* the covenant is henceforth suspended.

From this time forward we find among Israel a tabernacle of God, but in that tabernacle Jehovah no longer reigning as Israel's King; a priesthood, but no influence for good being exerted on the course of events by those priests; sacrifices, but no longer on the standpoint of the covenant, in the house of the Lord, but in that of the Patriarchs, offered likewise on the high places.

From the royal priesthood to the institution of the Mediatorship was a step backwards. Even further back is the Levitical priesthood; behind this the patriarchal worship of God, and at the end of this road idolatry, oppression and exile.

No, this is not yet the end. At the end of the long road on which the people of the Lord are led upon, they pass another Gilgal, where the reproach is rolled away – Golgotha – and another Bochim, the place of weeping, where God pours out the Spirit of grace and prayers unto the final goal.

A Paradise at the beginning, in Genesis, and a Paradise at the end, in John's Revelation, are the two termini of world history. *The dwelling of God among Israel,* and *the dwelling of God among the people who go forth into the gates of the holy city*, are the two termini of the history of the covenant.

2. ISRAEL'S VOCATION TO EXECUTE JUDGMENT

> You shall defeat them, then you shall utterly destroy them. You shall make no covenant with them and show no favor to them.
>
> Deut. 7: 2, NASB 1977

> Let them kneel down and sing God's praises
> While their right hand in vengeance raises
> A sword to end the profanations
> Of wayward heathen nations.
>
> Psalm 149, verse 3 (*Anglo-Genevan Psalter*)[2]

The inheritance originally promised and assigned to Israel extended from the river of Egypt to the Euphrates. Yet in the days of Joshua and of the Judges, Israel took possession of only a relatively small part, and even shared it, partly voluntarily, partly forcibly, with the original inhabitants of Canaan.

We had been under the impression that the sufficient explanation of these facts lay in the unbelief which made Israel refuse to expel the Canaanites to the north and the Philistines to the south of Canaan, in the disobedience which compelled it, contrary to the express will of the Lord, to make a covenant with the remnant of the nations whom the Lord had exterminated before it, and in the judgment by which Jehovah deprived it of His help, leaving it to itself, a judgment which would have been a judgment of extermination or of reprobation had the Lord acted according to right, since the *ban* which rested upon the generation of Canaan, as the history of Achan indicates, had been transferred to the people of the Lord.

Is there any reason to doubt the accuracy of this statement?

In the second and third chapters of Judges, at least, these facts are considered from an entirely different point of view. It is expressly stated in Judges 2: 22 that "I will no longer drive out before them any of the nations

---

[2] *Book of Praise: Anglo-Genevan Psalter*. Burlington, Ontario: Committee for the Publication of the Anglo-Genevan Psalter, 1972.

Joshua left when he died. *In this way I will test whether Israel will keep the way of the LORD by walking in it as their fathers did.*" The same expression occurs, among other places, in Ex. 16: 4 regarding the manna: "Then said the LORD unto Moses, Behold, I will rain bread from heaven for you; and the people shall go out and gather a certain rate every day, that I may *prove them*, whether they will walk in my law, or no" (KJV).

In other words, Jehovah caused the heathen to maintain themselves in and around Canaan for the same purpose for which He fed Israel in the wilderness. It was therefore *necessary* and *desirable* that this should take place. There is no statement at all that this is a penal judgment, that this is a question of the disastrous consequences of sin, of something that could and should have been different. It is entirely consistent with what we read in Judges 3: 1–3, namely, "These are the nations that the LORD left *to test* all the Israelites who had not known any of the wars in Canaan, *if only to teach warfare to the subsequent generations of Israel*, especially to those who had not known it formerly: the five rulers of the Philistines, all the Canaanites, the Sidonians, and the Hivites who lived in the mountains of Lebanon from Mount Baal-hermon to Lebo-hamath."

Is it not as if the Lord in His wisdom had arranged everything so that Israel would land in the school of self-knowledge and come under the discipline of tribulation? What from one point of view we have to regard as a punitive judgment and therefore as a revelation of God's wrath, is from another point of view a proof of His favor, a sign of His faithfulness, a gracious disposition, not in response to anything that Israel did or did not do, but to what it had to become.

What surprises us in this, or at least gives us food for thought, is not the fact that in the places cited, that which elsewhere is associated with Israel's disobedience is here attributed to Jehovah. This is entirely consistent with what is also found elsewhere in Scripture. The hardening of Pharaoh, the sin of David in numbering Israel, the betrayal of Judas, are attributed to man as the *secondary*, to Satan as the *cooperating*, to God as the *primary* cause. The Lord also directs the sinner by giving or leaving him to himself, even by bringing him into temptation. Evil, which on the one hand is entirely man's responsibility, nevertheless also occurs according to the determinate counsel and foreknowledge of God.

God would simply not be God if He allowed Himself to be determined by the actions of the secondary cause.

The motto of King Edward VI – a hand reaching out from a cloud and holding the globe by a golden chain – contains, in connection with the legend "Nihil sine Deo!" (nothing without God), a brief compendium of the entire reign of God. Nothing without God! Neither the small nor the great, the good nor the evil, we say as well.

Still less does the striking feature of the aforementioned statements lie in the fact that they regard the evil done by man, the judgment brought upon him, as something that is often turned for the better by God. This lies in the nature of things and is worthy of God. We already knew this in our childhood when the history of Joseph aroused our interest. We later found it expressed in many ways on many a page of Holy Scripture.

God brings forth light out of darkness. Chastisement, though in itself no cause for joy, bears the peaceful fruit of righteousness. God led His people by "a straight path," Ps. 107: 7, though that path seemed so long, so difficult, so unnecessary, and rather a detour. He who does not serve Him willingly will be compelled to use by Him as a tool.

The same truth is presented in these various statements from this side and from that. If there is something strange, something puzzling in all this, we attribute it to our short-sightedness. God's thoughts are not our thoughts. There is no fathoming His mind.

In connection with the appearance of the Angel of the Lord at Bochim, what strikes us in the judgments, Judges 2: 21–22 and 3: 1–3, is simply the *complete silence regarding the sinful acts of Israel, that is, of its unbelief and disobedience.* What appears from a superficial consideration of events to be related exclusively to Israel's refusal to carry out the commandment to exterminate the Canaanites in all its severity, and thus in a certain sense to be considered accidental, was not only contained in God's hidden counsel, but also so entirely in the nature of the matter, in Israel's condition, i.e., in the sinful condition of man estranged from God, that the question: why were the pagans not driven out? may well be answered by "because the purpose of the covenant could not be accomplished, because the plan of the Lord could not be carried out unless Israel came to learn self-knowledge in the school of temptation and was brought to God under the discipline of tribulation."

So this, then, is that to which we have to pay attention. When we pay attention to both the *nature* and *purpose* of the covenant and to the *stipulation* thereof, it becomes clear to us that Israel cannot reach its destiny – in other words, that the kingdom of God cannot reveal itself among this people, or what amounts to the same thing, that fallen man cannot be redeemed – unless the way upon which Jehovah leads His people actually proceeds from Gilgal to Bochim, from Jerusalem to Babylon, from Bethlehem to Golgotha, the Mount of Olives and the Upper Room, that is, to the glorious revelation of the New Covenant.

Everyone would see this at once, had they not formed – this is especially true of the theology of the end of the last century and the beginning of this one – such misconceptions about the Old Covenant and the rule of God in Israel.

Some believe that these were calculated for the Israelite people in the period of their infancy and constituted the sensory expression or inklings of spiritual conceptions that only after a long development could be understood from a different and higher standpoint. In recent years the realization has been made that this representation cannot be reconciled with many facts communicated to us in the historical books. The structure of the history of Israel, especially of its religious and political life, does not fully conform to the specifications and outline of it given in "the law."

We need not concern ourselves with the inference that many scholars, including Kuenen, Wellhausen, Robertson Smith, derive from this, namely, that the forms of the Old Covenant and of the rule of God described to us primarily in the five books of Moses, that is, in "the law," are of later date, that they are to be regarded not as a guide but as the fruit or outcome of Israel's development. This viewpoint cannot be maintained with even a semblance of justification if one does not wish to distort that history, tear it asunder, and do violence to it in every respect.

But there is another inference which I think is more obvious, namely, that the above-mentioned depiction of the Old Covenant as an educational institution is contrary to what we can learn from the law and the history with regard to its nature and purpose as well as to the essence of theocracy.

From the point of view of the *hidden* will of the Lord, the Old Covenant was destined to pass into the New; it was, as expressed in Heb. 8:

7ff., "obsolete and near to disappearance" because of the condition of fallen man. Viewed on the other hand from the standpoint of His *revealed* will, it already contained everything promised to the fathers, everything the sinner needed and faith expected. But it contained this *shrouded in shadows*. In the same way that the Glory of God dwelt among Israel – a light, a fire, hidden by the forbearance of God in the heart of the cloud that was the sign of the divine presence – there also came about communion with God, that is, the atonement.

In other words, the law was never fitted for a normal state of the people.

Think for a moment of Israel, not as it was, but as it should have been: a people "living by faith," a people not faithlessly breaking the covenant of their God but walking in the ways of the Lord, and we imagine heaven descending to earth; we imagine God dwelling in the midst of His people; we imagine the shadows vanishing and the glorious reality which they concealed becoming visible to all eyes.

Something of this was already seen when, at the first coming into Canaan, "the Commander of the LORD's army" (Joshua 5: 14) the same Angel of the Lord who had led the people in the column of cloud through the sea and the desert, appeared to Joshua in human form to give him orders and take charge of things.

Consideration of the terms of the covenant brings us to the same result. Israel was called to exterminate the Canaanites, overthrow their altars, burn the forests in whose shade they had served lust – under the name of religion – and destroy the idols. Seemingly an easy task, a task entirely in keeping with its interests, along with that which certain theologians (in elucidating certain facts in its history, e.g., the act of Ehud and Jael and of some statements in e.g. the so-called curse [i.e., imprecatory] psalms) like to explain as its bloodthirsty nature.

Such-like viewpoints make it impossible for us to understand the Holy Scriptures, and to explain the Age of the Judges.

Let us turn the matter around and assume that the condition to which God linked the possession of Canaan could not possibly be fulfilled as long as the people remained in their natural state.

When Jehovah commanded Israel to exercise judgment upon the nations of Canaan, He thereby demanded *the highest* that could be required of man. Canaan was under the curse of reprobation. It is beyond our scope to explain this appalling fact. One thing is certain, this curse is an aggravation of the judgment that Noah once pronounced on the youngest son of Ham: "Canaan would be a servant of servants to his brethren!" This too was fulfilled in the Gibeonites, who were destined to be woodcutters and water carriers, that is, to the service of the altar. But the curse of Canaan taken as a whole, on the other hand, was aggravated. The opposite of what we note in the history of Levi took place with him. "Cursed be their anger," Father Jacob had spoken of him and his brother Simeon on his deathbed. "I will disperse them in Jacob and scatter them in Israel" (Gen. 49: 7). Simeon experienced the full meaning of that curse; but for Levi, it was turned into a blessing. Levi was indeed scattered, but as a priestly tribe among the tribes of Israel.

The curse of Canaan, on the other hand, was *aggravated*, as we said. Through his own fault. God does not wrong man. Canaan will not be able to rise in judgment against Jehovah, saying, "Thou, O Lord, hast made me the victim of thy sovereign will for evil unto me!" Abraham's seed was to be oppressed for four hundred years in a land that was not theirs, so said the Word of God, in the day when the Lord made the covenant with the father of believers (Gen. 15: 13). But "the iniquity of the Amorites is not yet complete"; only then could Israel be led out of Egypt. Only the fourth generation could return to the land, of which God had said, "To your descendants I have given this land" (Gen. 15: 13–18).

In the light of this word, then, the entire history of Canaan falls under the viewpoint of the forbearance of God. That the Patriarchs dwelt in this land, that Abraham, Isaac and Jacob called on "the name of the Lord" here, that the king of Sodom was not allowed to say, "I have made Abraham rich," it all has to do with the Lord's intention to give time and certainly many an exhortation to repentance to the nations over whom judgment would be brought. That they were not ignorant of the purpose of Israel's coming is evident, among other things, from the song of Moses and Miriam: "The nations will hear and tremble; anguish will grip the dwellers of Philistia," and again, "those who dwell in Canaan will melt away" (Ex. 15: 14–15). It is also evident from the history of Rahab, and stamps her act, which from any other viewpoint would be considered a reprehensible act of faithless and cowardly betrayal, as an act of faith (Joshua 2: 2ff.).

God has come to execute judgment on Canaan.

That is what the trumpet sound that causes Jericho's walls to fall proclaims. The blast of the trumpet accompanied Jehovah's descent on Sinai to give His law (Ex. 19: 19). When the "trumpet of the jubile" (KJV) sounds on the Day of Atonement in the fiftieth year, Jehovah comes as the Goel, the redeemer of the wretched people who have no blood friend or blood avenger, no redeemer (Lev. 25: 9). As soon as the "trumpet shall sound," the dead will be raised and God Himself will appear *for judgment* (1 Cor. 15: 52).

The conquest of Canaan is God's work; He Himself drives out the inhabitants of Canaan before Israel (Ex. 34: 11). The sign of His presence is borne at the head of the army. "Behold, the ark of the covenant of the Lord of all the earth will go ahead of you into the Jordan," says Joshua (Joshua 3: 11).

The eradication of the Canaanites takes place, as it were, independently of Israel. Its purpose is not to make room for Israel. God eradicates them and *thereafter* gives His people the inheritance of the heathen (Ps. 111: 6). The conquest of Canaan is God's work, not in the general sense in which we are to attribute to Him everything, even that which occurs through secondary causes contrary to His revealed will, but in the entirely special sense whereby we are to see in it a revelation of His judgmental activity.

Only after this has been established can we draw our attention to another fact, namely, that *He chose Israel for this work, granted it to become a co-worker of God therein, and commanded it to place its sword in the service of the Judge of the whole earth.*

This takes us one step further in the history of man's redemption. Until now, the Lord has used the forces of nature to execute His judgment: water in the Flood, sulfur and fire in the destruction of Sodom and Gomorrah, the Red Sea in the destruction of Pharaoh. Now He uses man, the redeemed, Israel, the people of the covenant for this purpose.

Is here indeed, as we said, a task assigned to Israel that is weighty for man and, left to himself, incapable of execution by him? Man is, alas! willing enough to use the sword in his own interest. The first crime mentioned in Scripture is fratricide. The first fruit of poetic inspiration communicated in that Scripture, if we except Adam's greeting of Eve, is the song of the sword (Gen. 4: 23). It is one thing to raise that sword in his own name, in his own interest, and something else altogether to raise it in the name of the Lord.

Faith is demanded to the very end. It requires utter devotion. Deeply must he be imbued with God's wrath against sin; the image of the Holy and Righteous One must be deeply engraved in his soul before things get this far with man; that is: in the right way, unto the true end; and above all, *perfectly*.

We learn to understand something of this when we hear Enoch, the seventh from Adam, prophesying of the coming judgment, and consider how God took him away, because his faith, that is, his appeal to the righteousness of the Lord, would have precipitated the judgment that God, in His forbearance, who waits until the uttermost, wished to delay (Jude v. 14).

We see it in Elijah, who no longer announces the judgment on Israel, but begs for it. "He prayed earnestly that it would not rain," the Apostle tells us (James 5: 17).

We are in fact compelled to notice it in Moses, when he – the very same one who offered himself as a curse offering for his people, the one who desired to be cast out of God's book for his brethren according to the flesh – commands the sons of Levi, "Each of you men is to fasten his sword to his side, go back and forth through the camp from gate to gate, and slay his brother, his friend, and his neighbor" (Ex. 32: 27, cf. v. 32).

We grasp something of it, despite the opposition of our own hearts, when we feel in many psalms the glow of a holy wrath against sin, a zeal for God's name and an awareness of God's incorruptible justice, standing in stark contrast to the Eli-character of the church even in our time and of each member of that church in particular; the character of the man who has forgotten judging and punishing and wrathfulness and – be it said with holy earnestness – cursing, because these traits of God's image have been virtually obliterated in his soul by selfishness, inertia, carnal love.

But what are we saying of this image of God as it appears in sinful men; to Christ "He has given ... authority to execute judgment, because

He is the Son of Man" (John 5: 27). In this character He will one day appear on the clouds of heaven, and the same thing that Enoch prophesied about God coming in judgment "with myriads of His holy ones" (Jude v. 14) will be fulfilled in the congregation of the Lord. "Do you not know," the apostle Paul exclaims to her, "that we will judge angels?" (1 Cor. 6: 2–3).

"The God of peace will soon crush Satan under your feet" (Rom. 16: 20).

But then it will first have become completely conformed to "the image of the Son" (Rom. 8: 29).

Natural sympathy enables us to imitate Christ the Consoler, that is, the Savior in the gentle aspect of His revelation, at least as far as outward acts are concerned. But something entirely different is required for *judgment.* Sin must then have revealed itself to us in its true form, as the abominable, the desecrating, the doom-worthy thing that must be expunged from before His holy face.

Sometimes something lives in the souls of God's children that compels them to this holy activity, but to this indeed applies what the Heidelberg Catechism says of the life of faith, "even the holiest men, while in this life, have only a small beginning of this obedience" (Q. & A. 114).

Jonathan Edwards relates that once, after spending a long time in great anxiety about his state for eternity, and having tried in vain to appropriate the promises and consolations of the gospel, unexpectedly and for a reason unknown to him received a deep insight into the majesty, sovereignty and justice of God; an insight which was accompanied by a profound conviction of sin. He saw it, he wrote, in its curse-worthiness, and in such a way that he vindicated the judgment which he, as it were, carried within himself. But to his amazement he also perceived that at the same time a blissful feeling of fellowship with God flowed through him, a feeling in complete contrast to the conviction in which he had stood for a moment, that he himself was lost. He had seen God and his soul was saved.

Something similar was experienced by a mother in the dream. She was often very distressed because of the unconverted state of her children. Some of them showed themselves to be enemies of God and His service, and the thought that they were lost tore at her mother's heart.For her there was no salvation that was not shared by those she loved! What would it profit her to depart and be with Christ if she had to be separated from them forever!

On her sick- and death-bed, though, she had a profound dream, and in that dream came a face. Judgment Day had come. The Judge appeared on the clouds of heaven, all His saints with Him, and among them all she as well. The court was set. The dead, small and great, stood to be judged according to what they had done in the body. "Depart, ye cursed," sounded the voice of the Savior, her King, whom she loved with the unspeakable love of her soul, "into the eternal fire prepared for the devil and his angels!" At that same moment she saw her children to the left of the throne, enemies of Him before whom every knee must bow... and a solemn "amen!" that came audibly from her lips sealed the sentence. She awoke and preached the vengeance of God to hers, who had remained numb to the proclamation of the Lord's wonderful love and grace, but learned to tremble before "the wrath of the Lamb!"

To participate in the *judgment of God* is indeed the highest calling man can have. In the shadows of the Old Covenant, this is depicted by the Cherem, the ban. The ban too is a sacrifice offered the Lord. That Israel understands this is evident from many events in its history.

From many examples only this one. When the king of Arad attacked the people after Aaron's death, therefore just before they left the desert, and took some prisoners, Israel made a vow to the Lord and said: "If You will deliver this people into our hands, we will devote their cities to destruction. And the LORD," we further read, "heard Israel's plea and delivered up the Canaanites. Israel devoted them and their cities to destruction; so they named the place Hormah" (Num. 21: 1–3).

This passing of judgment is the highest revelation of faith and therefore the *first demand* with which Jehovah comes to His covenanters.

Under this condition Saul receives his crown from the hand of the Lord. He must banish Amalek but succumbs to the temptation to spare Agag and the best of the spoils. In so doing he reveals his carnal disposition, his unbelief.

In battle, many are defeated and sometimes the defenseless are killed. Man can be so cruel. But the battle against the enemies of God, by which God's judgment is brought upon them, has nothing in common with this. The least exception that one dares to make in this passing of judgment, as with Saul and Achan, proves that one acted from a wrong principle and did not live under the conviction of the mission which one was called to accomplish with the sword.

On the same condition, Israel is also given possession of Canaan. In Achan it had before it the appalling example of a man who transgressed the law of the Lord and did not shrink from bringing upon himself the curse with which the cursed thing which he had appropriated brought him into contact. All the people participated in the punitive exercise in the valley of Achor; it was performed not only in its name but also by it, that the guilt of this abomination might be averted.

And yet, Israel is later guilty of the same sin, Israel as a whole and each tribe in particular. Achan had preserved something inanimate, something which in itself could be considered desirable and, if not for the place where it was found, actually was. *They* spare the generation of those whom God had ordained to destruction. The children, the powerless, those who were found without weapons in hand, men and women from whom they hoped to derive some sort of benefit, it matters not: we discern here the *arbitrariness* that nullifies obedience, because an obedience that does not go beyond that which is consistent with one's own interest or understanding is simply not obedience; we see here the *carnal mind* that does not submit to the law of God; the *loftiness of heart* that corrupts God's judgment, the enmity that wishes to be more merciful than God and implicitly accuses Him of arbitrariness and cruelty, and we find in it a revelation of man's condition before God.

Faith is wholeheartedly hostile to *all* sin and has pleasure in *all* righteousness. It is precisely in this utterness that it exhibits its actual being. Pharisaism, on the other hand, knows how to venerate the mint and the cumin, in the fulfillment of certain duties it pushes scrupulousness to the limit; but it has many a proviso. It knows to give and take, and in a word, like Ananias and Sapphira, it takes away from God that which belongs *entirely* to Him.

A single weak link thwarts the purpose of the chain; a single crack in the bell silences the chime; the saving of some few Canaanites nullified the covenant between Jehovah the King and His people Israel. But for this very reason, in connection with what has been said about the nature, purpose and condition of the covenant, there is no longer any doubt in our minds that Israel's sin, by which the purpose of the covenant was thwarted, cannot be called accidental in the sense that we might imagine the possibility of the opposite, as if it were a momentary impulse, an involuntary omission, a thoughtless act. On the contrary, it may be called necessary, again not in the sense that the people would not be guilty, having acted passively in regard to it, but so that it was connected with sin as such, with the unbelief that constitutes the inner essence thereof, with the misery that keeps redemption out of man's reach as long as the conditional covenant is not replaced by an unconditional covenant, i.e., as long as the requirement of God is not replaced by the gift of God, the law not replaced by the gospel.

A *conditional covenant*. Was the covenant God made with Israel of that nature? Such a covenant is called a covenant of works because the blessing it promises and brings depends on man's actions.

Did God renew *that* covenant with Israel in the wilderness after it had been broken by man in the fall? This cannot be inferred from the fact that God gave His law at Sinai. The law is the revelation of God's immutable will; it is eternal. Grace does not nullify it. The issue is not whether God demands something of man, but whether this demand is also the condition upon which He intends to grant the promised salvation.

After the fall, this is to be denied with respect to the law. God accepts Israel, e. g., His people whom He redeems, leads, feeds, brings to Himself, before He asks anything of that people. The law is the form of gratitude, and yes, as such the means of acquiring many blessings, for "in keeping them is great reward" (Ps. 19: 12) but the promise of Canaan, the relationship between God and Israel *precedes* it. Instead, it might be inferred from the demand discussed in this chapter, namely, that the Canaanites be eradicated. Here we really have a condition the fulfillment of which, if not possession, at least free possession, if not the condition, at least the normal condition of Israel depends.

Yet it is clear from many details that this condition, although it is in *the form* of a covenant of works, in essence is of a different character. This is already evident from the fact that the punishment of complete rejection is not made dependent upon the breaking of the covenant but is threatened first for *the forsaking of Jehovah,* i.e., *idolatry*. But above all it is evident from the statement that, according to God's hidden will, Israel's disobedience and punishment were to serve to bring the people into the school of temptation and under the discipline of tribulation.

God deals with man according to His revealed will, i.e., He places him before the perfect: the perfect requirement, the perfect promise, the perfect blessing. He does not say: I know that man will disobey, that he is incapable of exercising faith, that he will descend from the height on which I place him to a lower position, for which reason I will put no higher demand upon him than that which he is able to fulfill at this time. This way of doing things would simply put an end to all history. No; He makes His demands, announces His intention, points to the final goal, but includes in His counsel, His plan of redemption, the disobedience, the apostasy which will gradually be revealed.

God wishes to spare Nineveh. Jonah knows this. It is the very reason he refuses to accept the commission to this city. Will the pagan repent and live while Israel listens to no admonition and rejects the preacher of repentance? Yet the preaching which, under the Lord's rigorous discipline, he later makes in the streets of Assyria's capital says "After forty days Nineveh shall perish!"; and this revelation of God's will becomes the very means by which the purpose of God's forbearance is accomplished.

Saul was not the elect of the Lord, was not the man destined to rule Israel; his kingdom would not, could not endure. This is proven by Jacob's prophecy about the scepter of Judah. This is also evidenced by the fact that Zion was kept by the Jebusites, by God's will as it were, until this fortress and thereby the key of the land passed into the hands of David. God gave this king in his wrath. But none of this takes away from the fact that Saul is subjected to a trial; nay more, that he is anointed by Samuel and animated by the Spirit, that he is treated, recognized, honored and empowered by God as king. He fell through his own fault; his rejection is a punishment for his disobedience. Yet we know very well that his conduct toward Amalek is entirely character-based and, like Israel's breach of the covenant, *necessary* in connection with his inner existence.

By the same rule, God demanded that Israel eradicate the Canaanites. That demand was just. Did Jehovah not have the right to demand blind and unconditional obedience? Had He Himself not executed a judgment of Jericho and of the confederates at Gibeon and Merom? Yet the path by which Israel will fulfill its destiny has already been determined from the beginning. Sin, temptation, punishment, and tribulation are made subservient to it.

That the grace of God works by such means, that in this way it proves necessary, is wished for, makes its appearance, and that its most glorious revelation in Christ is thereby brought nearer, is proof that in the Old Covenant as well we are dealing with a *covenant of grace*.

In chap. 2: 22 and 3: 1, only the beginning is pointed out of the way which, as has been said, leads from Bochim via Babylon to Bethlehem. That the Christ who will later appear and suffer in the flesh is already at work in the midst of Israel, it is this, be it said once more, which makes the covenant of God and the former administration to be known as a *covenant of grace*.

This is not revealed first later, but first now. It was already shown when the people at Sinai were unable to hear the voice of the Lord and instructed Moses to stand between them and God. "Then the LORD said to me, 'They have spoken well. I will *raise up for them a prophet* like you from among their brothers. I will put My words in his mouth, and he will tell them everything I command him. And I will hold accountable anyone who does not listen to My words that the prophet speaks in My name'" (Deut. 18: 17–19).

So not Moses but another is the Mediator who stands before the people with God and brings the word of the Lord to that people. There the final goal is pointed out. In the history of Israel, in the Age of the Judges, we observe that goal being brought closer step by step; and indeed by these four means, indicated in the places cited above or directly related to them: punishment – temptation – need – and redemption.

3. OTHNIEL—EHUD

Judges 3: 8–31

God takes care when suffering comes,
That he does not fall down completely,
That he may not get a leg broken,
It is God who guards him.

Ps. 34: 10 (Psalter of 1773[3])

Regardless of whether one opposes and rejects it or agrees with it wholeheartedly, the confession that man is "wholly incapable of doing any good, and inclined to all wickedness," that I too am "prone by nature to hate God and my neighbor" (Heidelberg Catechism, Q&A 5, 8) stands in direct contradiction not only with what we observe in others but also with what we think we know about ourselves.

There is indeed much in our experience and in the history of mankind that to a certain extent substantiates it. Depths of enmity, abysses of misery often become visible when we look into the mystery of our own being or learn to peek into the heart of our neighbor. But all that we learn along these lines in no way justifies *the absolute judgment* of Holy Scripture from which this confession is derived and on which it relies.

If we start from experience, if we consult our consciousness, we are entitled to distinguish between this act and that one and to assume that there is much good left even in the most criminal person – that what is intended is sometimes better than what is carried out. Our knowledge of our neighbor is, admittedly, highly defective. We look at what is before our eyes and know little of the hidden motives of men, which are known to us only insofar as they become manifest in word or deed.

Equally deficient is our self-knowledge, since the danger of self-deception swells the moment we are called upon to pass judgment on ourselves.

But admitting all this, we are left with the immediate testimony of our *consciousness*, which opposes that of Holy Scripture. Is it not true, then,

---

[3] This refers to the Dutch "Berijming" (psalms put to verse) of 1773, here translated into English.

that we would do good even though evil is present with us (cf. Rom. 7: 21)? Are we aware of this tendency to hate God and our neighbor?

Hence, the contradiction we are referring to here is very natural and understandable. And yet it does not argue against the testimony of the Lord in His Word, to which our confession attaches the seal of our assent.

It is true that no one "knows the thoughts of man except his own spirit within him" (1 Cor. 2: 11). But it is no less true that "God is greater than our hearts, and He knows all things" (1 John 3: 20).

What is our consciousness? The surface of our being, illuminated by the sunbeam. It is like the surface of the ocean. Only near the shore can the bottom be seen. For the most part, even to our own eye, our existence is shrouded in darkness. Light does not penetrate here; how much lies beneath the undulating expanse of water that only becomes visible if one deliberately descends into the mysterious depths!

What is our feeling? It is like the invisible fluid, electricity, which conceals an irreconcilable contradiction the existence of which is only betrayed when it is dissolved by friction, i.e., by the influence of circumstances, and thereby becomes knowable.

What is the relative good that we are aware of possessing? The good that the prodigal son brought from the father's house before it was consumed; or the evil of sin in the form of a seed that has not yet developed and sometimes takes years, even generations, to mature, or sometimes under given circumstances is never fertilized, so that the possibility it carries within it never materializes.

This, and much more we could add to it, fully explains why the judgment of Holy Scripture does not coincide with ours. The explanation of what we express here is found in experience, in history, and in the Word of God as well. Peter wants to follow Jesus into death. He does not doubt his willingness to do and bear all, when his love for the Master is put to the test. Against the prophecy, "you will all fall away on account of Me" and "this very night, before the rooster crows, you will deny Me three times" (Matth. 26: 31, 34) stands the statement of his consciousness. Judas will betray his Lord. The seed from which this disastrous fruit in the end will come is already present. But there is neither in his behavior, nor in his feeling, nor in his consciousness even the slightest thing that revealed its existence either to the eye of his fellow disciples or to his own, when he enthusiastically joined the circle that awaited the Kingdom of Heaven, when, at the apostasy of the great majority of Jesus' followers, the question "Do you want to leave too?" was answered in his name as well, "Lord, to whom would we go? You have the words of eternal life" (John 6: 67, 68).

The revealing light of the Holy Spirit must shine in our hearts before the testimony of Holy Scripture concerning man and thereby the confession of his misery is confirmed. First sin, then ruin, and finally unwillingness or enmity are made known in that light.

Someone has done what is evil in the eyes of the Lord. But while he is willing to acknowledge this, the cause of that evil is sought first in the circumstances in which he found himself placed. "The woman whom You gave me," it is said, "she gave me fruit from the tree, and I ate it" (Gen. 3: 12). But as he probes deeper, he experiences that the source of that evil lies in the heart, that is, in nature. He confesses and realizes his powerlessness more as a misfortune and as something he has to put up with than as a guilt, and has the impression that he would be different if he could do what he would like to do. At last he also loses confidence in his own willingness, and thereby embarks on the way to understanding what it means to be "saved by grace."

"Tell me: in what way did you come to salvation in Christ?" asked the teacher on the occasion of the examination preceding admission to the Lord's table of a very uncultured member of the congregation who was to confess his faith at an advanced age.

"The Lord and I both did something," was the reply.

A look of understanding and surprise was exchanged between the preacher and the elder when the question was posed, "Well, what did *you* do?"

"I," said the simple one, "did nothing but resist. God pulled, I would not follow. God called, I refused to hear. At last He became too strong and overpowered me; that is how the work was divided."

Apparently, the simple one had progressed far in the knowledge of the work of salvation.

The study of Israel's history in the Age of the Judges brings us to similar results. Its unbelief reveals itself in the disobedience that makes it violate the commandment of the Lord. But judging superficially, we would say that this has not yet proved that nothing good dwells in it, not declared that it will *in no way* submit to God's law, not shown that the promise of the Lord will not be fulfilled under the Old Covenant!

Hear, then, with what decisiveness the people reject idolatry! "Far be it from us," it says to Joshua at Shechem, "to forsake the LORD to serve other gods" (Josh. 24: 16). The *outcome* will show what awaits this people, how little they will be able to maintain themselves in the position of patriarchal faith that they yet occupy at present.

But that outcome is the fruit of Jehovah's work on them. It is the work for man's salvation, in which is distinguished:

1. The activity by which Israel is discovered to itself and compelled to reveal its sinful condition to itself. The means used for this is *temptation.*

2. The discipline by which Israel experiences the consequences of sin and learns to notice the punishing hand of the Lord. The means the Lord uses for this is *affliction by enemies.*

3. Conversion, by which they are repeatedly brought back to God. We have to consider it as a fruit of the *struggle*, of the *need*, and of the *law.*

4. The redemption by which God reveals His mercy and faithfulness; this is wrought by the chosen instruments of God's will, i.e. by the *Judges.*

1. What is temptation?

This is implicitly stated in James 1: 13–14: "When tempted," says the apostle, "no one should say, 'God is tempting me.' For God cannot be tempted by evil, nor does He tempt anyone. But each one is tempted when by his own evil desires he is lured away and enticed."

God *cannot* be tempted by evil, because it finds no point of reference in His holy Being. "God is light, and in Him there is no darkness at all" (1 John 1: 5).

It is different with man. In him dwells lust, that is, the pull toward sin. It exists even if it remains hidden. Everything that awakens it, that forces it to reveal itself, is a temptation. Temptation is to the moral world what the chemist's keys are, by which he learns the hidden properties of substances wholly or partly unknown to him, and thereby the sort to which they belong.

At first glance, gunpowder and coal dust have much in common. However, the burning fuse enables us to determine in a given case which of these two substances we have before us.

In the same way, we get to know people as well as ourselves. If lust is present, it will ignite under the influence of given circumstances. Ergo: two people find themselves in the same situation: on the one, that situation exercises no influence at all, but on the other it brings about temptation to do evil. The sight or smell of hard liquor is very apt to make the erstwhile drunkard stumble, yet does not endanger the temperance of him who has never been addicted to drink.

Diogenes was incorruptible. No matter how much Alexander had at his disposal, he was incapable of tempting the philosopher. He could give him nothing, for he desired nothing; deprive him of nothing, for he possessed nothing.

Opportunity does not make the thief, but it makes him known. Only when the disposition is fertilized by the occasion does it come to the sinful act.

This is also why God is said to tempt no man. God, the Holy One, cannot take pleasure in that which is contrary to His own Being. His *purpose*, therefore, is never to cause man to stumble. That is the work of Satan, who knows our weakest side and knows how to work on it.

However, this does not take away the fact that the *circumstances* in which we find ourselves under the guidance of God's providence can become *temptations* for us, so that humility and self-knowledge put the prayer on our lips, "Lead us not into temptation."

A sinner cannot go anywhere to escape temptation. Everything that serves to test faith and exercise strength, in other words, the objections and difficulties that life brings, give him cause for dissatisfaction, make him murmur or cause him to rebel against God. On the other hand, prosperity, the blessings that come his way, force him to forget God and lead him to be ungrateful.

So it lies in the nature of things that association with the Canaanites, who remained in the land of promise, tempts Israel. The law is spiritual while Israel is "of flesh, sold into bondage to sin" (Rom. 7: 14). Under the name of "Religion," the service of Baal (i.e., the sun-god, the creative force of nature) and of Astarte (i.e., the moon-goddess), is comprehended not only nature-service – idolatry in all its forms has this character – but flesh-service, i.e., sensuality in its grossest and most disgusting manifestation.

In passing, we have to count this service among the abominations that brought judgment upon the peoples of this land. When the distinction between good and evil, right and wrong, is obliterated, man is hopelessly lost. Evil reaches its zenith *in this,* that good is called evil and evil good. The so-called religious festivals of the Baalites were joined to the life of nature, the changing of the seasons. The deity was worshipped under images that denote precisely what remains of the pure knowledge of God when the moral qualities, the virtues, known through personal supernatural revelation, have fallen away from the image one forms of God, viz. *power* that finds its image in the bull calf. Sensual lust, which had already seduced Israel's youth into the service of Baal-Peor in the fields of Moab, now too exercises its temptation. The gods of Canaan become, in a word, a *snare* to Israel.

A snare: especially because their influence makes itself felt first in the sphere of social life. The servants of Baal and Jehovah come into contact there, and the influence of idolatry extends far beyond the circle of actual religious life. It is to this unnoticed and often imperceptible influence that Israel first succumbs. "Thus the Israelites continued to live among the Canaanites, Hittites, Amorites, Perizzites, Hivites, and Jebusites. And they took the daughters of these people in marriage, gave their own daughters to their sons, and served their gods" (Judges 3: 5–6).

With some thought, it will become clear to us how temptation has done its work here. Even more so because its method remains unchanged even today. Religion is a fortress that does not fall into the hands of the enemy without a fight. Therefore, the first work of that enemy is to occupy the outer works. Friendship, social intercourse, the habits and customs of domestic and social life are highly accessible and are not directly related to strength. The greatest danger, in a word, threatens from the side of natural life.

Unfortunately, mixing with the pagans benefits not Israel but paganism. Health does not communicate itself, but infirmity. Without knowing it, one comes into contact with idols in their most attractive, least repulsive forms. It is so difficult – what am I saying? – it is utterly impossible to mark the boundary at which the lawful ends and sin begins. Those who wallow with the Canaanites find themselves in a contaminated atmosphere and fall under the spell of a life infused with idolatry, with all its attractions for the natural man.

When the enemies laid down their arms, Israel thought they had rendered them harmless. They paid no attention to the danger that threatened them from the side of their gods. They succumbed to the temptation. This was the "victory of the vanquished." But this defeat in the area of moral and religious life was self-inflicted.

Self-inflicted? Is this entirely correct? "God cannot be tempted by evil, nor does He tempt anyone," we said on the basis of the apostolic word in James 1: 13. In Judges 2: 21–22, by contrast, the very thing in which we thought we saw a consequence of Israel's disobedience is attributed to Jehovah Himself. "I will no longer drive out before them any of the nations Joshua left when he died. *In this way I will test* whether Israel will keep the way of the LORD by walking in it as their fathers did."

Thus our consideration of temptation is incomplete as long as we see in it only a consequence of man's sinful condition, and not also a disposition of the Lord, a *revelation of His judicial activity*.

It is perfectly true that Israel falls into temptation as a result of its own fault and negligence. Sin is entirely the responsibility of the creature. But this does not mean that this creature is in any way independent of God. God is not powerless against evil as something He wanted to prevent but couldn't; no, He uses it and forces it to reveal itself in its own character.

If Balaam, knowing that God is righteous and Israel is doomed, wants to go with Balak's envoys to curse the Lord's people, he later receives the *command* to continue on the path he has taken. Now he goes, not contrary to the will of the Lord, but in accordance with that will. In this we must see a punishment, a judgment.

Not only that. When Balak and Balaam intended evil for Israel, God turned it for good. Jehovah opened the mouth of the dumb yoke-bearing beast, and in the same way put his words in the prophet's mouth. Balaam goes to curse, and comes to bless.

God is not controlled by circumstances, He controls them. We see this in the history not only of Balaam, but also of Pharaoh and of Judas. How striking, to dwell on Judas alone, rings out the word with which the Savior sends the traitor from His presence! "What you do," it says, "do it quickly!" The betrayal is accomplished at Jesus' command. In that command He speaks as King, as Judge. Well! He who tempted no man leads Israel into temptation; viz., He does not go forth to drive out the Canaanites, and thereby sets a snare for them. But the decision He announces here is not arbitrary, something that could have turned out differently. It is *the announcement of the punishment that Israel's disobedience fully deserves.*

Insofar as He thereby sets in motion the entire train of events that finally lead to Israel's rejection as a people, it is a revelation of His judicial activity. But what moves more particularly into the foreground now is the fact that this stands in the closest connection with the *development of His plan of redemption.* The refusal to wipe out the Canaanites is the expression of that God-hostile existence that makes Israel impervious to being redeemed unless God glorifies His grace to it. If this is to happen, then sin must reveal itself not in a certain form but in its *actual essence,* then what still exists in its seed must bear fruit, then sin must pave the way to tribulation, to chastening, to redemption.

How wonderfully the various workings interlock here! The history of salvation is that weaver's masterpiece of which a German poet has said that one stroke ties thousands of threads together. The same God who in the indicated fashion brings His people into temptation, also places them under *discipline.*

2. Four generations had to come and go before the iniquity of the Amorites became full (Gen. 15: 16).

Does – we are tempted to ask – the harvest of sin ripen so slowly in the fields of human life? Surely this is not due to the seed, nor to the soil in which it germinates, that is, not to man's sinful inclination, man's wrong disposition, nor to man himself in his state of alienation from God! It is only and solely due to the *grace of the Lord,* which halts evil in its development, not only in Israel but also in the pagan world, as the above example shows. It is called common grace, because it only restrains evil and prevents whatever good remains in man from his former state from completely suffocating, but it does not exert any salvific effect. Often, however, it serves to prepare the way for particular grace and redemptive activity, and passes into it or flows together with it.

It revealed itself from the first moment in which man fell. God Himself established enmity between the sinner and his tempter; He prevented him from surrendering himself entirely to Satan, Gen. 3:15a, brought him under the discipline of labor and suffering, vv. 16, 17, 19, opened to him the prospect of redemption, pointed out the means of reconciliation, and made him know by experience not only His forbearance but also His justice, v. 21 and ch. 4: 6, 7, 12.

In the history of Israel during the Judges as well, we discovered the traces of its manifold activity. In more than one way it *suppresses* evil. In the first place by the *discipline of domestic life and public opinion*. "The people," we read in Judges 2: 7, "served the LORD throughout the days of Joshua and of the elders who outlived him, who had seen all the great works that the LORD had done for Israel." Left to themselves, the younger generation would certainly have preferred Canaan's gods and Canaan's religion to that of their fathers. The tabernacle lacked the visible sign of the presence of God. In their eyes, the shadow service, of which that tabernacle, as the palace of Israel's King, was the centerpiece, became a succession, if not of meaningless forms, at least of forms without purpose.

In all this, only that has significance which constitutes the essence of every religion and what is imperishable in it, that which has existed from ancient times, even in the days of the patriarchs. Precisely because of this, however, the line between true and false religion is less sharply drawn. They, like the forefathers, served Jehovah on the heights. Do not the inhabitants of the land do the same? Let one call Jehovah "my Baal" (Hosea 2: 16) and the line is obliterated.

But at this point the experience and knowledge of the elders still stands in the way of sin among the youth. They have seen the great works of the Lord; they experienced the severity of judgment for forty years in the wilderness. The public assembly at Bochim is still fresh in their minds. Their discipline, word and example are not in vain. Many a family man in those days was certainly mindful of the Lord's command: "Only be on your guard and diligently watch yourselves, so that you do not forget the things your eyes have seen, and so that they do not slip from your heart as long as you live. Teach them to your children and grandchildren" (Deut. 4: 9).

Now as long as all this forms no exception but instead can be said of the people as a whole, sin lacks the freedom of movement it requires for its growth. The individual is always under the dominion of public opinion, and for the time being this keeps and draws the younger generation in the track trodden by the fathers. When the rumor spreads that the tribes who obtained their dwelling places beyond the Jordan have built an altar on the bank of that river, the whole assembly is ready to destroy them and their land (Josh. 22: 12). When the atrocity that took place at Gibeah of Benjamin comes to Israel's attention – the event occurred in the earliest time after the settlement in Canaan, although the story of it is included as an addendum at the conclusion of the book of Judges – the indignation of the tribes is sustained and Benjamin is almost completely annihilated (Judges 20: 48).

In another addendum we are informed how idolatry took root in the tribe of Dan and the household of Micah, evidence that we are here dealing with a fact that can only be explained from the extraordinary circumstances of this chapter, the 18th of Judges.

What opened the door? "Joshua son of Nun, the servant of the LORD, died at the age of 110. They buried him in the land of his inheritance, at Timnath-heres in the hill country of Ephraim, north of Mount Gaash. After that whole generation had also been gathered to their fathers, another generation rose up who did not know the LORD or the works that He had done for Israel. And the Israelites did evil in the sight of the LORD and served the Baals" (Judges 2: 8–11).

In the second place, the development of evil is countered by the *constant struggle that Israel had in order to maintain its existence in Canaan.* When God expelled the sinner from Paradise, He actually showed great mercy to him. There is no better means of arresting the progress of sin than the constant struggle for existence, the struggle against the thorns and thistles of life. Lust has no more faithful ally than emptiness. From this point of view, the fact mentioned in Judges 3: 2 that Jehovah did not proceed to exterminate Israel's pagan neighbors and the original possessors of its land in order that He might "teach warfare to the subsequent generations of Israel," is of great significance. Everything that requires effort serves to exercise our strength, counteracts corruption, forms character and prevents man from giving himself up entirely to evil.

This is especially true of exercise obtained in battle against enemies. He who is in constant danger cannot live for pleasure. Life makes other and higher demands. Nor can he live for himself, but is forced by a desire for self-preservation to seek fellowship with others. Battle demands ceaseless vigilance coupled with courage and display of strength, in a word the exertion of all one's powers, but with it teaches not only self-confidence but also dependence. Especially when, as in Canaan, this struggle is man to man.

Scripture only informs us of the fact that powerful tribes were found both inside and outside the borders of Canaan who disputed Israel's possession of its inheritance. But little thought is needed to make one see that this very struggle for the land one inhabits and the bread one eats, for household and life, was better suited than anything else to strain and exercise the powers of mind and body that were demanded, to stand firm in the face of guile and violence.

When we read in Judges 1: 34–35, "The Amorites forced the Danites into the hill country and did not allow them to come down into the plain. And the Amorites were determined to dwell in Mount Heres, Aijalon, and Shaalbim. But when the house of Joseph grew in strength, they pressed the Amorites into forced labor," then this calls to mind the scenes as they are reported to us in the history of Scotland and Switzerland. The history of our own Eighty-Years' War and of Prussia after the Revolution and the downfall of the first French empire, and that of the United States of America after the Civil War, can teach us how God uses the struggle for existence or independence to raise the life of a people to a different and higher level and to bring out the hidden power of that people.

What in itself and in all manner of ways is undesirable and useless becomes a blessing for the sinner. A blessing namely in the sense in which we call the storm a blessing because it purifies the atmosphere. God used the difficulties and sorrows of the desert journey to both punish and educate the elders. Now He uses the turmoil, danger, uncertainty and effort inseparable from Israel's condition in Canaan for the same purpose.

Were it possible, Israel's fall would have been stemmed by this. Now it is only delayed and interrupted. But these common effects of God's grace are in the closest connection with His activity of *redeeming the sinner*. They reveal God's long-suffering and wisdom, and also pave the way for a new revelation, namely, of the Righteousness of God, which not only makes Israel fight against the enemy but also delivers him to that enemy, so that he may be dominated and oppressed by him.

After temptation and struggle, we must also discuss

3. Oppression.

In Judges 3: 8 it is said that Jehovah sold his people into the hand of Cushan-rishathaim. We could thus save ourselves the trouble of tracing the natural causes of Israel's humiliation and downfall. "Who gave Jacob up for spoil, and Israel to the plunderers?" we hear Isaiah ask. And the prophet's answer: "Was it not the LORD, against whom we have sinned? They were unwilling to walk in His ways, and they would not obey His law. So He poured out on them His furious anger and the fierceness of battle. It enveloped them in flames, but they did not understand; it consumed them, but they did not take it to heart" (ch. 42, vv. 24–25).

When the people were smitten at Ai, its elders threw themselves on their faces before the ark of the covenant. Israel could not be defied by any power in the world; sin alone could bring it down. This conviction makes Joshua speak. If his people are smitten then it is an indication that fellowship with Jehovah has been disrupted, that Israel has been cut off from the source of its strength.

The faithful Israelite always spoke in days of trouble and distress: "I was mute, I did not open my mouth, Because it was You who did it" (Ps. 39: 9, NKJV). However, hidden in this display of God's righteousness is a revelation also of His forbearance, not least also of His wisdom.

> The Lord's works are very great;
> Who has ever delighted therein,
> Searches them diligently and steadfastly.
>
> Psalm 111: 2 (Psalter of 1773)

The King of kings has many servants who, willingly and unwillingly, knowingly and unknowingly, do His good pleasure, along with many instruments, and – what becomes especially visible in Israel's history – He has arranged everything in Israel's social condition, in its civil relations, even in the disposition of nature, in such a way that the violation of the law of the Lord immediately, that is, even apart from the special intervention of the Lord, has the most disastrous consequences for its prosperity, its unity, its flourishing, yes even for its popular existence.

Israel, to cite something by way of example, is a people divided into tribes. Faith in God, obedience, religion are thus inseparable from faith in oneself, that is, in one's origin and destiny. As soon as it gives up its firstborn right for the concoction of earthly pleasures, the brotherly bond between the tribes is broken. From now on they have conflicting interests and intentions, they do not care about each other and only self-interest is able to rouse them from their languid rest. The twelve-fold cord has been unraveled and can be loosened and torn thread by thread.

Israel knows this, and learned it by sad experience in the Age of the Judges. That is why it later wanted to establish an external bond of unity instead of this natural one, willed by God. "Give us a king!" it was said in the days of Samuel, "like the other nations" (1 Sam. 8: 5). It is the need for unity that expresses itself in this way. One rejects the good and seeks to partake of its fruit by other means. However, even if, through the forbearance and grace of the Lord, this unity is not only established but, thanks to His special intervention, is cemented by common and visible deliverance, cf. 1 Sam. 11: 1ff., it will endure only temporarily.

Going with Saul were "the men of valor whose hearts God had touched" (1 Sam. 10: 26). But the man from Benjamin is not heartily acclaimed as king by the heads of the other tribes. When the scepter later passes into the hands of Judah, it is envied by Ephraim and lamented by Benjamin. And conversely, Jeroboam knows very well that the separation of the one Israel into two independent kingdoms cannot exist if he does not succeed in tearing them apart in a religious, i.e., spiritual, sense. The prophets both in Israel and in Judah know and maintain religious unity as well, despite the political difference.

The altar on Carmel counts twelve stones, just as the laver in the temple stands on twelve oxen. Every Reformation activity brings the tribes together again. The messengers of Josiah and Hezekiah invite the northern tribes to the Passover feast at Jerusalem, and the temple is restored from contributions gathered throughout the land.

In the Age of the Judges more than in that of the Kings, it comes out how the people are divided, weakened and, consequently, defeated and oppressed by the natural and necessary operation of sin. To the enemy, Israel's religious condition opens up the prospect of overthrowing this people, invincible as it may be in the power of its God. The condition of the people means that that enemy possesses a foothold and starting point, if only in Mount Jebus. Allies and spies abound among the Canaanites. The land is so fertile and the promise of booty so great that there is no lack of incentive to attack, even on the side of self-interest.

There is, besides, an incentive in the enmity between the servants of idols and the people of the true God, which drives the nations toward Canaan. It is about the honor of their gods, the same consideration that once caused Pharaoh to exclaim, "Who is Jehovah that I should obey Him?" and that caused the Philistines to place the ark in the temple of Dagon.

"Mine heritage," says the Lord in Jeremiah 12: 9 (KJV), "is unto me as a speckled bird, the birds round about are against her."

As long as Israel remains faithful to the covenant and walks in the ways of the Lord, the enmity shown to it applies to the God it honors. We see this in the attack of Amalek at Raphidim, in the opposition encountered by Daniel and Nehemiah. But as soon as it forsakes God, they also hate it for what it itself is. This hatred of the Jews does not really date from our days but is rooted in the nature of a people who are compared by their own prophets to the wood of the vine, which is unusable and anything but attractive as soon as it does not fulfill its purpose.

This and much more that could be added proves that there was reason enough to dispute Israel's peaceful and free possession of its inheritance. As the invisible hand of the Lord stopped the waters of the swift-flowing Jordan where it flows between steep mountains on either side so that they did not continue to flow down, following the law of nature, to the Dead Sea which takes them up, so the Lord had to arrest Israel's enemies and prevent them, as it were, from attacking His people.

This is evident not so much from the first occupation of Canaan by Cushan-rishathaim, as the Scriptures call him (if we may judge from the almost identical name in the Persian charters, he is the same one who undertook a conquest to Syria and penetrated into Egypt) as from the next conquest by Eglon and all subsequent attacks.

As for the oppression by this aggressor of the Near East, in Judges 3: 8 it is said that "He *sold* them into the hand of Cushan-rishathaim king of Aram-naharaim." The expression indicates that He acted, leaving aside the details, just like the sons of Jacob who surrendered Joseph into the hands of Ishmaelite merchants. It was entirely their doing. The traveling party would have passed if they had not agreed to make this sale.

Forty years later, Israel was beaten by Eglon. But now in Judges 3: 12, "He gave Eglon king of Moab *power* over Israel." The initiative therefore emanated from Eglon. Even so, Jehovah made his efforts successful. Eglon conquered the land in the strength of his unknown ally.

Yet in both cases, the actual cause of Israel's degradation is the same. "So the Israelites did evil in the sight of the LORD; they forgot the LORD their God and served the Baals and the Asherahs" (Judges 3: 7). It was God's hand that pressed heavily on them day and night. Only in the nature and duration of their indignity can a difference be noted. The first tribulation lasted eight, the second, which came forty years later, eighteen years. Cushan-rishathaim turned the country into a province, probably without making any change in the government. Eglon settled in the country.

Generally speaking, it can be said that each subsequent tribulation was more severe than that which immediately preceded it, and also posed more danger to Israel's independence and survival. The pressure gradually intensified. In the administration of God as much as in that of man, *tribulation, punishment* has great significance. "Before I was afflicted, I went astray," says David, "but now I keep Your word" (Ps. 119: 67).

A wonderful thing. What visible connection exists between that serving of the Baals, spoken of in Judges 3: 7, and this invasion, e. g., of Moabites, allied with Ammonites and Amalekites, driven by the pursuit of profit? Conscience seeks and finds this connection. No, as soon as man is ready to see a punishment in suffering, disappointment, affliction, as soon as he does not stop at the instruments of God's will but discerns the hand of the Lord in them and recognizes His gracious purpose in doing so, that is, as soon as suffering ceases to be for him an accident, an abuse, a sad consequence of all kinds of mediate causes, then also is the purpose of punishment accomplished.

A wondrous affair is punishment! The sinner knows to do good and does not do it. He is admonished and warned but hardens his heart. Neither the threats nor the promises of the Lord impress his mind. But hardly does he lie there flattened in the dust, when – should God gives the grace of repentance – his will is bent and the natural hardness of heart is transformed into the condition of the defeated and contrite spirit in which God Himself wishes to take up residence.

A certain little boy experienced this when he claimed he *could not* do something his mother demanded of him. It was a very minor matter and yet he felt completely powerless to do so. "Je ne puis pas," he maintained, even when a light punishment had been imposed on him. Hardly had the punishment been made heavier and yet heavier, however, than a change became noticeable, first in the tone of his sobs and cries, then in his attitude. It was not long before he was heard to exclaim, "O Maman: je vais pouvoir; je vais pouvoir!" – I can! The child felt power returning. What had been difficult for him, indeed impossible, seemed to become a foregone conclusion. This is what punishment accomplished.

There is no causal connection between a particular sin and an ordinary event that follows it sooner or later. But conscience sees a connection because the tutor, the schoolteacher, the head of the household bring the two together. Joseph's brothers are in distress; they are living through fearful moments in Egypt. But now suddenly the image of Joseph comes to mind as he was dragged away there by the rough hands of foreign merchants, dragged and driven to a land where nothing but misery and humiliation awaited him. "Then they said to one another, 'surely we are being punished because of our brother. We saw his anguish when he pleaded with us, but we would not listen. That is why this distress has come upon us'" (Gen. 42: 21).

"Seventy kings," groaned Adoni-Bezek, "with their thumbs and big toes cut off have gathered the scraps under my table. As I have done to them, so God has repaid me" (Judges 1: 7). Nevertheless, the Lord takes care that the connection between offense and affliction is often such that, as the example of Adoni-Bezek proves, the most inveterate sinner must recognize: this is the finger of God!

During and after the civil war between the Southerners and Northerners in the United States, many atrocities were perpetrated upon the blacks and their protectors by the members of a secret society, that of the Ku-Klux. They not only acted in the most secretive manner, but also took care that each victim, felled by their murderous hand, received a sign on the forehead to make known by whom and for what purpose they had been deprived of life.

The Judge who Himself secretly executes the sentence upon the sinner also has his sign, known to all who will notice, clearly showing by whose hand, at whose charge and in consequence of what evil this punishment is brought upon the sinner at this time, in this manner, in this form. It is often a small thing, a striking similarity, something accidental by which the intent of a particular event is indicated. At Ebenezer, in the same place where the ark was taken, Israel later inflicts the crushing defeat on the Philistines, 1 Sam. 7. In the field of Naboth where the curse was pronounced on Ahab's house, Joram falls, struck by Jehu's arrow, 2 Kings 9. The same city of Jericho which God delivered to Israel without having fired a single arrow against it or hurled a single stone against it, became the seat of Eglon. In Judges 3: 12, 14 he is called the king of the Moabites. From the fact that he did not live at Rabbath-Moab, cf. 2 Kings 3, but at Jericho, as well as that he obtained Canaan with the help of other tribes, viz. Amalekites and Ammonites, v. 13, it may be inferred that he was a courtier or perhaps a prince from the royal house of Moab, who founded an independent kingdom on the other side of the Jordan. But we know too little of those relations to grant ourselves the right to speak with decisiveness here; we conclude that the designation "the king of the Moabites" *must* be understood in the sense of "one king from among the Moabites."

But however this may be, Israel once lived in tents in the flat fields of Moab. Nothing could harm him, for his God was with him. And now from that same Moab comes a multitude that oppresses it for eighteen years, settles in the land and, what in this case is the sign of its rejection and deep humiliation, holds in its hands the key to Canaan, once given by God Himself to His people Israel.

This is the finger of God, this is the hand of the Lord, this is God Himself who has bared His arm against His people!

To see this, to know this, is the most painful thing of all, but it is also that from which Israel, if properly understood, could take courage. Hope could thereby be revived within it. "God has smitten me," said a child of the Lord; "He has chastised me severely, but He had to come close to me to do it, and I have experienced how wonderful this is."

The song of faith is often a lament like the 42nd psalm, which speaks of depths, vortices, abysses of misery. But when David sings of the waves and waterfalls that "trouble his distressed soul" (v. 4, Psalter of 1773) *that* is the bright spot for him, the consolation, the ground of confidence that it is "Your waves and Your waterfalls" that pass over him. His life is not a game of chance. He is not a plaything of the enemies, though he is their "string music." The same God who wounds will heal, who afflicts will comfort, who causes to cry out in distress will save. "My Savior and my God," the song ends. Punishment was not an end, just a *means* to an end. The hour of salvation strikes as soon as that goal is attained.

4. Consequently, chastening coincides with *redemption*.

As soon as Israel "cried out to the Lord," He repented of the evil He had brought upon His people. He had surrendered it, withdrawn the visible sign of His presence and thereby effectively suspended the relationship that existed, albeit in the form of the Old Testament shadow service, between Him and Israel. But He did not thereby abandon His people, did not forget His covenant, did not change His plan. He was only accomplishing it by another way, the only conceivable way, and the salvation which He now graciously dispenses is in the closest connection with that final goal, is an image of it, and serves to pave the way to that redemption.

In the night visions of Zechariah (ch. 1), the hostile powers that scattered Israel are represented under the image of four horns, and the redeemers whom the Lord employs to frustrate the power of those horns are represented by the image of four smiths. For each horn there is a blacksmith, i.e., a workman calculated for the task assigned to him.

The redemption of which the book of Judges gives consecutive report is the revelation of the Lord's manifold wisdom as well as grace. First comes Othniel, the lion of God, of Judah's tribe, which was to be first in all things. He was the conqueror of Kirjath-Sefer or Debir, for which he received Achsa, the daughter of Caleb, for a wife; the son of Caleb's younger brother, among the last of the generation that saw the deeds of the Lord and of the house that was highly honored by God. Then Ehud, of Benjamin, the tribe that by then might already have been brought close to ruin, and in any case was smaller and less influential than Judah, though at all times closely associated with it.

We would not take notice of the decline to be noted here if it were not maintained in succeeding judges. Othniel "judged Israel" before he led him against the enemy, Judges 3: 10, i.e., he brought the people under the discipline of the law. Of Ehud it is only described that he "redeemed" Israel by his valiant act, v. 15. The Spirit of the Lord "was" upon Othniel. In that inspiration, at least for the purpose to which he was called, lay something lasting. Of Gideon we later read, Judges. 6: 34, that the Spirit of the Lord "clothed" him, an expression in which lies the idea of protection. Of Samson, Judges 14: 6, 15: 14, that the Spirit of the Lord became "mighty" over him. The power suddenly came from above and outside and then was taken back.

Ehud did not act under the inspiration of the Spirit. In view of the means by which he employed himself to redeem Israel, it is at least not without significance that his name is missing among the heroes of faith in Heb. 11, and especially that with him, precisely the addendum indicating the origin of the power of the other Judges is missing.

Othniel "went out to war," v. 10. He faced Cushan-rishathaim and, although the details of that battle are not given, it is implied that miracles of valor were wrought by Israel under him, and that the God of hosts fought with and for him. Ehud only acts with decisiveness and boldness, gives evidence of determination and love for his people, and is used and blessed by the Lord, but exhibits the character of his tribe and confirms the prophecy, Gen. 49: 27: "Benjamin is a ravenous wolf; in the morning he devours the prey, in the evening he divides the plunder." He calls Ephraim to his aid to occupy the springs of the Jordan, thereby cutting off communication between Canaan and Moab and completing the slaughter of the enemies.

And yet, whatever distinctions are found between the one redemption and the other, they always have the same purpose, namely, the revelation of God's virtues, the conversion of the people to the God of the fathers, the suppression of sin, the preservation of Israel, in a word, the knowledge of misery, redemption and gratitude.

4. DEBORAH AND BARAK

Judges 4 and 5

Of chariots, horses and heroes
Our enemy is stout;
We shall rest on the honor and greatness
Of God, who preserves us.

Ps. 20: 4a (Psalter of 1773)

The greatest possible diversity is to be observed in the visible world: in the realm of sound, in language and thought, in the field of the arts of whatever character, in a word, everywhere in the universe. But the thinking and inquiring mind everywhere seeks unity in diversity, reducing it to its simplest constituents, and finds that it consists of some few basic materials, sounds and forms that occur in all kinds of compositions and under all kinds of points of view.

It is no different in the spiritual world, no different in history. In every chapter of Israel's history at the time of Judges, for example, we have to speak of *sin, punishment, redemption* and *gratitude*, i.e., of the transgression of which Israel is guilty, of the suffering which it undergoes, of the chastening which paves the way to its redemption, and finally of redemption itself, with all that it entails.

In all this, however, a bare unchanged, i.e., monotonous repetition of what happened earlier is found exclusively *on the side of man*. While God never does the same thing twice, man always falls back into the same errors, the same sin, the same rut. Contemplation of the Lord's deeds puts the word of Paul on our lips : "O, the depth of the riches of the wisdom and knowledge of God! How unsearchable are His judgments, and untraceable His ways!" (Rom. 11: 33).

The observation that Israel falls again and again into previous sins within almost the same passage of time and in much the same way reminds us of the Savior's complaint about the unbelieving and perverse generation among whom He lived. That complaint is, as it were, the echo in the New Testament of the exclamation which Jehovah repeatedly sounded under the Old, viz. "How long will you refuse to keep My commandments and instructions?" (Ex. 16: 28; Luke 9: 41).

With the single exception of Gen. 5: 24, the well-known words "and he died" are expressed in the genealogy of the first humanity contained in Gen. 5 as an invariable conclusion as if a refrain of the lamentation of the sons of Adam, highly poetic and profoundly solemn in their appalling monotony. In this respect, there is no distinction between man and man, between one generation and another.

We find something similar in the book of Judges. Poignant yet full of earnestness and indescribably melancholy, the phrase rings in our ears, recurring and referring to the continuity of life estranged from God.

1. Israel's sin.

"The Israelites," we read in Judges 4: 1 as we read in v. 12 of the previous chapter and shall again in 10: 6, 13: 1, etc.: "again did evil in the sight of the LORD."

In this age as well, the consistency of life in sin is repeatedly interrupted by God's grace, its progress for a time even seemingly halted. And this redemption that God effects in the midst of His apostate people is preceded by initial repentance and followed by initial reformation. In other words, each time around God sets Israel before a new beginning and thereby opens the way to restoration.

Alas! All this belongs to those effects of common grace spoken of in the previous chapter, by which the possibility of future and perfect redemption is determined and moral destruction is prevented from bringing about man's ruin, but brings about no conclusive change either in the character of man's nature, in the purpose of his striving, or in the continuous course of his history. This grace curbs, suppresses, controls evil, and restrains the creature from surrendering to it wholly and for good, but does not eliminate evil.

Sin is like the horse in the Greek myth that causes a fountain to spring up by its hoof-beats. Once begun, the activity of sin continues until God has made in Christ, the second Adam, that wonderful new beginning by which man can be truly restored to the image of God, because the second Adam has not become like the first, a *living soul*, but a life-giving spirit, 1 Cor. 15: 45. Until then His redeeming activity does continually throw a dam into the stream of man's destruction, but behind that dam the water stands, then accumulates, and then climbs higher. Behold! it only gains in strength; soon it will flow not only against but along and over that dam. With irresistible violence it will soon drag away everything that has for a time impeded its course.

The great error in judging people, including ourselves, lies in this, that every action is overly considered in isolation. How foolish! There may be no visible connection between the bubbles that form in the standing water of ditch or pond, under the influence of heat, and if no gas is produced on a cold day, they are completely absent. But whether few or many in number, seen yesterday or today, they betray the fact that in the water or in the soil itself there are plant or animal substances in a state of decomposition.

Does sin cease to exist as soon as it ceases to express itself in words or deeds? With just as much justification, one might think that the king has left the palace as soon as he no longer shows himself on the balcony to the people or does not show himself at the window. As soon as an evil that might have made us fear for ourselves withdraws from the eyes of the world, the hope revives that it is at least on its way to disappearing for good. We know very well that a grain of wheat may have lain in the sarcophagus for ten, twenty centuries without losing its productivity. But unless we have adopted the lessons of history, yea also of our own experience, i.e., have learned not to stop at *sins* but to penetrate to *sin*, namely, to the root and source of evil, we are inclined to regard the wrong that for a time seemed unfruitful to be unfruitful as such.

History, experience, as has been said, teaches us something entirely different. The pious Norwegian princess Bridget, canonized[4] by Rome, at the age of sixty-eight was tormented by inclinations and persecuted by imaginations that had been completely suppressed early on by a life of deprivation and abstinence to such a degree that she seemed to have died to the flesh. God used this humbling experience as a blessed means to give her insight into the work of redemption as early as the thirteenth century,

---

[4] Hoedemaker adds the adverb "onbegrijpelijkerwijze," "incredibly," probably because he shared the view that Bridget was a proto-Protestant.

the century in which she lived, and to cause her to utter what only became more generally understood two or three centuries later.

The children of Israel carried on doing that which was evil in the eyes of the Lord "after Ehud died" (Judges 4: 1). Here, then, we have implicitly explained why the people, after remaining faithful to the service of Jehovah for forty years, once again sank back into idolatry. The nature of that people was not converted but only prevented from revealing itself. One can lift up a rock; one can even bring the water through pipes to the top floor of a house, the former by hand or with the aid of an implement, the latter by the well-known law applied in our waterworks; but gravity pulls the rock down, and the water of its own accord seeks its level as soon as the impediment is removed which, though it temporarily made it obey some other law, did not bring about a change in nature. That a people is subdued, or as Scripture says, feigns obedience, need not surprise us. This has been seen at all times to a greater or lesser degree. It applies to individuals and families as well as to entire nations.

The cause of amazement is only the fact that a single man, and then a man like Ehud, who was not under the guidance of the Holy Spirit to the same extent and in the same manner as other Judges, was able to exercise this effect. For the Judge possessed no office in civil government; he stood in no relation to the ordained priesthood. Very true. But he was the organ of Jehovah through whom redemption was brought about. And this redemption was not due to personal heroism but to the grace of God, and therefore stood in the closest connection to conversion, i.e., the return in any case from idolatry to God, and inseparably from this to the law, insofar as it could be maintained in the still abnormal state.

Among other nations, too, an individual man, as a result of personal qualities that make him stand out in the eyes of his tribesmen or peoples, often succeeds in having himself recognized as chief and raised on the shield. But the peculiarity in the Judges was precisely that they acted as reformers, either before or after redemption.

Neither shields, bows, daggers,
Brave peoples of war,
Wisdom, courage nor strength,
Can ever in battle

Deliver any prince
Apart from the Lord's power.

Psalm 33: 8 (Psalter of 1773)

Israel knew that. Israel had to know that, if the meaning of the work of God were not to be lost to it. The misery it had endured was still fresh in its mind. But inseparable from this was also the conviction that new deviation would result in new misery.

In 1 Sam. 16 we find an example of how the Judge was wont to act. From what is said of Deborah, it is evident that people came to the Judge in difficult cases to seek justice and to be taught the law. But in some cases he also appeared in every place his presence was required. When the rumor of some atrocity or other came to him – when it appeared, for example, that a tribe, a family, a city was indulging in some sin – he came clothed with authority derived from his relationship to the law, to Jehovah himself, and found support in the better disposition of the "faithful in the land" to administer justice and exercise judgment.

In the chapter just quoted we read, "So Samuel did what the LORD said, and came to Bethlehem. And the elders of the city came trembling to meet him and said, 'Do you come in peace?'" (v. 4). One man thus counted as the soul of the whole people. In him we find kingship, to speak by analogy with the priesthood, "not after the law of a carnal commandment" (Hebrews 7: 16, KJV), i.e., not by virtue of an office hereditarily possessed by him, but according to the law of an imperishable life, i.e., as a divinely ordained *personality*, elected, called and empowered to this end.

Take away Othniel, take away Ehud, and the moral and religious collapse follows which had long been prepared in secret and was only prevented by the power of their word, their example, their influence and their multifaceted activity.

We once observed a huge vessel on the ramp before it was launched. It rested in the trough in which it was set up on the heavy blocks that held up the keel, and was fastened with heavy ropes and chains from all sides. One hammer blow drove out the wedge that loosened all those ropes and blocks, and with a speed that multiplied by the moment, the hulk glided toward the element in which henceforth it was destined to move.

How big must the stone be that held up the rocks, the cracks and crevices of which long ago indicated the place where a landslide would take place? Take care should you have to pass below the threatening spot! Hold your breath! The slightest thing can hasten the fall of the whole. A pebble put in motion by a bird, the bang of a gun, the thump of a heavily loaded wagon can be fatal.

Ehud dies – and Israel proceeds to follow its sinful inclination. "Has a nation," asks the Lord in Jeremiah 2: 11, "ever changed its gods, though they are no gods at all? Yet My people have exchanged their Glory for useless idols." Miraculous, appalling blindness of sin. "When they chose new gods," says Deborah (Judges 5: 8), "then war came to their gates." So they *chose* them. Willfully and voluntarily they left the spring of living water to carve out troughs, broken troughs that hold no water (Jer. 2: 13).

If we need any further explanation of this sinful enterprise, a reason to explain what is so highly unreasonable, then this may be added to what has been said already. It was thoroughly pagan to think that every country had its own gods as well as its own kings who ruled it and exercised within its borders a power which they did not possess outside, an opinion also which was diametrically opposed to the God-concept of the patriarchs and of the Israelites. A God who is Creator of heaven and earth is the God of gods. "All nations are His." But as long as the revelation of Jehovah was limited to a particular land and a particular people, as long as Israel could not fulfill its proper calling to bring the words of God entrusted to it to the other nations as well, that long the same motive existed for it as, to a certain extent, existed for the settlers who inhabited the depopulated cities of Samaria and cultivated the desolate fields of the ten tribes, which, in the face of the adversity they encountered, moved them to ask for a priest from among the exiled who would teach them "the requirements of the God of the land" (2 Kings 17: 26). This was superstition, but a superstition into which the people estranged from God naturally progressed.

The very exclusiveness of Israel's religion provided an incentive to abandon it. It was so easy for the pagans to assign to the service of Jehovah a relative right. In fact, this was entirely in the spirit of their system. Against this generosity, Israelite thinking stood out unfavorably. Even Solomon fell into this snare of syncretism toward the end of his reign.

Ehud dies – and forgotten are the experiences of earlier years, forgotten the oppression, the distress, the salvation. The stream of destruction no longer finds an obstacle but drags along in its furious momentum everything that could have slowed its course.

It would have been terrible if Jehovah, after the repeated deviation, now withdrew His hand. The people would then have enjoyed peace like the pagans roundabout. Prosperity would then have been its portion. It would have rejoiced in unprecedented prosperity... but would forfeit its significance, lose its right to independent existence, and finally go down in unrestrained mixing with the nations.

Jehovah remembers the covenant and comes to His people with His judgments. Sin is followed, this time as well, by

2. Punishment

Israel does not sin cheaply. What the nations do with impunity, it is punished for very severely. Jehovah admittedly did not yet deal with it according to desert. The apostate people still remain in the land desecrated by their whoredoms. Only much later does the word go out: "What right has My beloved in My house?" (Jer. 11: 15).

God now punishes with compassion, as a father does. But by virtue of the connection that exists between the Lord's punishments and Israel's sins, it is now taken further along the road that leads to its utter rejection. The punishment is gradually *intensified*.

If the first enemy is from afar, the second from the immediate vicinity of the borders, then the third dwells within the land as it was originally given to Israel for inheritance. "Servants rule over us," we later hear the prophet Jeremiah lament; servants and enemies and archenemies likewise, we may say. A century earlier, Jabin, the wise one, was the head of the alliance of the Northern Canaanites. He was defeated at Lake Merom and his capital Hazor burned with fire, Joshua 11: 1–11. His descendant, bearing the same title, now emerged as an avenger of his lineage.

He himself lived at Hazor in the far north, in the same place where stood, and in part may still be found, the ruins of the former capital. But his warlord Sisera brought down most of later Galilee, the tribal territory of Naphtali, Zebulon and Issachar, and settled at Harosheth-hagoyim, "the forge of the nations." Nine hundred iron chariots with scythes in the axles were manufactured or kept there.

It was he who oppressed Israel, "harshly" we read (4: 3), this time not eight (3: 8) or eighteen (3: 14), but twenty years.

The message casts a veil over the suffering that the Lord's people were now enduring. Scripture does not serve to satisfy our curiosity. But the fact that Sisera is a Canaanite who suffered so much by the sword of Israel, and by right ought to have been eradicated, tells us, in connection with the expression "harshly oppressed," more than enough. Verily he spares not the enemy who is now in his power and at his mercy. And if we wish to infer anything more from the few details in the message, chapter 5, and the song of Deborah in the next chapter, we have only to divine what spirit animates the noblewomen of his regal mother. "Are they not finding and dividing the spoil?" ask the wise women in a consoling manner. "A girl or two for each warrior, a plunder of dyed garments for Sisera, the spoil of embroidered garments for the neck of the looter?" (Judges 5: 30).

The daughters of Israel and their possessions have not been safe in these hands. That ten thousand men, mainly from the oppressed tribes, stood ready to follow Barak despite fear of the great superiority, not least of the iron chariots, serves in part to prove that the oppressed had been brought to the brink of despair. But everything else we learn of the condition only serves to show us to what depths of misery Israel has sunk under this domination.

"Was there also a shield seen, or a spear among forty thousand in Israel?" exclaims Deborah. So the people are disarmed. Not for the first time, and not the last. Ehud made himself a sword (3: 16), which seems to indicate that Eglon had formerly taken the same precautions as Sisera does now. The Philistines will follow suit. Samson's hands fashion his only weapon, and later the fresh jawbone of a donkey serves that purpose.

Already at the beginning of the tribulation, before Deborah arose, "in the days of Samgar" who beat back an incursion of the Philistines without any other weapon than an oxgoad with a long iron spike (3: 31), "the highways were deserted and the travelers took the byways" (5: 6). There was, so to speak, no safety in the land. Each did what was right in his own eyes. There was no law but that of the strongest and of the craftiest.

The land is full of dark murderous caverns,
From whence violence cuts us with wound upon wound.
Psalm 74: 19 (Psalter of 1773)

Tribe against tribe, house against house, stranger against native, on every road a snare, a pack of robbers in every forest, every rock, gorge or mountain pass! Woe to man, woe to the land, when discipline is absent, when justice is not demanded and there is no one who gives to that justice a mouth to testify, lends it an arm and a sword to uphold itself.

In times like those described by Deborah, one gets to know man from his evil side and, going on experience, would be easily converted to Hobbes' doctrine that *egoism is the essence of man*. Homo homini lupus! Every man a wolf to his neighbor!

Sometimes it seems to come true. But we do not adopt it. Man is not a tamed wolf but the fallen image-bearer of God, who still exhibits the remnants of that image but cannot do without the discipline of the word and the working of common grace, if he is not to be controlled by that poisonous thing which, through the serpent that coiled itself around the tree of knowledge, injected in him, along with covetousness and pride, hatred of God and neighbor.

In her song (5: 10), Deborah calls upon the nobles and the judges, the laborers, the shepherds and the villagers (v. 11) to "recount the righteous acts of the LORD." In doing so she clearly implies that they each in their measure and in their way have suffered from the iniquity of men. But even here the pen cannot rest describing the sad condition of Israel as it passed under the judgment of God. The coming of the judgment of the Lord is like the unleashing of the elements; water, fire and storm-wind then conspire and threaten with destruction all that stands firm.

When Titus threw up his ramparts against Jerusalem, treachery blew around in the streets of the holy city; famine fell upon the sorely afflicted population; the sad scene was illuminated by burning buildings; fellow countrymen sharing the same fate came to blows in the face of the flames, and the plague rushed in to join the feast of death and destruction.

The trials, the punishments, the judgments never come alone. The Lord's judgment is not a wave that comes crashing against the shore, but a flood that pushes up the waves, one by one, in immeasurable rows, to be followed by still more – until God Himself says "enough!" and makes heard His word of power, "Thus far and no farther!"

Consider for a moment what sadness was involved in that lack of a brotherly bond and brotherly loyalty by which, according to the song of Deborah herself, Israel in the hour of redemption was prevented from advancing as a single man to the help of the Lord with the heroes (5:23). Reuben remained seated among the stalls of the flocks, his zeal expended in endless deliberations without power or purpose, in reflections that never proceeded to actions because self-interest always retained the decisive voice in his deliberations (vv. 15–16). Gilead remained beyond the Jordan. Dan in the ships, Asher at the sea places amid his dismantled fortresses and cities in ruins (v. 17). Meroz refused to come up. Of Judah and the southern tribes there is not even a mention. Nothing is heard of them, not even a word of complaint. They are completely out of sight.

But what does all this tell us? That unity is lacking, and with unity health. What was seen in Israel are the signs of approaching death. If a part of the body must be tied off or die by itself, if there is not enough warmth to cause the blood to flow from the ends of the body, then the people's life is not well, for that people is one.

Indeed, the symptoms of disease in the Israelite people at the time of Deborah and Barak are familiar enough to later times that everyone is able to grasp their significance. People complain about division, lament it, and know very well that it is inseparably accompanied by humiliation and weakness, the harbinger of certain destruction.

The tribes under the yoke of Jabin probably also knew this. Yet if change is to come, there is one thing to be convinced of, namely, that the symptom of disease cannot and ought not be combated directly, but rather in the underlying disease that it reveals. It does not benefit the fever sufferer to artificially warm the members that tremble and shiver from cold or to temper the heat that makes them glow by cool and refreshing drinks. For this brings about only relief, not recovery.

Let Israel return to God; let him remember the covenant made by Jehovah with the fathers, and a new life shall shimmer through him, a new strength shall awaken in him, he shall again feel himself one body with many members, joined together under one head.

But the saddest thing of all, and what makes Israel's condition, humanly speaking, utterly hopeless is not mentioned with a single word either in the messages in the 4th chapter or in the song in the 5th which explains them. The silence here is eloquent.

Of the *tabernacle*, the *priesthood*, the *high priest,* not a word! "In the five books of Moses, in the Sinaitic legislation," scoffs Wellhausen, "we find a complete description of the way in which the Jewish State should be arranged. There is nothing missing, neither in the laws, nor in the institutions, nor in the ordinances. Everything forms a closed system of religion and statecraft, so closely connected that one cannot be thought of without the other. But hardly have we come to the Age of the Judges when all this is as if blown away. Fiction gives way to reality."

It is, unfortunately, all too true. Not that the tabernacle and priesthood never existed. Evidence abounds that they did not fail even in the time of the deepest decline. Instead, it is that no power emanated from all this. With Eli we find the regular service of the tabernacle but also the indirect indication that the priesthood must have been in decline, since in him it passed from the line of Eleazar and Phinehas, to which Jehovah had attached His promises, to that of Ithamar.

The salt lost its savor.

The sanctuary is, as it were, the heart of Israel. But that heart ceased to beat; the only thing that could lend unity and strength was missing from the miraculously constituted people. For this very reason the Lord God had to work by other means, special means, and give the extraordinary office of the Judge as a gift of grace to Israel, as He later gave the Nazirite and then the Priest-Prophet Samuel for the salvation of the people.

But thus we gradually have arrived at what is to be discussed in the third place:

3. Redemption

"Then the Israelites cried out to the LORD" (Judges 4: 3), and the Lord heard them, we add in thought. We could also go further and say, "Even before they call, I will answer" (Isa. 65: 24).

Wonderful forbearance and grace of God!

That the Lord hears after repeated apostasy is already a great deal. The expression, "then cried out," conjures up before us the picture of a child who refused to listen to his father, was not restrained from evil by threat, remained insensitive even under light punishment, but once the punishment became aggravated and unbearable, first came to repentance, begged for forgiveness, and was immediately heard.

Jehovah does not punish out of a desire to afflict. He is readily forgiving. Once the proud neck is bent, once the hard heart is shattered, then the punishment has taken effect and the possibility of restoration is given. It proceeds with Israel as with David in the 32nd psalm. "I said," we read there in the 5th verse, "'I will confess my transgressions to the LORD.'" It is still only an intention. It had not yet come to the deed. "And You forgave the guilt of my sin." There is no interval, no transition, no time of waiting, of probation.

That the Lord hears when the sinner comes to Him impelled by need, is even more. Even man is inclined to reconciliation when the wrong that has been the cause of alienation is recognized, acknowledged, confessed and regretted. But the heart closes immediately when there is ground for the supposition that even now this reconciliation would not be sought if self-interest, requirement, necessity did not urge the acquisition of it.

How entirely different is Jehovah. To Him alone does one come "driven by need for help" (Ps. 146: 3, Psalter of 1773).

That the Lord is already preparing and effecting redemption before the cry of anguish of penitence is heard teaches us how God forgives: royally, divinely, not after man has taken the initiative, as if confession had to serve to bring about a change in the mood, the disposition of the Lord, but in the majestic repose of His decree according to which He continues to labor and by virtue of which, even before the hour of redemption has struck, He already prepared the means and instruments by which it is brought about.

Deborah, the wife of Lappidoth, or, as those who take these words – torch, spirit or glow – not as the name of a man but figuratively as a further indication of the character of the prophetess, Deborah, "a woman through whom holy zeal glows," has already begun to judge the children of Israel. They come to her tent on the mountain of Ephraim, between Barna and Bethel, to ask for law and justice.... That is already the beginning of redemption. It begins in Israel itself. Sisera and the iron chariots are only the hands of the clockwork controlled by the inner cogs of religious and moral life. When the Lord bestowed Deborah, in the essence of the matter He had already given an undeserved and unexpected outcome. As soon as the clouds have become full, they pour out torrents of rain; as soon as the law has done its work, the power of the Lord will be seen in the destruction of the enemies.

FROM OTHNIEL to Ehud to Deborah traces a descending line.

It is precisely in this that the Lord reveals His manifold wisdom; in this the humiliation of Israel is indicated. When religious life has sunk to the lowest level, God honors woman by putting her in man's place. She does not dwell on secondary causes but penetrates to the final cause; i.e., she lives not from the deliberations of the reasoning mind but by the utterances of feeling, the heart, intuition, the immediate awareness of the spiritual, the higher.

Already under the Old Testament, there was neither man nor woman in Christ. For woman also to have prophetic inspiration and a judicial vocation is the sign of the universal priesthood of believers under the Old Testament, a ready proof that faith, i.e., truth, freed woman in a region in which she was treated as a plaything or beast of burden, and in a time when she was not considered the equal of man. Yet we must beware of seeing in this choice of a woman, be it said with respect, an arbitrary decision of Jehovah, as if there were men who could have replaced her.

God never does anything that is unnecessary; He never breaks the order of things without cause. So in the choice of Deborah we see a proof that Israel has truly sunk to a low level, although we immediately add here that the Lord also reveals therein His omnipotence, clearly shows that He is bound to neither tribe nor class nor sex, and thereby also wishes to teach us that the prophetic office is the foundation and essence of the judgeship.

Here is a woman who cannot place herself at the head of the army, a woman who herself honors the orderings of God when she commands Barak to bring about the redemption of his people; not a heroine of freedom, not a Joan of Arc or a Kenau Simons Hasselaar, but one who prophesies, judges, and places herself in the background when the moment arrives in which the redemption Jehovah already initially wrought among his people will become visible.

The rabbis find in the name Lappidoth a poetic description of the name Barak (flash of lightning); on the basis of this similarity, they further assert that Deborah was Barak's wife. But the message in Judges 4: 6 makes a different impression. "She summoned Barak son of Abinoam from Kedesh in Naphtali," etc. Barak is of Kedesh in Naphtali, one of the tribes that suffered the most from Sisera; he is a man of faith, up to the task of savior.

The man also of weak faith? He does not doubt the divine calling. Nor does he shy away from the difficult and dangerous work assigned to him. He only fears that his own influence will not be great enough to draw the thousands of Israel to himself, unless, that is, the Greek translators are right in their explanatory addition when they have Barak answer: "If you will go with me, I will go, for I do not know the day when I will defeat Sisera," v. 8. Still, he felt the lack of prophetic inspiration and thus the need for clear guidance as to what he had to do, and how he was to do it.

A weak faith therefore, whereby in the consciousness of his own incapacity he dared not count on the gift of the Spirit, which would certainly have been provided directly to him had he exercised faith. Evidence that here as well a decline is to be noted. Othniel was animated by the Spirit of the Lord. Ehud received no outward calling; Barak would not have come if the word of the Lord had not been made known to him from the mouth of Deborah.

ON MOUNT TABOR the ten thousand men stand ready, an army through which God intends to effect redemption. The nucleus of that army is formed by Naphtali and Zebulun, 4: 6, 10. These tribes, as has been said, had suffered most from the enemy. Yet many had also come up from Benjamin, Issachar, and Ephraim, 5: 14, 15. Surprising in this regard is the announcement in v. 14 which shows Amalek at the vanguard of the enemies. Could Sisera have been an Amalekite? From the first attack it endured in the desert, Israel always suffered from Amalek.

In the plain at Taanach, on the waters of Megiddo, 5: 19, where the alliance of the Canaanites in the north was crushed by Joshua, where the great battlefield of and for Israel has always been and, in view of Rev. 16: 16, the final battle will be settled, the enemy is now gathered. He counts on victory. One of the noblewomen of Sisera's mother – by a truly Oriental trait, his wife is not thought of – married life is not so construed as to present her as the mourner – can think of no other reason as to why the tidings of the battlefield are not forthcoming than that "The spoils must be divided after all." Which is why in the song of Deborah, with a trace of fine irony, she is called "the wisest of her noblewomen" (5: 29, Dutch translation).

He might also safely count on victory, for no more favorable opportunity could be afforded him to deploy his full fighting force than precisely in this broad and clean plain of Esdrelon. After all, Barak was completely surrounded on the Tabor, rising like a solitary cone in the middle of the plain. Perhaps it was this latter consideration that compelled Sisera to abandon another tactic. At least this can be inferred from the promise expressed in Judges 4: 7.

Foolish Barak! Truly, the heart of the bravest in the little army of Israel might well succumb when it saw below it in the plain those nine hundred dreaded iron chariots arranged in the most perfect order, braced like an impenetrable wall of movable scythes. Once they had failed to drive out the Canaanites, "because they had chariots of iron" (1: 19). Now they are set to hurl themselves down on them, facing death and destruction!

No, God also chastises His people by His benefactions. Everyone in that army who exercises faith knows that God has drawn Sisera there! The battlefield becomes a field of slaughter. The gods on which the enemy relies become his destruction. The Lord Himself calls to them as in Micah 4: 11–12: "But now many nations have assembled against you, saying, 'Let her be defiled, and let us feast our eyes on Zion.' But they do not know the thoughts of the LORD or understand His plan, for He has gathered them like sheaves to the threshing floor." Or, as in Isaiah 8: 9: "Huddle together, O peoples, and be shattered; pay attention, all you distant lands; prepare for battle, and be shattered; prepare for battle, and be shattered!"

The Lord thunders from the heights. The waters of the stream Kison are swollen with heavy rains. Hail and tempest terrify horses, charioteers and warriors together. Terror! Run for your lives! The God of Joshua lives. Those very chariots on which it relied, and which Israel feared, bring about the downfall of Sisera's well-equipped army.

The farther north one goes into the plain of Esdrelon, the narrower it becomes, until not far from the place where Harosheth-hagoyim (cf. 4: 2) was thought to be found, next to the brook Kishon, almost no space is left for a road, in some places not even for a footpath. There riders and horses dashed together at a furious pace and in irreparable confusion, through and over and with each other, into the watery grave into which Israel's enemies were now swallowed for the second time. "From the heavens the stars fought; from their courses they fought against Sisera. The River Kishon swept them away, the ancient river, the River Kishon. March on, O my soul, in strength! Then the hooves of horses thundered—the mad galloping of his stallions" (Judges 5: 20–22).

The song of Deborah and Barak echoes that of Moses and Miriam: "The enemy declared, 'I will pursue, I will overtake. I will divide the spoils; I will gorge myself on them. I will draw my sword; my hand will destroy them.' But You blew with Your breath, and the sea covered them. They sank like lead in the mighty waters" (Ex. 15: 9–10).

Not only was redemption wrought on this day, but that redemption paved the way for Jabin's downfall (Judges 4: 24).

How highly poetic is the turn with which the singers, after the climax of the song in 5: 22, immediately turn to Meroz, a city the name and place of which cannot even be found, with the dire word:

"'Curse Meroz,' says the angel of the LORD. 'Bitterly curse her inhabitants; for they did not come to help the LORD, to help the LORD against the mighty.'"

An appalling sin was the restraint of Meroz, which – although probably located in the middle of the oppressed lands – refused to join Barak's army; it was the sin of the eldest son in the parable, of the royal officer at the redemption of Samaria in the time of Elisha, of the Pharisee who says to himself, "If this man were a prophet, He would know who this is and what kind of woman is touching Him" (Luke 7: 39).

The city in which one spirit moves the people, one need presses upon it, one salvation awaits it, yet does not know how to sympathize and commiserate, is like the tree in the spring which, when every branch and twig are greening, does not bud but in its stolidity bears a proof of its barrenness, and already carries within itself the curse pronounced upon it.

4. Gratitude

What is gratitude? A feeling of appreciation for benefits enjoyed which finds expression in words or actions? That is only one of the forms in which it manifests itself. It is the bond that binds the afflicted, the redeemed, to his redeemer and benefactor, compelling and obliging him not only to appreciation but also to devotion.

The Heidelberg Catechism brings under gratitude everything that follows salvation and results from it. Its first, most immediate expression is praise, thanksgiving! Surely the purpose and the fruit of salvation is to know God and make God known, to magnify His virtues, to glorify His name.

The afflicted one exalts the Lord in his song. "Praise befits the upright." They naturally reach for the lute and harp, and in their singing pour out their full hearts before God and men, to praise the virtues and deeds of the Lord among the children of men, Ps. 107. And so, in the church's treasure of hymns we have the blossom and first fruit of the new and higher life of the children of God. Had Israel's psalms and hymns of praise been withheld from us, that life in its true nature and unfathomable depth would have remained largely hidden from us. We would have come to know of it only through its manifestation in deeds. But now it is laid bare before us, and we know that our predecessors in the race to the finish have known the same God to whom our hearts go out; have felt the same beatitude that we partake of or wish to partake of; possessed the same precious faith with us and did not dwell on deliverance from earthly pressures and salvation from temporal distress, but penetrated to the spiritual background of it all, the restoration of fellowship broken by sin.

Even if the accounts of Israel's history were mutilated or reworked, its psalms are neither one nor the other, and in them we have the quintessence of that history, a hallmark of its proper meaning. Israel's prophets are also its poets; they have seen what was hidden from others, and later express what others feel.

"On that day Deborah and Barak son of Abinoam sang this song" (5: 1ff.). That song, like the song of Moses, resonates in our hearts.

There is only one stanza that can make us wonder whether this Israelite woman was sometimes animated by a spirit other than that of Christ and His congregation in the days of the New Covenant. Jael, the wife of

Heber the Kenite, is called blessed because it was given to her to smite the oppressor of Israel, when as a fugitive he came to seek refuge in her tent, and a hospitable reception was accorded him, vv. 25–27.

Consider closely the fact glorified by the prophetess in this manner. The Kenites, the Midianite kinsmen of Moses who visited him in the desert and, encouraged to do so by the man of God, joined the host after the conquest of Jericho, had marched southward with the children of Judah and settled near Hebron, Judges 1: 16. We later find a line of Kenites in the vicinity of Harosheth-hagoyim. True to its ancestral way of life, it lives in tents. Israel's oppressors leave it unharmed, a proof that their lust is not aroused by what the Kenites possess, nor their enmity by what the Kenites are. Neither in the eyes of the Canaanites nor in reality were they merged with the people of Jehovah. Nor were they later, nor are they to this day.

A miraculous appearance in history, those Kenites! A wandering people they were and remained, like their fathers before them. Where we meet the Kenite, we discover in him the desert-dweller who is in his place beside Jehu on the chariot in which he goes to Samaria to execute the judgment of God on the house of Ahab; but not in his place within the walls of Jerusalem, where he temporarily takes refuge, yet without conforming to the customs of the townspeople in whose midst he dwells, 2 Kings 10: 15, Jer. 35.

That Jael reaches for one of the iron spikes that hold the cords by which the simple covering of the tent is fastened all around, when she saw the enemy of Israel there helpless at her feet – that the thought arises in her to get him out of the way, and that this thought determines her action, is very understandable in a Kenite, and in a woman. She acts as avenger of Israel in the character in which the song of Deborah views the defeat and downfall of Jabin's army. "Praise the LORD," read the opening words of that song, "for the *avenging* of Israel" (Judges 5: 2, KJV).

We only know that for twenty years Sisera was the instrument of the violent oppression of Israel, 4: 3, during which time Jael would have witnessed horrors without number, heartbreaking scenes. Her woman's heart rebelled especially against this man who feared neither God nor any man, and who was thereby the nerve, indeed the soul of all that was ever undertaken against Israel and perpetrated on the virgins and the graybeards, the men and the women of a people who, even in their deep humiliation, remained the people of God to her, year after year, day after day. It is love for the oppressed, indignation on account of the oppression, hatred of the oppressor, that prevents any feeling from coming to mind except the one which inspired the familiar deed.

Some scholars hypothesize that Jael's intention, when she saw Sisera come to her and she harbored him, was pure, but that later, under the influence of the Spirit of God, she acted contrary to the compassion that first moved her and the customs of her people and the immutable requirement of the moral law which prescribes fidelity and truth. To save the character of Jael, there is here attributed to the Lord even that which must be put to the account of man.

No. Only a woman, a woman like Jael, a Kenite woman, who has suffered so much in and with others, is capable of working out the salvation of Israel by such means. Woman, in general, knows no secondary considerations; she knows only her goal, and also allows herself to be completely controlled by that goal. It is that goal, that goal and the outcome both, that are praised by Deborah. Here there is no question of blessing in the higher, spiritual sense usually attached to this word. Jael is blessed above *tent-dwelling* women, i.e., the women of her tribe. In what that woman did, Deborah sees the disposition of the Lord, the fulfillment of her word to Barak, and the good hand of the Lord over His people.

What would have availed the defeat of His hosts if the ringleader had not been removed? It is the Canaanite, the Amalekite, who is here exterminated. "So may all Your enemies perish, O LORD! But may those who love You shine like the sun at its brightest" (Judges 5: 31).

5. GIDEON

Judges 6–8

You have too many people.

Judges 7: 2

At Ophrah in western Manasseh, not far from the border of Ephraim, in the days of Joash head of the Abiezrites, there was located a well-nigh inaccessible height where the people of this place or region sought to shelter wife and child as well as livestock and property, whensoever an enemy invasion forced them to do so, for as long as the invasion lasted, while in the narrow passes and on the steep slope they defended both themselves and their own against an overpowering enemy.

How this unfolded, the historian has not explicitly informed us. But we can imagine once we realize that entire hordes and tribes of desert dwellers, well over a hundred thousand warriors strong, crossed the Jordan year in, year out, to plunder the land and take everything of the harvest or livestock that lay within their reach.

Joash at least had to mourn the loss of sons seized in the defense of the entrances of the fortress, who were carried to the enemy's headquarters at Tabor and slaughtered (Judges 8: 18). His family was certainly not the only one to have thus been plunged into mourning.

On the fortified height here spoken of stood an altar of Baal with a gigantic image of Astarte, the moon goddess, with or without a forest (for the word "forest" is also used where there is mention only of the tree which by certain carved features was dedicated to the deity, or of the column which depicted or represented her). In other words, following the example of the pagan inhabitants they had placed both that stronghold and the entire region under the protection of Canaan's gods.

The Jebusites, for example, had brought their gods onto the walls of the fortress when David was preparing to conquer it. David called them the "blind and lame" (2 Sam. 5: 6ff.). He knew that an idol is nothing, 1 Cor. 8: 4. Israel had learned to sing:

Their idols are silver and gold,
Made by the hands of men.

They have mouths, but cannot speak;
They have eyes, but cannot see;
They have ears, but cannot hear;
They have noses, but cannot smell;
They have hands, but cannot feel;
They have feet, but cannot walk;
They cannot even clear their throats.
Those who make them become like them,
As do all who trust in them.
O Israel, trust in the Lord!
He is their help and shield.

Ps. 115: 4–9

But what a startling revelation of Israel's deep decay at Ophrah we receive from this perspective, whereby the people of the living God know no better refuge than the same gods the futility of which Jehovah had demonstrated before all observers two centuries before, at the crossing of the Jordan, the taking of Jericho, in the battle of Gibeon and Megiddo.

Demonstrated? For we read in Judges 1: 27: "At that time Manasseh failed to drive out the inhabitants of Beth-shean, Taanach, Dor, Ibleam, Megiddo, and their villages; for the Canaanites were determined to dwell in that land."

Precisely. We see here how sin begets sin. The expression "for the Canaanites were determined to dwell in that land" at the conclusion of the verse just quoted clearly indicates that they had developed greater power in the area of Manasseh than elsewhere, that here, in other words, they could lay down the law. As long as Manasseh did not recognize that *its own unbelief* prevented it from taking possession of the inheritance appointed to it in the power of God, the temptation was open to attribute to the power of Baals and Astaroths what was due to its own fault.

Idolatry must truly be deeply ingrained if, even in times of severe strain and bitter suffering, one knows or seeks no refuge other than in those same abominations which brought the judgment of reprobation upon all Canaan; deeply ingrained, if a people have the courage to demand from a father, the head of the family, the life of a son, perhaps the only one left to him, because he had stood up for the honor of Jehovah, the God of the fathers, who had wrought deliverances and to whose special intervention they owed the land they inhabited.

But from all this there is something for us to learn, not only concerning Manasseh or Abiezer, or even concerning man as such, but concerning God in His being and works. In a previous chapter we saw that the relation in which Jehovah stands to Israel, according to the nature of the covenant, is determined by Israel's relation to the law. Each time we find the word of David fulfilled: "To the faithful You show Yourself faithful, to the blameless You show Yourself blameless; to the pure You show Yourself pure, but to the crooked You show Yourself shrewd" (Ps. 18: 25–26).

While in His being God is immutable, in His appearance He must change when man changes. A father who makes the disobedient child experience his displeasure does not cease to love or to be a father. The same love that, when the child was obedient, made itself known in a smile of affection, a kind word, a caress, a gift, now reveals itself in the form of wrath in the punishment that the child suffers, in the estrangement that his wrongness caused.

It is unnecessary to dwell on all this; it lies in the nature of things.

In Judges 6–8 we learn not only that God's being is unchangeable but that His plan, His idea of redemption is likewise.

An earthly father, to whom we have compared Jehovah, although he always continues to love his child, is entirely determined in his mood, his dealings, his actions and his activity toward that child by the way in which that child behaves. It is different with the Lord God. He majestically goes on doing His work, demonstrating His grace, readying redemption, even when, or as long as, man does not know Him, does not acknowledge Him, does not bow before Him.

We see something of this in the love of the mother who, even though the good-for-nothing son has done enough to break her heart, and even though he has left her in misery, not only leaves a place in her heart but also in her care, and is always deliberating how she will arrange one thing and another to his pleasure and for his sake against the day when she will be allowed to take the prodigal into her arms again.

There is, for example, the touching story of a mother in Scotland whose only daughter had chosen the way of sin and could be seen wearing the prostitute's garb on the streets of the capital. How, after every attempt to bring her child back to her peaceful home and to the path of virtue had been met with unwillingness, she kept the door unlocked, the light burning, and the room heated in winter, for years on end, because the unfortunate one might sooner or later come to herself and realize her disastrous condition, and then, if she lacked the courage to flee to her offended mother, fall prey to despair and make an end of her sad life. Her precautions, which so many had mocked or resented, were finally rewarded! Incomprehensible motherly love and motherly care, which, independent of all that the child is or does, always remains the same!

Inadequate reflection, we may add, of the love of God for His own, demonstrated "even when they were still sinners," when they served idols, when they remained unrepentant and did not ask after Him. "I call you by name; I have given you a title of honor, though you have not known Me," said God to Cyrus, his anointed (Isa. 45: 4), and says to everyone who becomes a partaker of the heavenly calling.

There are fixed stars so far removed from our entire solar system that the astronomer who considers them with the trained eye can never detect any change in them. Indeed, they seem to come no closer when the earth in its orbit around the sun has reached the point closest to the object of contemplation. In relation to those stars, ninety-five million miles on this side or ninety-five million miles on the other side of the sun make no difference.

This image presents itself to our attention when we see that the entire process of Israel's history is governed by God's counsel and will concerning our redemption. "For as the heavens are higher than the earth, so My ways are higher than your ways and My thoughts than your thoughts" (Isaiah 55: 9).

We see this in Israel's sin and punishment. And no less in its redemption.

1. Its sin.

"And the land had rest for forty years" (5: 31). That is how long the land rested after the first deliverance by Othniel (3: 11), and how long it would rest after Gideon (8: 28), while for Deborah and Barak a twice forty-year rest went before (3: 30), and for Judah at the time of Jephthah and afterward, a forty-year tribulation would follow.

Is this number meaningless, or is it the expression of an idea of God? No doubt the latter, and in passing be it said also indirectly, a proof not only of the unity of the book of Judges, questioned as it is by many scholars, but also of the unity of Scripture. The number forty denotes the age of transition, whether this is the transition to judgment or to redemption. Both, therefore, are only provisional and as such are for man an age of trial or temptation. Anyone who takes the trouble to check all the places in Holy Scripture where the base number four occurs will find that it is the expression of earth, space, man and the human factor in revelation and, as a result, will be on the way to find either the above or a similar explanation for the number forty.

Here we confine ourselves to factual occurrences. The duration of the rainfall at the downfall of the first world, Gen. 7: 12; of Moses' sojourn on the mountain in the presence of God, Exod. 24: 18; of the absence of the twelve spies, Num. 14: 34; of the Lord's temptation in the wilderness, Matt. 4: 2; of the time between the resurrection and the ascension, Acts 1: 3; of the judgment on the apostate people in the wilderness of Paran, Num. 14: 33; the four hundred years which passed after the covenant with Abraham and before the entry into Canaan, Gen. 15: 13, cf. Exod. 12: 40; the one hundred twenty, that is, three times forty years in which God's forbearance bore with Noah's contemporaries, Gen. 6: 3; the four times four hundred, that is sixteen hundred stadia of blood flowing in Rev. 14: 20; and all possible combinations in which this number occurs, furnish proof that we are dealing here with one of the data which determine the course of history; that the revelation both of man's sin and of God's righteousness, just as the coming forth of the leaves and blossoms of some plants (although unlike them, not under the law of natural necessity), is the fruit not of chance or of arbitrariness but of the revelation of a higher law in the spiritual world, namely, the law according to which God works.

The forty-year rest being alternated by an era of tribulation, for example, is a clear proof of the inadequacy, the provisional nature of the redemption that God brought about through Barak and Deborah. Sin and affliction stand to one another as root to fruit, as cause to effect. Now salvation is complete and lasting only when, with affliction, sin is also removed or reversed.

It matters little on which side that redemption begins. To the stricken one lowered through the roof, the Savior says first, "Son, your sins are forgiven!" and then "Get up, pick up your mat, and go home" (Mark 2: 5, 11). By contrast, the blind man's eyes are opened before Jesus asks him, "Do you believe in the Son of Man?" (John 9: 7, 35). But that it is possible to be initially saved from some of the consequences of sin without becoming a partaker of full salvation is shown by the words of the Savior to the sick man at the bathwater in Bethesda: "Stop sinning, or something worse may happen to you!" (John 5: 14). Besides, it lies in the nature of things. Only when we have obtained "the redemption of our bodies" (Romans 8: 23) is God's work for and in us complete.

Israel, through Deborah and Barak, as before in the days of Ehud and Othniel, was brought back under the discipline of the word and immediately delivered from the hand of "those who hate him" (Ps. 68: 1). But this did not bring the people to another life, under a new covenant.

What is life? Activity from an internal principle, in keeping with the nature and extending to the purpose of the animated whole in which that life is found, as a principle of growth and of show of force. It is distinguished, among other things, from everything that is mechanical, put into motion from the outside, and which automatically comes to a standstill once the force communicated to it has run its course. A stone is hurled high into the air, but from the moment it leaves the sling it already comes under the influence of gravity, which finally and in fact quite speedily overcomes the communicating force that temporarily propelled it.

Carnal Israel was under the law of sin, of temptation, of habit, of the flesh. God temporarily conquered the power of evil and placed the people at the entrance of a better time and a different life. Not even forty years have passed, however, and already the labor of the Lord's mercy and forbearance must be replaced by the revelation of His wrath, that is, of His justice. Forgotten is the previous distress, forgotten are the Lord's benefits. His mercy leads not to repentance but to hardening. If this continues, the people are lost, sinking completely into nature-service. Hear what the people say: "I will go after my lovers, who give me bread and water, wool and linen, oil and drink" (Hosea 2: 4).

And so the Lord says, "Therefore, behold, I will hedge up her path with thorns; I will enclose her with a wall, so she cannot find her way. She will pursue her lovers but not catch them; she will seek them but not find them. Then she will say, 'I will return to my first husband, for then I was better off than now'" (Hosea 2: 5–6). But He who saves is the same as He who punishes; both actions stem from the same principle, have the same purpose, and serve the same plan of redemption.

2. Misery

According to an ancient legend, the Roman Sibyl, i.e., the sacred prophetess of Cumae in Italy, came to Tarquinius II with nine books, filled with oracles and prophecies, for which she demanded an exorbitant price. When the king refused to negotiate, she burned three books, asking as much for the six as before for the nine. Tarquinius was again unwilling to discuss the sale, so she again burnt three books. Only then did the fear that another refusal would make him lose everything move him to meet her demands without further ado, so that in the end he was in much worse shape than he would have been if he had complied immediately.

Tarquinius in this meaningful story is the picture of the sinner who lightly rejects the offer made to him, the demand made upon him, and must at last bow down with the conviction that his unwillingness made him gain nothing, but forfeit much.

As Israel again falls away, the punishment is again aggravated. True, this time the tribulation does not last more than seven years, but it is also of such a nature that the people would have been utterly ruined if the Lord had not provided an expedited outcome. "And if you reject My statutes," said the Lord in the desert, "despise My ordinances, and neglect to carry out all My commandments, and so break My covenant, then this is what I will do to you: I will bring upon you sudden terror, wasting disease, and fever that will destroy your sight and drain your life. You will sow your seed in vain, because your enemies will eat it. And I will set My face against you, so that you will be defeated by your enemies. Those who hate you will rule over you, and you will flee when no one pursues you" (Lev. 26: 15–17).

This threat was fulfilled when Israel was "greatly impoverished" because of the eastern Midianites, Judges 6: 6. Despite the natural protection of the Jordan River where the enemy could only cross the so-called "fords" in a few places, despite the strong, almost impregnable fortifications to be found especially in the mountainous regions, Israel succumbed to a people it had reduced to subjection two centuries earlier when it was still wandering in the desert Paran, Num. 31: 7. A mixed population of wandering herding tribes came not to possess the land, not to settle in the habitations of Israel, but to massacre and plunder it.

Locusts form one of the most terrible plagues in the East. "The land before them is like the Garden of Eden, but behind them, it is like a desert wasteland—surely nothing will escape them" (Joel 2: 3). This plague can be compared to the now seven consecutive years of repeated incursion of the desert dwellers, including Israel's ancient enemies, the Amalekites. The people are not oppressed but starved, ruined in every respect. To what end did they sow, when there was the certainty that others would reap? To what purpose do they labor while lacking all confidence? Israel does not pay tribute but has become a slave who must serve the uncivilized peoples of the East without pay, peoples who ask only for booty and have not even learned to save out of precaution and self-interest what could be of service to them in future years, but who with the fruit also annihilate the tree. What Israel preserves must be hidden away with deliberation, often before it is ripe, in burrows and carefully covered subterranean passages.

Is it any wonder that Gideon, called "strong hero" by the stranger who settled under the oak tree near Ophrah, feels all the humiliation of his labor? He threshed wheat not on the threshing floor in the open field but at "the winepress," to "hide" it from the face of the Midianites, Judges 6: 11. That is the work of the slave, the sign of Israel's deep fall, and as such a curse, a seal of its rejection. God has forsaken His people. It has become Lo-Ammi, no longer my people, Hosea 1: 9.

That thought is deflating. Soon he and all his countrymen and tribesmen and villagers will seek to protect with their blood themselves and their own, even that which will be scarcely sufficient to preserve them in life. What violence cannot accomplish, cunning and treachery will. Under such circumstances, where are pride and confidence; where are displays of strength, courage, faith and hope?

"All worshipers of images are put to shame—those who boast in idols" (Ps. 97: 7).

And Jehovah has given his people into the hand of the Midianites! This tribulation is His work.

And Jehovah remembers the covenant, and does not chastise the children of men from the heart! Surely, the blessings and the punishments of the Lord come from the same source and have the same purpose.

One of the stories told by the well-known evangelist Dwight Moody transports us to the beach where a large crowd had gathered to witness the calamity that had befallen a ship near the shore. The doomed vessel was already sinking below the water line and a large part of the crew, after struggling for a shorter or longer time with the high rolling waves and with death, disappeared into the depths. A single stout swimmer, however, approached the beach. He is watched with bated breath as he comes closer and closer, sometimes disappearing into the deep whirlpools and floating seaward, sometimes carried on the waves, but who, as one can clearly see, is almost completely exhausted and now and then seems to be on the verge of giving up the impossible and submitting to the inevitable.

The spectators are powerless. Among them no one is found who is up to the task of offering any assistance to the unfortunate man who arouses all pity. Yes, there is one, an experienced sailor of stout stature, who has already more than once been the means of saving human lives. He stands there, continuously keeping his eye on the drowning man, but otherwise without giving a single sign of life. A dull murmur indicates the dissatisfaction felt because of his attitude, while the glances that are occasionally cast upon him express the expectation that this time, too, he would offer salvation.... A few moments dallying and the fate of that unfortunate one would be decided for good. Behold, he no longer struggles. He lacks even the strength to utter a cry of despair ... he sinks away .... Nay, his savior is with him, has seized him, and lays him down unconscious as he gains dry land, where skillful hands are already busy reviving the spirits of life.

It was not fear, not lack of sympathy, but only the knowledge that the shipwrecked man could not be saved if he still had enough strength to drag his rescuer into the depths with him, that moved the latter to stand so long from afar, to wait so long with the help that could only be given in the extremity.

The latter is what we wish to apply from this image to the ways God keeps with His people. The Lord too awaits the extremity. Israel must no longer be in a position to resist its Redeemer. Seemingly left to itself, a plaything of the enemy, a sure prey to destruction, there is an eye that watches it and a hand outstretched to its aid. God knows its distress, its danger, and stands ready to help.

Tribulation is only the ploughshare that tears open the hard ground, in order for the seed of humility to be cast therein and the fruit of salvation to be borne.

3. Redemption

The work of salvation is like building a house on swampy ground. There is much labor to be done before the actual building can rise. The ground is cleared and the foundations laid down on a floor of upright piles, of which only the tops are visible.

If God wants to redeem a people or a person from the consequences or punishments of sin, then He lays the foundations, hidden from the eye of the beholder, in true self-knowledge, humility and heartfelt conversion. While one asks whether the Lord has forgotten to be merciful, and while he shrinks away under the lashes of the floggers, the actual and most difficult work has already begun. Not only is He working in secret to bring into readiness the instruments by which the goal is to be accomplished, but He is also working to pave and prepare the place where He will use them.

The Savior appears at the first Passover after He is revealed to Israel, in "my Father's house" (John 2: 16) to "purify the sons of Levi" (Malachi 3: 3) and "bring justice to the nations" (Isaiah 42: 1), the nations for whom Israel has no place in the courts of his God. One hoped, expected – and, it was believed, nothing else was needed – the overthrow[5] of Roman authority, the coming of the kingdom of God, the kingdom of peace, of God Himself to rule over His people. Is there no one, then, who has an eye for the striking fact that this work is in full swing as Jesus wove his

[5] The original text reads "onderwerping aan" (submission to), which is contrary to the line of thought here. Most likely this is a typographical error, and the text should read "omverwerping van" (overthrow of), which is what we use here.

whip of cords? The judgment begins, not in the governor's palace, but in the house of God, not with the Italian Regiment (cf. Acts 10: 1), but among the elders of Israel.

So it was in the days of the Midianite tribulation. From the depths the people cried out for salvation to the unknown God who had made Himself known to their fathers. The harvest is ripening. The Passover feast is imminent. The enemies are ready to cross the Jordan. But Jehovah will show that He, from of old Israel's Redeemer and King, is still the same as in the days of old, that He has very well heard the cries of His people, cf. Ex. 3: 7. He has risen to help ... and sends not a judge, not a warrior hero, but a *prophet,* Judges 6: 8.

To what end? To work the very first thing required to salvation, knowledge of misery and therefore also knowledge of truth. Not only had the people deviated from the ways of the Lord. A judge who administered and upheld the law would then have been sufficient. But it had sunk so deeply that it no longer knew how to distinguish truth from error, religion from idolatry. The key of knowledge had been lost. "Therefore I have hewn them by the prophets," says Jehovah (Hosea 6: 5), "I have slain them by the words of My mouth, and My judgments go forth like lightning."

It is this operation that God is now conducting on His Israel. The man of God goes from tribe to tribe, from place to place, pointing out to the people the true cause of their misery. He has no other calling. There is nothing in his preaching of redemption, of salvation. On the contrary, his word is apt to pitch them in despair. God alone can save, and this God they have angered and rejected!

Yet the few who, as "the quiet in the land," have kept alive the memory of Israel's past and proudly expected a better future from everything that seemed to argue against it, saw in the appearance of this prophet proof that Jehovah was still interceding with his people, and a harbinger of better times.

And let us thank God heartily,
His Word again possessing.
Summer is even at our door.[6]

Luther's faith was expressed in the chant from which these words are taken, when the first Dutch martyrs Hendrik Vos and Jan Van Essen sealed the testimony of truth with their martyrdom. What the great Reformer uttered certainly lived in the hearts of many in the Israel of Gideon's day (cf. Zech. 11: 11). The name of this man of God has not been preserved. Of the effect of his preaching, nothing is reported to us. We only know that it was in the closest connection with what else was seen in Israel and performed in Ophrah-Manasseh.

The word that makes the guilty people see a judgment in their suffering is a word of hope. He who smites can also heal; He who surrenders His Israel to the enemies is also powerful to deliver from their hand. Did we speak of preaching that gives way to despair? As soon as one gets God in view, hope revives, even if one is not aware of it, or at least does not dare to acknowledge it.

The same reasoning with which the Savior refutes the Sadducee is also valid against despondency and despair. "He is not the God of the dead, but of the living" (Matth. 22: 32). Whoever stands in relation to the Eternal Living One must possess eternal life. The immutable God is also the all-knowing, the all-powerful, the all-wise, the faithful one.

In the preaching of the justice of God lay the same comfort that Rabbi Akiba, according to a profound story in the Talmud, drew from the judgment on the ruins of Jerusalem. Rabbi Elijah wept when he saw a fox ambling on the demolished walls of the holy city; but Rabbi Akiba laughingly asked, "Why did you weep at this sight, O master in Israel?" "It is written," was the reply, "'For the sake of Mount Zion, which is destroyed, on which the foxes run'" (Lamentations 5: 18). "This gladdens me," Akiba then said, "if God's threats are fulfilled, his promises will not miss their fulfillment." The prophet is only a forerunner of the judge, the savior, whom God has chosen.

---

[6] From verse 12 of *Flung to the Heedless Winds* by Martin Luther (1523), translated by John A. Messenger (1843).

1. Who is the judge?
2. Where does his work begin? What does it prepare the way for?

1. One finds that judge in Manasseh, the tribe perhaps more entangled in idolatry than any other.

God, who calls Luther from the monastery and arrests Paul on the road to Damascus, knows how to bring forth from the house of Joash, however small among the thousands of his tribe, the guide who will pasture his people Israel. Othniel the prince of Judah was succeeded by Ehud from Benjamin; Ehud was succeeded by a woman in union with Barak from Naphtali; succeeding these, the poorest of the least considerable line from Israel's smallest tribe, Judges 6: 15. As grace descends deeper to seek her servants, to that same degree she also shines more gloriously. She truly descends here. This is evident not only in the choice of Gideon but also *in the manner in which he was called.*

Othniel felt the prompting of the Holy Spirit when he acted to judge Israel. Ehud responded to an inner voice. For Barak it was enough to learn through the prophetess the task to which the Lord had called him. But Gideon needed the appearance of the angel of the Lord, and more than one miraculous sign.

How often do we, men, misconstrue things! The more extraordinary and wonderful are the means by which it pleases the Lord to work or strengthen faith, the greater a privilege we consider it. As if the Lord Jesus had not said to Thomas, "Blessed are those who do not see and yet believe" (John 20: 29). Was it a privilege for Peter that the vision of the sheet with the unclean animals fell to him? It was a proof of the Lord's condescending goodness, which even by such means shames his unbelief and removes his misunderstanding. But it would have argued for the apostle's spiritual insight if less had been enough to bring him into conformity with the Lord's intentions.

It is necessary to point this out, because otherwise one would easily take for an ascent what we have to see as a descent. One falls so lightly into the opinion as if the revelation Othniel received were lower than that with which Gideon was endowed. The opposite is true. If the latter received it, it was precisely because he needed more to come to the exercise of faith; consequently, he stood lower. Gradually, the truth expressed by the Apostle in 1 Cor. 1: 27–28 receives further confirmation.

However, as this becomes clearer to us, we have to guard against a new misunderstanding to which we, one-sided creatures, so lightly fall, viz., that the insusceptibility and unworthiness of those whom God chooses also relates to what they have been made and have been turned into by God. In that case the sovereignty of God would be glorified but not His wisdom in choosing.

The proverb says that God can strike a straight blow with a crooked stick. Who would dispute it? It is no less true, however, that as a rule God uses *suitable* instruments, i. e., creates them, chooses them, forms them, *makes them suitable*. God calls but does not choose in time. His works are known to Him "from eternity." Already in the generations He is working in all kinds of ways to prepare the call and the called.

Ruth and Rahab did not enter the genealogy of Jesse and David by chance. Abraham, Moses and Paul are men suited and formed for their task. Regardless of how surprising the choice of Gideon seems to us – his is another case whereby Israel cannot boast: "My hand has redeemed me!" – no one would dare claim that he was not the right man in the right place. The name of his father Joash, "Jehovah is strength," is already striking from this point of view.

Gideon himself believes in Jehovah, even though he is in a pagan environment. The greeting of the stranger who has settled down under the oak tree while he is threshing the corn puts the complaint on his lips: "Please, my Lord… if the LORD is with us, why has all this happened to us? And where are all His wonders of which our fathers told us, saying, 'Has not the LORD brought us up out of Egypt?' But now the LORD has forsaken us and delivered us into the hand of Midian" (Judges 6: 13).

He not only possessed a royal stature (8: 18) but belonged to the lineage that had already suffered much from the foreigner, certainly not for lack of courage and strength in the defense of its homesteads. Gideon's policy works out every time, as when he chooses the night to carry out the divine charge, 6: 27, or when he divides his select band on the height from which one looks down upon the enemy's camp and seizes the convenient means to confound an army composed, like theirs is, of distinct tribes united only temporarily by the bond of a common interest, and indeed with their families, livestock and cattle, chs. 7: 8, 16, 17ff.

How much courage did Gideon show when he pursued the still mighty army of Zebah and Zalmunna, which had crossed the Jordan, not like their allies Oreb and Zeeb at Beth-barah, but farther south at Beth-shean, fifteen thousand men strong, chs. 7: 24, 8: 5, 10, 12. How perilous was his undertaking is shown by the answer to his request for bread given by the people of Penuel and Succoth, ch. 8: 6, 8. How serene was the milder answer with which he turns away the wrath of Ephraim, ch. 8: 2. How much decisiveness does he show in punishing the people of Penuel and Succoth, who had shown that they were cut off from the body of the Israelite people, ch. 8: 14, 16.

Above all, how he shows that he was an Israelite of the true stamp, having penetrated deeply into the spirit of theocracy, when he turned down the royal dignity with that word which throughout the ages has resounded like a trumpet blast, Judges 8: 23: "But Gideon replied, 'I will not rule over you, nor will my son. The LORD shall rule over you.'"

This was the man fully up to the work that God had given him to do. Let us consider that work.

2. His first work, namely the eradication of the Abiezrites' idol.

God came to him when, deeply downcast under the influence perhaps of the tidings that the Midianites were approaching, he sought to bring some provisions to safety, 6: 11. He came in human form in like manner as He appeared to Abraham in the oak groves of Mamre, Gen. 18, and to Joshua at Gilgal, Josh. 5. God made Himself known to him, initially when He "turned to him" (v. 14), signaling in an unspecified manner that He was dealing with a heavenly messenger, and further when – the force of the original cannot be reproduced in the translation – He used the sacred *Jehovah name* to encourage him. Indeed, to his question, "Please my Lord, how can I save Israel?" 6: 15, the answer is, "Surely *I will be with you*," therefore implying "because I am Jehovah, He who is and who will be," v. 16.

The last doubt was removed from Gideon's mind when he presented the Angel with victuals – according to the Oriental manner, *boiled* in a pot for instant use, *roasted* in a basket for the journey – with an ample quantity of unleavened cakes, v. 19, and saw the gift accepted as an *offering* that was consumed not, as he might have expected, by fire from heaven, but by the flame that rose from the rock when the stranger's staff touched it, proving that He who came from heaven was beside him. Yet with this, he was also consecrated and called to be a witness of the living God.

Thus, in His condescending grace, the Lord had communed with Israel's future savior. But the altar of Baal stood on high and had to be removed: he received an express command to do so "on that very night," 6: 25. This command presupposes both that Jehovah had become his God and that it was not enough to erect an altar next to that of the idol. "Build a proper altar to the LORD your God," we read further, "on the top of this stronghold. And with the wood of the Asherah pole you cut down, take the second bull and offer it as a burnt offering."

God can never be the second. He is the only one; the only one who has a right to be served in Canaan.

Two comments in passing.

The fact that the Angel of the Lord did not consume food has been taken as a sign that the correspondent writing in this sixth chapter had outgrown the childlike position in which Gen. 18 had placed us. There in the oak groves of Mamre, we are told, the angels who came to Abraham consumed the meal, while at Ophrah, Gideon did not expect this to happen.

One should remember that Abraham was in a covenant relationship with God and was allowed to have fellowship with the Lord, which was sealed by this meal, while in Gideon's case God had broken the covenant with Israel. Gideon feels that his life is forfeit. The realization of the holiness of God and his own unworthiness, of which no trace is found in the stories of the pagans concerning the dealings between gods and men, causes Gideon to exclaim, "Oh no, Lord GOD! I have seen the angel of the LORD face to face" (6: 22). God Himself speaks the word of reconciliation: "Peace be with you. Do not be afraid, for you will not die!" 6: 23.

This leads to the second observation.

There is no mention here of the law or of the sacrifices offered according to the law in the tabernacle. Gideon is graced with a revelation and builds himself an altar in the place where it fell to him, called Jehovah Shalom – the Lord is peace. As has been rightly seen, Gideon here is not living and acting under the *Sinaitic covenant*. He who is puzzled by this overlooks, as has been said before, how inconceivable it would be to suppose that this covenant would have remained in force while the relationship which it presupposes has been disturbed, and the purpose with which it was instituted has been utterly thwarted, namely, to serve as an institution of salvation, as a means of communion with Jehovah.

The tabernacle, the worship, the law had been left just as had been the tree of life and the Paradise of God – so that they might be a prophecy of future restoration, a sign of hope for man who had been driven out of this Paradise, whose power was no longer from the tree of life.

Gideon stands in the patriarchal position. The first step to arrive at the renewal and redemption of the people is the removal of idolatry. This then is where he has to begin his work. Redemption begins in his own house. He is called to act reformationally.

That is how God always acts. The duties which we first have to fulfill are right in front of us.

That Gideon acts cautiously at night is not only understandable but does not detract from his faith. He who takes his first faltering steps on the path of life is led on step by step. He who, like Nicodemus, comes to Jesus by night will confess the Crucified One as his Master in broad daylight.

How much reason Gideon had to proceed with great caution, the outcome demonstrated. The people of his city want to kill the bandit who has defiled the image and sacrificial place of the deity, 6: 30. But his son's courageous act of faith, now that the case has been decided and the impotence of the deity proved, has had a revelatory effect on Joash. He resigns himself to what he would surely have prevented had it not been done without his knowledge. It is not he, says the father, who overthrows the altar of Baal, but he who stands up for Baal, who leaps into the breach for him, as if he were incapable of defending himself, who dishonors himself.

Jerubbaal! Baal contend with him! With fine irony, Gideon is given over to the vengeance of the offended king of heaven.

On the hill now rises another altar. It is the standard, as it were, that the captain of Israel's armies has planted before all eyes. Jehovah takes His rightful place. That is what everything comes down to for Israel. That is the great work to which Gideon was called. Everything else is now a matter of course. Israel can now sing, "The Lord is the leader of those who help me!"

The service which God demands is never negative, but always positive. It does not consist in the removal of the idol, but in the restoration of the altar to the true God. With the wood of the idol the seven-year-old bull is offered; it is "the second," intentionally in view of the seven years of tribulation, or perhaps of the covenant of which the number seven is the expression, designated by God Himself, 6: 25.

The stones for this altar were brought by Gideon, which was the main reason he needed his ten servants. The altar to the Baal could not serve for this offering. It was defiled. But out of the ashes of the life of self-denial rises the glow that consumes the God-pleasing sacrifice.

From this we learn what use we have to make of our idols. On the estate of a prominent Englishman who had recently returned from India, an idol was placed by the gate, not far from the public road, holding a mission box into which many a passerby used to deposit his gifts. Similarly, Gideon made Astarte subservient to Jehovah, and the work of Israel's restoration was thus begun.

3. To what does this pave the way?

To Israel's deliverance.

While the Angel of the Lord was appearing under the oak tree at Ophrah, the Midianites were approaching, Judges 6: 33. The next day, when the altar of the Lord was restored in honor, they crossed the Jordan. Not many days later they were encamped in the plain of Jezreel, from which, avoiding the mountainous regions northward and southward, it was possible to move through the largest and most fertile part of Canaan, and along the coastal lands to reach even the cities of the Philistines.

Yet the people who dwelt in Canaan were not the same as that which had been oppressed by wandering shepherd tribes for seven consecutive years. By the one act of faith of Gideon, nay, by the one revelation of the Lord that preceded it, everything had changed.

A beautiful Greek myth tells of the giant Antaeus, son of Neptune, the god of the sea, and Terra, the goddess of the earth, that he was invincible as long as he remained in touch with his mother, so that each time he was thrown to the earth he received from her new and greater powers. Knowing this, Hercules lifted him and held him up in the air, there to crush him in his muscular arms against his own breast. The believer is an Antaeus who derives his powers not from the earth, from which he was taken as a man, but from God, in whose image he was created and recreated.

Israel has been brought back into contact with its God and has received the word of reconciliation. At Ophrah stands an altar that in its name, Jehovah-Shalom, does more to revive hope than a mighty army of well-equipped auxiliaries. "Conscience," says the English poet, "makes cowards of us all!" An evil conscience renders the bravest cowardly and weak. It is the same thought that the poet expresses in this way, Proverbs 2: 8: "The wicked flee where there is no persecutor, but every righteous man is bold as a young lion."

Israel knows well that its prosperity, its recovery, its existence depends on its relationship to Jehovah. Idolatry consumes its strength, deprives it of all resilience and all courage. This is indeed the case, all the while that it boasts against the Lord, puts its trust in the Baal and would like to kill its noblest sons because they have committed sacrilege against the worthless "dung god."[7]

There are such contradictions in a poor human heart.

Indeed, all this is true of Israel as long as it continues to possess any knowledge of its own past. Apostates lack the naivete with which those who have not possessed the knowledge of the truth commit sin. But now God has returned in mercy. A single man in a remote town of the half-tribe of Manasseh has received the assurance, "Peace to you, do not fear; you shall not die!" (Judges 6: 23). That is not a word for him alone; it is the message that God is sending to all Israel.

And the Old Testament is supposed to breathe a different spirit, bring a different teaching, preach a different salvation, set different conditions, demand and awaken a different life than the New! How superficial is this reflection! How it contradicts the ongoing history of Israel! Israel certainly did much to warrant the grace of God! Was not Jehovah the same who had sent the prophet to teach the people the meaning of tribulation; was He not the same who came to Gideon, who did not know Him, had

---

[7] The word used for "idol" in the Dutch translation.

not awaited His coming, and very well realized that he, sinner, would not be able to see God and live?

Did the future judge of Israel himself also bow the knee before Baal? We think we have good reason to doubt this. The common working of God's grace prevented this. Yet he belonged to a generation that had surrendered to the abominations of the Canaanites. Joash, his father, had neither the courage nor the power to prevent the evil that was destroying Israel. The destruction of the altar on the height and whatever else took place both there and under the oak tree *followed upon the word of peace* and was performed in the power of the Lord by the one who was the first to be inspired. In terms of dogmatics, all this pertained to the work of sanctification.

The Midianites entered Canaan in as great numbers as before, to the same purpose as before, but they found another people; for with the tidings that once again the dreaded scourge did not fail to materialize comes the news of what great things the God of the fathers has done to and through Joash's son. This causes the 32,000 men from the northern tribes, even though they apparently have not counted the cost and cannot withstand the danger when it threatens them more closely, to meet the captain of the Lord's army – though "his thousand is the poorest in Manasseh" – with a willingness that even Barak and Deborah did not encounter. Likewise Asher, who did not show up then, but this time around did, 6: 35.

This alarmed the enemies and filled them with an unknown and inexplicable fear. Soon after occupying the heights around the camp of the Midianites, Gideon descended with Purah, his servant, to their guard posts and there heard the dream which a man told his companion, the dream of the barley bread – the bread of the poor – which rolled down from the heights of the mountains – where, as they knew, Gideon had gathered his own – into the army of the Midianites, struck against the captain's tent and knocked it over. "This is none other," spoke the companion, "than the sword of Gideon the son of Joash the Israelite man; God has given the Midianites and all this army into his hand" (Judges 7: 14).

Only Gideon himself seems not to have shared the general expectation. The more the hour of decision approaches, the more need he feels to strengthen himself in the Lord his God and to receive anew the assurance that God will redeem Israel by his hand, as He had spoken, v. 36.

Is this not inexplicable in a man of faith? Heb. 11: 32. Does Gideon not contradict himself here when he expresses in one breath both that God has promised him His help and that he wanted to obtain more certainty? Is this request for a sign not proof of unbelief and basically a denial of Jehovah?

If the life of faith were nothing more than the ability to draw inferences from data provided by the Lord in His Word, most certainly. However, it is of an entirely different nature than the purely rational reasoning which works by syllogism. "Your 'therefore,'" said Luther to a man of reason, who wanted to put cool calculation in the place of life with all its swings, its apparent contradictions, its unfathomable depths, "is a fool." Is it any wonder that the vine, moved by the slightest gust of wind, winds its creepers around any object that possesses firmness? Is it any wonder that the poor weak human heart, tormented by the sense of unworthiness and looking upon circumstances, succumbs again and again and takes refuge in the living God?

Therein lies the very essence of faith. It is with faith as with love. Not in order *to be* assured that the object of attachment loves in return, but because one *is* assured of this, does one wish to see and hear and feel that one has not deceived oneself. There is a doubt which brings in uncertainty because it does not trust God: the doubt of Achaz, Isaiah 7: 12, and of Zacharias the father of John, Luke 1: 18. But there is also a doubt of oneself, of one's own strength; a doubt equal to the shuddering of the sufferer who voluntarily surrenders himself to undergo a dangerous operation even when his intention to place himself in the surgeon's hands is in no way altered at the sight of the preparations.

Weak faith is also faith. In the fear which faith exhibits, which in itself is also proof of man's sinful weakness, lies an irrefutable characteristic of his sincerity, i.e., an indication that it is not born of ignorance. "Do you tremble?" asked a recruit with undisguised disdain of an old graybeard standing in line beside him, just prior to the onset of the battle. "Are you afraid for that old body of yours?" "Yes," was the reply. "And if you were half as frightened as I am, you would already be running away."

Gideon coveted a sign. Shall the dew – the image of the Lord's blessing – be on the fleece of wool – symbol of Israel conducting its business – and dryness on the earth around – on the other nations? 6:37. Yes! Perhaps the fleece retained moisture longer and the nocturnal earth did not remain dry. Will dryness, when God commands it, be on the fleece, and dew throughout the whole surrounding area? Jehovah not only grants his desire but gives him more than he asks for when He caused him to witness the nightly conversation between the two enemies.

God comes to the aid of Gideon's weakness but apparently also desires to shame it, in this giving to the church of all ages a striking lesson that every child of God must sooner or later learn by his own experience. Gideon fears because the number of his allies is so extremely small, so out of all proportion to the number of his enemies. He is mistaken; "The people who are with you are too many" (Judges 7: 2).

Let those who recoil in the hour of danger return home! They number twenty-two thousand. Surely courage on the battlefield is something different from courage shown on the parade ground! Many are the people of good will who, as sexton Nicholas Klim (the memoirs of whom Rabener has conveyed to us) could tell us, wanted to write such books and perform such bold deeds![8] Let them leave, the frightened ones! They lack courage, nay, faith and the true knowledge of God. God will soon know how to use them when the Midianites are defeated and scattered and Israel does not have enough hands to finish off its enemies. The Lord in His wisdom has a job for the twenty-two thousand to do. But that job does not have a place where hundreds and tens face hundreds of thousands.

Ten thousand men are arrayed around him. But again the word of the Lord comes to Gideon: "There are still too many people." God Himself by a clear sign designates the three hundred whom He has chosen to work for redemption. It is they who have not fallen to their knees but, whether standing or lying down (this the text leaves open), have drunk from the hand, ch. 7: 5.

---

[8] A reference to "Eine Todtenliste von Nicolaus Klimen, Küstern an der Kreuzkirche zu Bergen in Norwegen," in *Gottlieb Wilhelm Rabeners Satiren: Erster Theil* (Verlag Johan Gottfried Dyck, 1761).

A plausible explanation of the certainly not unwitting distinction here made by the Lord is given by the Rabbi Rashi. The servants of Baal, he says, were accustomed to pray while kneeling, 1 Kings 19: 18, Isa. 45: 23, and by an involuntary act betrayed the power of custom; all the more so, as the professors of Jehovah purposely avoided it.

With this little army Gideon will do valiant deeds. The outcome – he knows this, and we too have to learn it – depends not on the means at his disposal but on the Lord God who employs those means. And yet Gideon, though he knows this, acts in the consciousness that he is used not as a bare mindless and will-less tool, not as a puppet, but as a thinking being, a true secondary cause.

He chooses, as has already been said, the expedient means of confusing an army composed like that of the Midianites. The nightly attack, the shouts of war "for Jehovah and for Gideon!", the unexpected and unexplained sound of the breaking jars, the light of the torches seen at so many points, even the absence of the enemy, who "took his position around the camp" (7: 21), the sounding of the trumpets and the fear that combines with a natural distrust of their allies that makes them see in each other an enemy – what could be better calculated than all this to achieve the intended goal?

Faith does not exclude but demands the use of means and precautions. God Himself ensures that Israel has no room for boasting, by saying, "My hand has delivered Me." If God causes Israel now, and later, and yes ever to sing of "'salvation prepared for him," it will be in the words of the 115th Psalm (v. 1, Psalter of 1773):

Not to us, O Lord, not to us,
To Your name alone
Be, for thy faithfulness and mercy's sake
All honor and glory given.

6. THE CONSEQUENCES OF SIN IN BELIEVERS

Gideon's Ephod and the Kingdom of Abimelech

Let no vain care make you stray from the path of salvation;
In your way keep your eye on God,
Trust in Him, and the outcome shall not fail,
He will soon make your right, before every face,
Rise like the morning sunbeams,
And shine like the bright noonday.
Be silent unto God; wait for the end of the Lord's ways.
When here you see the wicked prosper
And by trickery obtain their desires,
Neither inflame your temper nor bear you sorrow;
Then begrudge them no imagined blessing;
Abstain from wrath, and seek not vengeance.

Psalm 37: 3–4 (Psalter of 1773)

God is great and we do not understand Him!

How then could we understand His thoughts and ways? We, who do not see everything, how could we see through everything?

The same applies to His Word and His work. Although, thank God, we need not complain "There is no priest who declares Him," yet we find mysteries, apparent contradictions, in everything the Lord says and does.

Herein lies a temptation for man to impatience and unbelief. Everything he cannot understand, cannot reconcile, becomes to him, as Scripture calls it, a vexation, a skandalon, that is, a stumbling block and a trap. Man is so easily vexed with God and the Christ.

We see this from the laughter of Sarah, the subterfuge of Moses, the counsel of the spies, the despondency of Elijah, the doubt of John the Baptist, the interference of Peter, the unbelief of the Jews. Our wisdom conflicts with the wisdom of God. If only we could learn to be silent about God and wait for the *conclusion* of the Lord's ways! Our trust in someone is not great if it fails the moment we cannot check and verify with Him. And yet, unless grace prevents it, this is the kind of trust with which we worship our God.

In Switzerland, the traveler is led blindfolded by his guide along the most dangerous points of a certain mountain pass. He is not allowed to see the dizzying depths into which a single misstep would bring his downfall.

Our human wisdom is foolishness before God. If we examine one by one the examples from Scripture cited above, we will find that there was reason enough in the circumstances of everyone we have mentioned to be vexed at the promise, command and guidance of the Lord. All suffered from the same error. They had not reckoned with God. Like Caesar, the Lord asks, "How many do I count for?" Which is why the highest reason is to entrust ourselves blindly to Him. Yet those who received the grace of faith were, in the midst of their objections and dangers, like sleepwalkers who walk with steady steps over the rooftops and along the cliffs. Afterward a shudder runs through their members at the thought of the overnight journey.

Did not Satan have the right to argue with the angel Michael over the body of Moses? Was not Moses a sinner? Was not his body forfeit to death? Was that accuser of the brethren not justified in making remarks about Joshua's appointment as high priest? Was not the charge he brought against Joshua in the presence of the Angel of the Lord perfectly justified? And God gives no justification for his actions! The time has not yet come when He will demonstrate His justice, that He will reveal how and why He can be just, even if it is that He justifies the ungodly. Wisdom would later be vindicated by all her children; for now, faith speaks, "The Lord rebuke you, Satan!"

Gideon, too, is vexed. To him, after the victory over the Midianites, a snare was set that he avoided. They wanted to make him king, to give him the glory of the redemption that God had wrought through him. That could not, should not be! He knew all too well that it had not been his courage and foresight by which he, the poorest of his father's house, had become the savior of his people. But although Gideon attributes the victory to God, this does not mean that he will also be willing to leave the future to God.

When the manna fell, there were those in the host who wished to lay some up for the following day. It lies in man's makeup not to enjoy the present unless he has a better guarantee for the future than the promise or proven faithfulness of his God.

What will become of the fruit of salvation if Gideon does not build a barn to secure and perpetuate it? The rock of offense stands in his way and he stumbles over it, dragging his family down with him. For there was a great gap in the way the Israelite state was set up, a gap which would certainly have been filled if Israel had not broken the covenant of God, which in its very existence gives unmistakable proof that God had provided something better for His people, and which, under the existing circumstances, that is, as a result of Israel's apostasy, must be considered a punishment and a temptation.

Israel had priests, but no priest-government. Prophets, but the prophet like Moses had not yet risen. Judges, either local government, namely the tribal leaders, or endowed with a special, extraordinary calling, but no hierarchical administration.

We should certainly call this a gap. A people divided into tribes and lineages all with their own territories and partly conflicting or at least divergent interests, had to be weak. True, purely spiritual unity would have been felt and preserved if the tabernacle service had been maintained according to the requirement of God's law. But one sin, as we repeatedly experience in life, is the fertile mother of another. Israel desperately needed a visible expression of and a fulcrum for its national unity, especially at the reduced position on which it now stood. Even when, as at the time of Barak, the tribes acted under higher inspiration to throw off the communal yoke by a communal act, Reuben, Asher and Meroz were left out, while more recently the conduct of Ephraim and the response of the men of Penuel and Succoth testified precisely to the lack of a true Israelite existence.

The opportunity was now propitious to put an end to such disharmony. Should and would he become king, the whole seed of Jacob would probably sooner or later have bowed under his scepter. But of this there is now, as has been said, no question. The true source of Israel's strength and the essential guarantee of independence lies, Gideon knows, in the grace and faithfulness of his God.

But why should he not remain active as judge *for the entire country?* This he could do, even without further appointment, by virtue of the right of the prophet, the advocate for the name and cause of the Lord. Everything would then depend on his personal influence. In this case he would have to give himself entirely to this labor, as Samuel did later, continually going from north to south, punishing sin and upholding justice wherever it was necessary. Would people hear him? Would people obey him? Certainly not, if the spirit of the people of Penuel and Succoth, as most likely was the case, had penetrated elsewhere. Little Manasseh, at least, finds no support among proud Ephraim and distant Judah, to whom, according to the ancient prophets, primacy is due. But why then should he not seek his strength in the God who had revealed Himself to him? If that revelation was a communication of His will, then surely he could expect that the spring which God's grace had opened for him at Ophrah would henceforth flow there?

Before Moses' death, Jehovah had appointed a successor at the request of his servant. "May the LORD, the God of the spirits of all flesh," so the mediator had spoken, "appoint a man over the congregation who will go out and come in before them, and who will lead them out and bring them in, so that the congregation of the LORD will not be like sheep without a shepherd" (Num. 27: 16–17). That Israel should have one head, lay then in the intention of Jehovah. Such a head must be there. He was indispensable. Why was he not there? Joshua did not perpetuate his office at his death, as Moses did before him, but left the future to God.

If Gideon once acted as head? He had no appointment. But is this vocation not contained in the revelation that came to him? After all, necessity knows no law! And the present situation is untenable. The people want a king, that is, they disregard the rights of Jehovah. Well then! Let Ophrah become the spiritual center of Israel and Jehovah Shalom – the Lord is peace – be worshipped. By this an incalculable evil will be prevented!

As far as we are able given the imperfect data we possess, we will attempt to put ourselves in Gideon's situation and follow the course of his deliberations. It is necessary to do this because much becomes clear to us that would otherwise remain inexplicable.

Let us, conversely, examine what argued *against* this view and prevented the execution of this plan. When Joshua, at God's command, took over from Moses the task of being the leader of his people, God placed

Eleazar the priest by his side. Surely Jehovah was Israel's king who revealed His will in special cases through the Urim and the Thummim. The permanent revelation of that will was found in His holy laws. By this the Lord ruled over His people, and that people was distinguished from all other nations on the face of the earth.

> He gave to Jacob his laws,
> Made Israel heed His words;
> He taught them to walk in his ways,
> Thus He would not deal with any other nations;
> They had to miss His testimonies
> And His covenant secrets.
> Let then God's praise rise to heaven;
> Let all that have breath praise Him!
>
> Ps. 147: 10 (Psalter of 1773)

True, those laws contained not only certain regulations with a view to particular cases, but also the broad principles to be applied according to circumstances. But that was also why the gift of prophecy had been granted. They were called seers who deduced the hidden counsel and will of God from the letter of the law and the spirit of events. They saw what remained hidden from others. We are amazed at the deep vision of those prophets and the truly spiritual – today one would say gospel-oriented – sense that animated them when, to mention just one thing, we find at the temple not only a court, but also a court of the nations.

God thus ruled through the intervention of those who interpreted His law and, through their deeper, spiritual contemplation, did not abolish it but fulfilled it. In some cases, on weighty occasions, this took place, as has been said, through the Urim and the Thummim.

There is no question of priestly rule. This in itself is evidence that the Israelite state was of divine origin. The history of no other nation can be compared to that of Israel in this respect. This fact is so telling, so full of meaning, that one would be compelled to join Wellhausen, Kuenen and others in denying the existence both of the law and of the Levitical priesthood should one not be prepared, starting from faith in the divinity of Holy Scripture, to find a more natural explanation – that is, to assume that the high priest had to be the *appropriate organ*, or rather, the instrument of revelation.

The high priest did not rule. He only carried the ephod. But God ruled through him. "The words of God were entrusted to him." Hence, the utterance of the Urim and Thummim is always directly regarded as a speaking by God. "After the death of Joshua, the Israelites inquired of the LORD, 'Who will be the first to go up and fight for us against the Canaanites?' 'Judah shall go up,' answered the LORD. 'Indeed, I have delivered the land into their hands'" (Judges 1: 1–2). "[Saul] inquired of the LORD, but the LORD did not answer him by dreams or Urim or prophets" (1 Samuel 28: 6). "Some time later, David inquired of the LORD, 'should I go up to one of the towns of Judah?' 'Go up,' the LORD answered. Then David asked, 'Where should I go?' 'To Hebron,' replied the LORD" (2 Samuel 2: 1).

It lay thus entirely in the course of revelation that Joshua would not, like Moses up to this point, act entirely independently, but that he would receive divine commands in the cases indicated above, through the priest. "He shall stand," we read, "before Eleazar the priest, who will seek counsel for him before the LORD by the judgment of the Urim. At his command, he and all the Israelites with him—the entire congregation—will go out and come in" (Numbers 27: 21).

This place now, namely the office held by Joshua, is what Gideon wished to occupy. He felt the necessity of becoming Nagid, i.e., Judge, leader of the people. Whoever overlooks this is unable to explain the answer he gave when he received the people's command. "But Gideon replied, 'I will not rule over you, nor will my son. The LORD shall rule over you'" (Judges 8: 23).

This does not mean, as it is usually interpreted, "God is your King and proceeds to reveal Himself as such." On the contrary: it was precisely the grievance that so little was seen of this kingship, so little power emanated from it, that the spiritual bond that held the twelve rods of Israel's people together in one bundle was broken.

In the closest connection with this, Gideon says, "Let me make a request of you, that each of you give me an earring from his plunder." We read further: "From all this Gideon made an ephod, which he placed in Ophrah, his hometown" (Judges 8: 24, 27).

This, then, was the reign of Jehovah that he meant. The irregularity that had existed in Israel since the days of Joshua, and only occasionally was somewhat lessened by the appearance of an Othniel, Ehud, Deborah and Barak, would be removed. Not only would there be a priest who *carried* the ephod, but also a judge who *queried* the Urim and the Thummim. God would again "answer" and Gideon himself would be vested with this divine authority.

Gideon thus did at Ophrah the same thing that Micah did on the mountains of Ephraim, not far from Lais or Dan, namely, set up a *regular worship of God*, cf. Judges 18. We can only assume that the service at Ophrah was comparatively pure. Micah had teraphim, carved and cast images, Judges 18: 14, while Gideon, who had received the revelation of the living God, was not directly guilty of idolatry. Surely, we cannot possibly suppose that a man who was so greatly privileged as he was, was immediately afterwards, as some interpreters assume, guilty of idolatry which had a great deal in common with the service of Baal.

For the ephod alone, as has been noted very much to the point, no seventeen hundred shekels weight of gold, not counting the moons, chains, etc. (Judges 8: 26), was necessary. But this certainly goes together with a priest, and with the priest a dwelling, probably in connection with the altar: "The Lord is peace," 6: 24, though because of the brevity of the narrative neither the one nor the other is expressly mentioned.

But at this point the questions multiply. The tabernacle, the Levitical worship, the Aaronic priesthood – where have they gone, now that a man like Gideon, receiving a revelation from the Lord and overthrowing the image of Astarte, establishes a separate worship service at Ophrah? To what purpose was another ephod made besides the existing one? Why at Shechem, in the capital of Ephraim, still nearer to Shiloh, assuming that the tabernacle stood there at the time, a temple erected in the same tribe, of Baal-Berith, the Covenant-Baal, so-called either because the Shechemites had made a covenant with him or because they had taken some things from the Jehovah service, so that he was worshipped after the manner of the covenant with Jehovah?

To these and more such questions which come to mind, Scripture gives no answer. However, the few details that are given us about the religious condition of Israel point only to the deep decay of the central sanctuary.

This is especially true of the Baal service at Shechem. All kinds of causes, partly the fragmentation of the tribes and their mutual envy, partly the political relations, not least the presumption of Ephraim, could contribute to discourage visits to the tabernacle. But the fact that Ephraim itself presided over idolatry in its own tribe is sufficient proof that little power for good emanated from Shiloh.

Not long after this time, as we shall see later, the priesthood passed from the line of Eleazar over to that of Ithamar.[9] So in this, too, we have indirectly the indication that God's judgment came upon Shiloh. That, furthermore, the followers of Baal-Berith were not content to practice their religion quietly is evidenced by the support they provided Abimelech from the temple treasury, 9: 45. It is in the nature of things that they were as hostile to Shiloh as they were to Ophrah.

In short, Gideon certainly had plenty of reason not to reckon with Shiloh any longer. But this was precisely the stumbling block spoken of in the beginning. His sin, though not immediately, directly and personally punished in him, was of the same nature as that of Uzzah when he propped up the ark.

We humans are so prone to play providence. When the right hand is on the head of the youth Ephraim and the left hand is crossed over it, resting on that of Manasseh, we involuntarily seek to put them in different positions. When the prophet tells me that I will soon be clothed with the royal dignity, the first thing I do is effect a rebellion against Solomon.

All this, while truly human, is also exceedingly sinful. If we walk in the way of the Lord and choose His revealed will as our guide for our actions and conduct, we may safely leave the management of our affairs to God. The ministers may be unworthy, but the offices which God has established remain in force. The ark may have been buried in the tent of Shiloh, but it is still there and will be restored to its rightful place in God's time and in God's way.

---

[9] Here the text has "Phinehas," which is obviously a mistake: see p. 63.

When the bed of the stream is dry, there is no need to dig a drainage channel alongside; as soon as the clouds give water, we will see the stream flow again between its appointed banks.

God's promises are attached to the shadow service; they will certainly give way to something else, but only when the body shall have come (cf. Col. 2: 17). Even if the incumbent, or the office, or the entire institution to which they belong stand to be affected by God's judgment, we have no right to make ourselves unauthorized executors of that judgment.

David knows this. Though Saul was rejected by God so that he should not be king, though David himself received the anointing and calling, far be it from him to attack "the Lord's anointed." Even the apostles of the Lord know this. Already Christ had been raised from the dead and preached as the Risen and Glorified One. The moment was approaching when the Lord's threat would be fulfilled: "Not one stone shall be left upon another." But Paul, the apostle of the Gentiles, goes into the temple at Pentecost (cf. Acts 20:16), and circumcision – in this there is no difference between him and Peter – remains in effect for the seed of Abraham. A few more years and the entire Jewish state will collapse, and Israel's place of sacrifice and appeal will be taken away.

Gideon had received an extraordinary calling to a particular work, but he was not free to intervene in the work of God. Had he not found so much cause for his undertaking in the miserable, truly untenable condition of the moment, we would not even be able to say that he was bothered. That would suppose that to some extent he acted with good intentions. This might determine our judgment of the person but not of the matter. Gideon was a believer, but this is no reason to say that he put forward the ephod by faith.

In the eleventh century, the time of the so-called Pornocracy, Benedict XII, a boy "accomplished in all vices" as the historian reports, had occupied the papal seat. Gregory VI therefore believed he was called to deprive him of the papal dignity, and did so by simony. Indeed, he bought him out and thus by purchase became the possessor of the office, which he wished to exercise for the benefit of the Church. However much one may excuse him, the act in question was ungodly and entirely in keeping with the time in which it was committed.

It is no different with Gideon's ephod. All Israel whored after it, and it became a snare to Gideon and his house, 8: 27. Instead of carrying through the reformation of the church according to the Word of God, regardless of its seeming impossibility, even regardless of near-certain failure, he shifted the spiritual center of Israel to Ophrah and thereby pronounced a death sentence on that which God Himself had instituted, a sentence on the tabernacle at Shiloh which Jehovah did not sanction.

But the punishment did not tarry. Who has sinned against the Lord and had peace? Gideon may reject kingship, but from the moment that Ophrah became the place of pilgrimage for all Israel, he began conducting a princely state. He had no less than seventy sons and many wives, 8: 30. One of these sons, who lived in Shechem and was completely estranged from his father's house, bore the name of Abimelech, "My father is king." One need not ask what spirit animated him, or let me rather say her, who gave this name, verse 31, and in what sense, in what frame of mind the child was raised who received that name.

By other means as well, the sad consequences of his action became apparent. The worship service at Shiloh was not lifted from its decay, allowing the priesthood of the national sanctuary gradually to lose more of its significance. But for its part the impure, unlawful service at Ophrah was incapable of counteracting the tendency toward idolatry. The Baal service persisted at Shechem even during Gideon's lifetime. After his death, "the Israelites turned and prostituted themselves with the Baals, and they set up Baal-berith as their god" (Judges 8: 33).

Baal fought against Jerubbaal and gained the victory. That we may speak of battle here is evident both from Abimelech's saying, "Is it better for you that seventy men, all the sons of Jerubbaal, rule over you, or just one man?" (9: 2), and from the fact that seventy pieces of silver were provided to this fratricide from the temple treasure to carry out his infernal plans, v. 4. It is even quite possible that they have made themselves ready to maintain their religion and herewith their authority, and that on that ground Abimelech presents his fellow citizens with the choice to serve either him or his father's sons.

But in this way, the kingship founded by him also comes up naturally for discussion. On the part of Ephraim many attempts were made, before and after, to arrive at a different arrangement of the state. This can be deduced from the fable which Jotham, the only remaining son of Gideon after the slaughter of his brethren, standing on the protruding rock of Mount Gerizim, close enough to the place to be heard in the pure air of that region but far enough away not to be caught, used to portray the conduct of the people of Shechem and show them the future.

Neither the vine nor the fig tree were willing to be uprooted to soar above the trees of the forest. The thorn tree alone had nothing to lose, but would now demand the impossible, that is, demand that those who raised themselves above him should from now on stand below him.

It is as natural that already in those early times Ephraim should have striven for supremacy, as that only a man like Abimelech would be willing to accept the scepter over a people like Israel.

How, to dwell for a moment on the first statement, the sins of the patriarchs had far-reaching consequences! Jacob's fondness for Rachel, for Joseph, paved the way to the separation of kingdoms. Ephraim never forgot his lineage. Joshua was from Ephraim, and Deborah lived and judged in Ephraim, giving sustenance to the longing of this tribe to be first in everything and to compete for dominion over the other tribes, even over or at least in addition to Judah, on whose shoulder Father Jacob, by God's will, had placed that dominion, and who was appointed leader by God Himself.

How, to tarry a bit longer with the latter statement, was earthly kingship contrary to the essence of God's government! But is this not to put it too strongly? Did not Balaam foresee earthly kingship when he said, "I see him, but not now; I behold him, but not near. A star will come forth from Jacob, and a scepter will arise from Israel. He will crush the skulls of Moab and strike down all the sons of Sheth" (Num. 24: 17)? Did not Jacob foretell, "The scepter will not depart from Judah, nor the staff from between his feet, until Shiloh comes and the allegiance of the nations is his" (Gen. 49: 10)?

Yes; and Sarah received the promise that "kings of peoples will descend from her" (Gen. 17: 16). And the expectation of Israelite kingship is so firmly established that the message in the genealogy of Edom: "These are the kings who reigned in the land of Edom before any king reigned over the Israelites" (Gen. 36: 31) must likely be explained from this. And Hannah rejoiced in what Jehovah will do to and through his anointed king: "The LORD will judge the ends of the earth and will give power to His king. He will exalt the horn of His anointed" (1 Sam. 2: 10). And Moses himself, in the so-called law of the king, Deut. 17: 14–20, gave provisions concerning the choice of the king and handed down regulations to which he would have to adhere.

All this is true, and we might even add to it; and yet none of this proves that earthly kingship is compatible with God's rule in its actual essence, any more than it, on the other hand, argues for the view of the learned practitioner of Old Testament scholarship who seeks to deduce from the places cited above that the books or the chapters in which they occur are of later date.

However autocratic and supreme an earthly sovereign may be, there is one area in which his poorest subject is completely independent of him, namely, the area of conscience, of moral, internal life. He judges actions, not the motives of those actions. God is a King in whose law it is written, "you shall love the LORD your God with all your heart and with all your soul and with all your strength" (Deut. 6: 5). He demands that His servants shall not covet, Ex. 20: 17.

Who would represent Him? God is the eternally living and omnipresent One. In what capacity could a child of man replace Him? As vassal, as viceroy, as king by the grace of God, as vicar? But both the one and the other presuppose on God's side the surrender of certain rights, remuneration for services rendered, at any rate an area in which man is independent of God.

Between God and man stands not a *king* but a *mediator*. But this brings us to the heart of the matter because it points out to us the defects of the earthly mediatorship and the way by which it acquires its normal shape and shows itself operative in the exercise of the three offices, namely of prophet, priest and king.

Moses is prophet and as such lawgiver, but neither a priest nor a king. That is a gap, a defect. He is not even a, that is, *the* prophet in the full and true sense of the word. At the time that the law was issued at Sinai, Israel asked for a mediator, saying: "Let us not hear the voice of the LORD our God or see this great fire anymore, so that we will not die" (Deut. 18: 16), Jehovah answered, "They have spoken well. I will raise up for them a prophet like you from among their brothers. I will put My words in his mouth, and he will tell them everything I command him" (vv. 17–18).

Note that God does not say, "I will take you, Moses, as a mediator and substitute for the people," but "They have spoken well." Why? Because "I will raise up for them *a prophet* like you." Can the imperfection of Moses' mediatorship more clearly be expressed, along with the future appearance of the true mediator, the great prophet, whom the Samaritans continued to expect – whereby the first revelation of the Christ was given to a Samaritan, John 4: 19ff. – but whom the Jews distinguished from the Messiah? (John 1: 21).

Nor is Moses a *priest*. The ground of the Aaronic priesthood lies in the sin both of Moses and of Israel.

Of Moses? Although the Lord had removed his objections and equipped him with the divine powers he needed for his mission to the king of Egypt, the servant of God rejects the commission given to him. "But Moses replied, 'Please, Lord, send someone else.' Then the anger of the LORD burned against Moses, and He said, 'Is not Aaron the Levite your brother? I know that he can speak well, and he is now on his way to meet you. When he sees you, he will be glad in his heart'" (Ex. 4: 13–14).

Of the people? When the universal priesthood of Israel was forfeited as a result of the apostasy at Sinai, to which Korah, Dathan and Abiram later laid claim, God freely chose Levi to "draw near" to Him. But the explanation of this choice lay solely in His own good pleasure. God rendered no account for this act. Aaron's rod, like the others, was cut off from its life support. In that barren wood on which was carved his name or the sign of his lineage, there was as much or as little life force as in the other eleven pieces of wood. That that staff blossomed and, as we may assume, continued to blossom, was a sign of election to the priesthood.

But Aaron and Levi never had the significance in the history of Israel which, considered superficially, was due to their position. If we mention Phinehas and Jehoiada, then we have named all the priests up to the time of the Maccabees who blessed Israel not only by their office but also by their personal actions. The service and the sanctuary, the examination of the letter of the law, and the fact that their personal interest was involved in the flourishing of religious life in Israel exposed the priests especially to the danger of formalism and self-righteousness when the prophetic inspiration was missed.

Nor was Moses a *king*. God spoke to him as a friend face to face and by appearance, not by obscure words, Num. 12: 8. But precisely because of this he lacked the independence, the governing power that characterizes kingship. Everywhere we are told, "And the Lord spoke to Moses."

Yet there had to be a king. Jehovah rules Israel in and through the "Angel of the Covenant." But as we saw, that Angel withdrew as a result of Israel's breach of the covenant. The Glory is no longer seen in Israel. Besides, the government of the holy God over and in the midst of a sinful people is something unthinkable. It comes about first in and through the perfect Mediator, the God-man. But now a light dawns on us.

The earthly kingship in Israel does not exist by virtue of divine institution but as a result of man's sin, by God's grace, which stoops so deeply, goes so far that it employs and miraculously turns for the better that which was wrong in itself. It is foreseen and foretold but not *prescribed*. It is from this point of view that the law of the king in Deut. 17: 14–20 is to be explained.

Of the judges and officeholders, it is said in Deut. 16: 18 : "You shall set them over you"; of the king, on the other hand, "When you shall have come into the land which the Lord your God gives you, and you shall possess it hereditarily and dwell therein, and you shall say: I will set over me a king like all the nations that are round about me," Deut. 17: 14. This law must therefore be placed on a par with the license to "give his wife a letter of divorce," provided by Moses to the Israelites because of the hardness of their hearts, Matt. 10: 4.

In the theocracy conceived according to its proper idea, there is no place for earthly as well as divine kingship. The dominion of God over man is broken by sin. His entire revelation is only a descent to man, the way to the Incarnation; and to this end, the kingship is precisely the transition.

It is unnecessary to pursue this line of thought further. The solution of the apparent contradiction, that is of the opposition between the rule of God and of man, is found in the sonship of Israel's king. "The LORD said to my Lord: "Sit at My right hand until I make Your enemies a footstool for Your feet" (Ps. 110: 1). "I will proclaim the decree spoken to Me by the LORD: 'You are My Son; today I have become Your Father'" (Ps. 2: 7). David's Son is David's Lord, Luke 20:42. "But about the Son He says: 'Your throne, O God, endures forever and ever, and justice is the scepter of Your kingdom'" (Heb. 1: 8).

Of Christ, then, applies what the poet sang:

Your riddles find their explanation
In Him, God's everlasting Word,
God's highest and most glorious revelation
In whom thou seest and hearest what is highest.
The Godhead, who made Himself visible,
Humanity in thy flesh and blood,
The God after whom the soul hungered,
Man as he ought to be.[10]

With this, however, we have jumped ahead of our history. A glance into the future was necessary to explain the present.

Nonetheless, we need not dwell long on Abimelech. However instructive his fortunes may be, he grew up like Jonah's miracle tree and withered away just as quickly. He was a traitor and was betrayed; brought the curse upon a people who rejected the blessing; was soon overtaken by the judgment of God, and even in his death showed that the glory of men was paramount to him; in a word, he arouses our interest here because and insofar as he was the provisional expression of the same spirit that later became manifest in the rejection of Samuel and of Jehovah and the appointment of Saul.

The difference between the two events lies in this, that the company of the inhabitants of Shechem provides evidence of a corruption in which there is no trace of the original, national life. Abimelech is on a par with the kings of the Canaanites, who ruled over a city or over a few nearby places. Shechem, except for what may have been adopted from the Baal service, has sunk entirely into paganism. Whereas it is the elders of Israel, that is, the representatives and heads of the tribes, who desire of Samuel a king, 1 Sam. 8: 6, and in the supplication which they cause to be heard,

[10] Source unknown.

not only accomplish the possibility which the law in Deut. 17: 14ff. postulated, but in the words which they employ, show that they *know* that law, 1 Sam. 8: 5, cf. Deut. 17: 14.

God "gives the king in his wrath"; His kingdom did not exist. But the very institution incorporated into the people's life upon the choice of Saul was maintained by Jehovah and constituted the transition to a new stage of the Lord's revelation in the work of redemption.

7. JEPHTHAH

Judges 10–12

Thy gentleness hath made me great.

2 Samuel 22: 36 (KJV)

Let us, O God of hosts!
Wait not fruitlessly for your assistance;
Turn away our haters;
Faithful shepherd! Bring us back;
Deliver us, show us the lovely light
Of your comforting countenance.

Ps. 80: 5 (Psalter of 1773)

If we became acquainted with the moral and religious life only from discussions, sermons and treatises on the usefulness of adversity, and from consolatory letters and discussions, we would imagine earthly life to be an institution for education, a foundation for improvement, a preparatory class for eternity, in which man is brought by paths of test and stress to where he must arrive under the wise discipline of the Heavenly Father. Perhaps we might even be of the opinion that those who suffered the most down here were also the most privileged and could expect the most abundant harvest hereafter from the tear-seed of misery.

In this connection, the well-known lines from Hymn 20: "He knows when either sorrow or joy benefit our minds!"[11] might give us the impression that a human heart were as susceptible to the workings of the Lord as the apothecary's or grocer's scales are to the weights placed in one scale or another. An ounce here, a gram there, a few more grains or drops, and the scales are in balance!

Is this view correct, or is it in direct conflict with our experience? Did not Jehovah say to Israel: "Why do you want more beatings? Why do you keep rebelling? Your head has a massive wound, and your whole heart is afflicted. From the sole of your foot to the top of your head, there is no soundness—only wounds and welts and festering sores neither cleansed

---

[11] *Evangelische Gezangen*, p. 39.

nor bandaged nor soothed with oil" (Isa. 1: 5, 6)? Does not the Lord complain, "All day long I have held out My hands to a disobedient and obstinate people" (Rom. 10: 21)? Do we not hear Him say, "If the miracles that were performed in you had been performed in Tyre and Sidon, they would have repented long ago in sackcloth and ashes" (Matth. 11: 21)?

These instances, which fully confirm what we can learn from history and experience, indicate the point of view from which we have to consider the suffering that comes upon us by a judicial or paternal act of God. Although it is an *expedient means* of rendering us contrite and bringing us to repentance, it is not therefore infallible. If the outcome – as is the case with the forces at work in nature – were predetermined by the lesser or greater suitability of the means employed, such means would receive the honor due to God alone.

Nothing in the world can fix the sinner; God alone can do this.

Despite the experiences Israel had gained over a span of what now came to three centuries, it had – viewed superficially – not only remained the same, but actually regressed in the half-century that lay between Gideon and Jephthah. We read in Judges 10: 6: "And again the Israelites did evil in the sight of the LORD. They served the Baals, the Ashtoreths, the gods of Aram, Sidon, and Moab, and the gods of the Ammonites and Philistines. Thus they forsook the LORD and did not serve Him."

We can only say that this was not the purport of the affliction that befell it, the forbearance shown it, and especially not the deliverances of the Lord. Seven forms of idolatry are listed in v. 6 and seven evident deliverances are listed in vv. 11 and 12. Both punishment and blessing always have a double effect, leading to both *repentance* and *hardening*. The same heat of the sun that melts the wax hardens the ground that has been soaked by the rain.

But none of this takes away from the fact that what is true of the Word of the Lord can be said of the leading of Providence and of the work of grace: "so My word that proceeds from My mouth will not return to Me empty, but it will accomplish what I please, and it will prosper where I send it" (Isa. 55: 11).

Although the great and decisive change that is the fruit of the working of the Holy Spirit under the New Covenant, Jer. 32: 40, has not yet taken place, the Lord does not do anything in vain, and the effects of all that

Israel has gone through are indeed seen in its life. We notice this each time we consider Israel after a lapse of time, not from a dogmatic point of view and not while dwelling on a few salient phenomena of its life, but by taking its history as a whole and its happenings in mutual connection. Not from a dogmatic point of view, for then we see only the absolute and not the relative in man. Israel, for example, is just as sinful, just as unbelieving and stubborn as ever, just as incapable of having fellowship with Jehovah as before. But that does not mean it has remained the same, or that no change is noticeable in its moral life.

This can be seen immediately on close inspection. It is similar to colors. One speaks of four colors and up to seven transitions; but the connoisseur discovers all kinds of nuances, and learns to distinguish cardinal from dahlia red, and both from shrimp pink and reseda green.

The Israel of Jephthah's day is not the Israel we came to know under Gideon. But one must try to take into account the impression it makes as a whole, and not focus blindly on a few specific phenomena.

When we take a seat on an express train heading south on a cold spring day which is to arrive, for example, in Brussels, we have a hard time imagining that the people there are enjoying the warm weather in the open air in front of the cafes and hotels. The fact is, it is another world.

So it is also with the world in which we find Jephthah. The repentance shown by Israel, the removal of the foreign gods, 10: 16, in a word the reformation we observe, presupposes not only more *religious knowledge* than was previously possessed even in Ophrah, but also the *regular practice of the tabernacle service*. But in order to become cognizant of this – as has been said – one must not dwell on a single phenomenon.

The announcement in v. 6 that Israel was not content to serve the Baal but indulged in idolatry in all its known forms might lead us to the conclusion that the people had now departed much further from God than before. In certain respects this is indeed the case; but still it does not prove what at first glance appears to be entailed in this. For progress in moral or religious life is not progress in a straight line, but zigzag.

Things do not progress here, as Longfellow would have it,

that each to-morrow
find us farther than to-day[12]

such that one can calculate the stages of our progress in accordance with the number of days we are traveling.

In fact, the opposite is often true. Progress sometimes announces itself through apparent regression. Just when pain is felt, the danger has passed. Just when one seems to be getting better, a breakdown occurs, the fever increases, or the life spirits visibly diminish. When the possessed person was brought to Jesus, the evil spirit threw him into convulsions. Is it not quite natural?

As soon as God strikes us with conviction, we regress. When the stronger one comes to spoil the strong man's goods, he resists. The fierce lightning and the booming thunderclaps immediately precede the clearing of the sky and the pouring down of the rain.

Israel has changed. Let us see

1. how this change was brought about,
2. how it became manifest,
3. to what it led;

and in connection with this, as it were in the light of all this, let us consider the character and actions of Jephthah.

1. When God's judgments come upon the earth, the people of the world learn righteousness (Isa. 26: 9).

Ophrah and Shechem were both affected by God's judgment. Appalling as that judgment may have been, the shock it brought about was probably beneficial. The apostle presents man struggling with the truth, and in such a way that he succeeds in subduing it and suppressing it, Rom. 1: 18. What do shocks bring about in our lives? They make us lose balance for a moment, so that the truth can assert itself against our will and our intention. What does the extraordinarily abundant and surprising catch on Lake Gennesaret have to do with Peter's soul? Yet he exclaims: "Go away from me, Lord, for I am a sinful man!" (Luke 5: 8). Is "Sirs, what

[12] *A Psalm of Life*, v. 3.

must I do to be saved?" an answer to Paul's exclamation, "Do not harm yourself; we are all here"? (Acts 16: 28, 30). No, but it reveals what dwelled in the depths of the soul of the jailer at Philippi.

Scripture tells us nothing about the events immediately following the extermination of Gideon's family, the destruction of Shechem and the death of Abimelech. But if shortly afterwards we discover a *completely different state of affairs,* the assumption is nevertheless that a certain connection exists between these facts. We are strengthened in this conviction by what we found at the beginning of the 10th chapter, which is the transition to the history of Jephthah.

There we read: "After the time of Abimelech, a man of Issachar, Tola son of Puah, the son of Dodo, rose up to save Israel," though no record of him is given. Is it not as if the Holy Spirit wants to show that He is free to animate the organs of salvation from all the tribes?

Here we are faced with one of those facts which later, such as at Saul's first appearance when the gift of prophecy was communicated to him, so often caused the people to ask, "And who is their father?" i.e., is the Holy Spirit attached to a particular lineage then? (cf. 1 Samuel 10: 12).

"He lived in Shamir, in the hill country of Ephraim" (Judges 10: 1). This last is especially noteworthy. After all, if we may consider Samir to be Shamir or Shemer, then the perimeter of Shechem, cf. 1 Kings 16: 24, was the center of his activity. In other words, God did not surrender the God-forgotten people but continued to work upon and preserve Ephraim. By what means? By spiritual means, but which by their very nature were accompanied by *judicial* actions. Especially in the time in question, and in the midst of the existing divisions and confusion, the sword also had to be brought to bear, and resolute deeds and decisive action were certainly not lacking.

To the activity of Tola – how remarkable that the burial places of him and the later judges are mentioned, cf. 8: 32; 10: 2, 5; 12: 7, 10, 12, 15 – is connected that of Jair, of whose history we are only informed that he had thirty sons, riding on thirty colts of donkeys, and that these sons exercised authority over thirty cities across the Jordan, called the Havvoth-Jair, ch. 10: 4. So his labor too becomes known to us only in its effects or outworking.

God is a great King who has all kinds of servants and causes all kinds of work to be done. "Does the plowman plow for planting every day? Does he continuously loosen and harrow the soil? When he has leveled its surface, does he not sow caraway and scatter cumin? He plants wheat in rows and barley in plots, and rye within its border.... This also comes from the LORD of Hosts, who is wonderful in counsel and excellent in wisdom" (Isa. 28: 24, 25, 29).

It is not said that the work of Jair and Tola and later of Abdon and Elon had lesser significance for Israel than that of Jephthah or Gideon, although we are not informed of any details in this regard. The fortress commander who by vigilance and fidelity preserves the key of the country, and the chargé d'affaires of the empire who champions the interests of his people at the court of a foreign power, are not mentioned in the history of their people in the same way as the gallant captain who has maintained the honor of the flag against a twice stronger foe; but at bottom do they therefore have less merit than he?

If we look back from the days of Samuel or even from those of Jephthah to the time of Gideon, we feel that in the interim much must have been wrought in silence. These founders, of whom only the name is given to us, were to their successors what Huss and Wycliffe were to Luther and his fellow workers.

Moreover, Jair was not alone. He was the head of a numerous family, a privilege that sustained him and the cause of the Lord. "Like arrows in the hand of a warrior, so are children born in one's youth. Blessed is the man whose quiver is full of them. He will not be put to shame when he confronts the enemies at the gate" (Ps. 127: 4–5).

That the tribes east of the Jordan were relieved from the pressure of the Ammonites after only eighteen years, while Judah continued to groan under that of the Philistines for *forty* years, is due, at least in part, to the influence exerted by Jair's descendants in Gilead. All this becomes clear to us as soon as we know that after Abimelech we are not dealing with successive but partly *concurrent judges*.

In the latter part of this period, Israel is oppressed from two sides. While the Ammonites are oppressing Gilead, the Philistines have taken possession of Judah. If we now compare the various time periods found in this and the following chapters, we find that Abdon died nine years after the battle of Ebenezer, 1 Sam. 7. The Ammonites indeed oppressed Israel for eighteen years, Judges 10: 8. Thereafter Jephthah exercised the judgeship for six years. Ebzan judged Israel in Bethlehem – not Bethlehem-Ephrathah, but another place in Issachar – seven, Elon in Zebulun ten, Abdon in Ephraim eight years; together, therefore, they served for twenty-five years. Hence when Abdon died, forty-nine years had passed since the beginning of the Ammonite tribulation.

Judges 10: 7 reads, "So the anger of the LORD burned against Israel, and He sold them into the hands of the Philistines and Ammonites." This seems to indicate that the enemies attacked from *two sides at once* (although chapters 10–12 speak exclusively of the Ammonites, while the Philistines are spoken of only in 13: 1). Assuming this to be the case, then it would mean that Abdon lived and worked for nine more years after the forty years of domination by the latter enemies, and further that Eli the high priest, as we shall see in the next chapter, was a contemporary of Jair and Jephthah, as well as that, like Samuel, Samson was yet born under the high priesthood of Eli.

2. What indicates the change?

Let the history told to us in Judges 10: 6ff. answer this. Israel had been guilty of idolatry in a way unparalleled in the heathen world. "'Cross over to the coasts of Cyprus,'" spoke the Lord later through the prophet Jeremiah, "'and take a look; send to Kedar and consider carefully; see if there has ever been anything like this: Has a nation ever changed its gods, though they are no gods at all? Yet My people have exchanged their Glory for useless idols. Be stunned by this, O heavens; be shocked and utterly appalled,' declares the LORD. 'For My people have committed two evils: They have forsaken Me, the fountain of living water, and they have dug their own cisterns—broken cisterns that cannot hold water'" (Jer. 2: 10–13).

The broken cisterns were not only the gods of Canaan but of *all other nations*. If the people of God forsake Him, they fall and sink much deeper than their neighbors. Peter not only denies belonging to the circle of Jesus' followers but curses himself until even the servants of Caiaphas recoil in dismay. The renegade not only denies the faith which once seemed holy to him but becomes a persecutor of those who profess it. A child of pious parents, when once he has broken the bonds of discipline that restrained him, indulges in excesses that even ungodly companions deem unbecoming. By a known law in the moral world, the best or that which was intended for the highest becomes the most dangerous or unworthy if it undergoes a deformity or corruption.

Nonetheless, the judgment did not fail to materialize this time either, and as before served both to halt the progress of destruction and to bring the people to repentance. For Israel did not need to seek the connection for what was done to it by the Philistines and the Ammonites. From the standpoint of paganism, the gods and the nations were equated. Therefore, from that standpoint it was not just the two peoples who oppressed it, but their gods, who in this way acknowledged the honor bestowed upon them voluntarily by a foreign nation, of its own accord. In this way it experienced sin to be a harsh mistress that rewards with ingratitude and unfaithfulness.

King Dionysius of Syracuse, according to an ancient story, once ordered a heavy gold chain of extraordinary length from a blacksmith against whom he held a grudge. When the poor man with great difficulty succeeded in carrying out the order and hoped to receive the desired reward, he was ordered to double the length. This took place twice, yes, three times, while each time the time he was given to deliver the required work was halved. But when he appeared before the king the third time, he had used up all his money in accomplishing the task assigned to him and his strength was completely exhausted by his overexertion. And what was the reward for such service? "Go," spoke the tyrant to his servants, "to the highest point of the highest mountain, let down the chain into the depths, and see to it that this miscreant hangs at the end to seek his reward in the abyss!"

This is the way evil treats its faithful servants, the way Kamos, the god of the Ammonites treated Gilead – for we lose sight of Judah for the moment. "'Your own evil will discipline you; your own apostasies will reprimand you. Consider and realize how evil and bitter it is for you to forsake the LORD your God and to have no fear of Me,' declares the Lord GOD of Hosts" (Jeremiah 2: 19). That chastisement, however, did not miss its mark. Not only did Israel "cry out to the Lord," but it also came to *confession of guilt* and *repentance*. What is more, whereas until now the reformation movement emanated from a single person who had been called and empowered by God to do so, and in such a way that the entire work of reformation stood and fell with him, we now see *the people as a whole repenting.*

When a movement becomes powerful enough, it goes beyond the circle to which it was first confined to become active as a force that drives an entire people in a certain direction. Few are then in a position to withdraw from the inspiration of the idea that dominates the whole. When Israel, after Joshua had allowed the trans-Jordanian tribes to go to their inheritance, heard tell that "the children of Reuben and the children of Gad and half the tribe of Manasseh have built an altar, opposite the land of Canaan, on the borders of the Jordan, on the sides of the children of Israel," Josh. 22: 11, they drew themselves up *as one man* to fight against the tribes that were apostate in their eyes. The same thing happened after the abomination committed by the children of Benjamin, Judges 20: 1. When Pekaliah king of Israel and Rezin the Syrian attacked Judah under Achaz, the king's heart and the hearts of his people were moved as the trees of the forest are moved by the wind, Isaiah 7: 2. Judah was one body moved by one soul. Again, when the prophet Joel called on Israel to do penance, his revival applied to all the people from the greatest to the smallest, cf. Joel 2: 15–17. The judgment on Sodom is justified in Gen. 19: 4 by the fact that *the entire people,* from all the way to the furthest end, surrounded the house.

Similar phenomena showing clearly that a people is not a chance aggregation of individuals in one country or under one administration but a unity composed of individuals which, like the single man, has its own origin, its own vocation, and, in spite of all differences, its own peculiar character, we find at all times in history. We discover them in the *migrations* of ancient times and in the *political movements* of the modern; in *the urge which in Israel led men from all classes and the farthest reaches of the land to the desert* where John the Baptist appeared, and did so with a power from which Israel's proud priests and deluded lawgivers could not escape, Luke 3: 7, John 1: 19; in the *days of the Reformation,* when entire nations rose up to break away from the power of error, when within the space of two weeks the theses which Luther had nailed to the door of the palace church at Wittenberg were read in the palaces of the great and the huts of the poor, "and it seemed," as a contemporary reported, "as if angels had written them down and caused them to be carried on the four winds, to the most distant spots, in the most inaccessible valleys where one usually remained cut off from the currents of time"; in *the force which drove the entire French people* to the borders amidst the cry: "à Berlin, à Berlin!"

There are times like those of Elijah and Elisha, of Isaiah and Jeremiah, and indeed, to come to the Age of the Judges, of Gideon and Samson, when the truth is felt and confessed by only *a few* in a nation, when it forms more or less confined circles. There it reveals its full power and from there it makes its influence felt to a greater extent. But as long as the *nation itself* is not brought back to God, that influence remains limited, the power of truth is broken and the goal of those who remain faithful to it is not achieved.

When Moody and Sankey, the well-known evangelists, after having worked for some time in the East End of London among the poorest of classes with wonderful success, transferred their activity to one of the theaters in the West End, where only the elite used to attend, Moody, when opening his new hall, in the presence of many royals and others, used the following image:

> Society is similar to an English fireplace. The grate is covered with paper, chips and lighters, or at least with highly flammable substances. These are the people in the out of the way corners, who ignite very easily.
>
> Once lit, the flame in the East End reached around to all sides.
>
> Above this one finds a second layer, made up of wood and peat; it represents the sedentary middle class, the merchants in the City, the trading quarter of London, who are more stolid and do not catch fire so readily, but on the other hand keep warm longer. To them, too, we have tried to bring the word of life.
>
> But on top lie the large pieces of coal, among which, however, smaller lumps are scattered. Only when these are reached to such a degree by the fire that all stations are ablaze, that their coldness gives way and the inflammable substances they contain are ignited, does the heat spread

through the rooms, and then not for a moment but for good. Such are the dignitaries, the nobles, the tone-setters, whom we now have in view.[13]

The conversion of the entire nation will come first in the days of Samuel, but what is now seen in Gilead, in the trans-Jordan, is an auspicious omen. They are the firstfruits of the harvest that we see ripening in the field of Israel's popular life, the harvest that will reward all the labor that has been expended on that land. When this harvest is brought in, we are on new ground, in another era.

The Old Testament is for us not only the *witness* of revelation, the story of what God has done to prepare and bring about redemption, but the *record of revelation itself* which encompasses every sphere of thought and ability and every area of life. In Holy Scripture we learn to know not only God and man, not only sin and grace, but also *life in all its circles and forms;* popular life, not according to the abstract concept embodied in the modern state, in which no account has been taken either of the origin, the history, or the vocation of the people, and in which its inner unity, which in our Christian, Protestant nations finds its highest expression in religion, is utterly overlooked – but popular life as it *really* is.

In Israel we not only see entire generations departing from God, but entire generations repenting. By this it is certainly not to be understood that every citizen, one by one, has come to true conversion, not to be understood as if in the days of Gideon it were not true what later the apostle said, "not all who are descended from Israel are Israel" (Rom. 9: 6); but it teaches us that both then and now all our laboring, praying and preaching must have for their object the *subjection of all the people to the truth,* according to the word of the parting Redeemer, "Therefore go and make disciples of all *nations*" (Matth. 28: 19).

The repentance of Gilead is a prophecy, a portent of the lamentation that Jerusalem will give voice to when Zechariah 12: 10 comes to pass: "Then I will pour out on the house of David and on the people of Jerusalem a spirit of grace and prayer, and they will look on Me, the One they have pierced. They will mourn for Him as one mourns for an only child, and grieve bitterly for Him as one grieves for a firstborn son."

---

[13] Source unknown.

"Then the Israelites cried out to the LORD, saying, 'We have sinned against You, for we have indeed forsaken our God and served the Baals'" (Judges 10: 10).

Israel not only feels that it is being struck, not only has discovered the smiting hand of the Lord, but also knows why the blows have been administered to it. It knows its iniquity, Jer. 3: 13. This is a sure sign that the punishment has hit the mark.

The unrepentant one holds up at secondary causes and provides a more or less accurate description of the unfortunate confluence of circumstances by which one or another misery has come upon him. If he ascends to the first cause, it is to blame God. "The fathers," it is then said, "have eaten sour grapes, and the teeth of the children are set on edge" (Ezek. 18: 2). But the true penitent discovers the very cause of all that befalls him, whether directly from God or through the agency of men, namely, his own sin, which found him "on the day of reckoning" (Isaiah 10: 3). He sees Absalom raging and bows before God's judgment; he hears Shimei cursing, and holds back the sons of Zeruiah who wish to punish him according to his merits, for this cursing is only the force that drives the arrow of conviction into his innermost being.

"I have lost four children," a woman once said to a pastor visiting her for the first time. "When the first died I was furious with the physician because I thought I knew he had not treated it well. When the second was taken from me, I was inflamed with anger against my husband because he had taken the lad on a trip in which he caught cold, and which therefore became the indirect cause of his death. The third was snatched from me, and I had no one on whom I could blame for the loss. Then I recognized the finger of God – but also felt how all that was in me rose up against God. In my eyes God was a tyrant, an arbitrary being. He tormented me – so it seemed – out of lust for torment. Was any sorrow equal to mine?

"O Wonder, there the blow fell again. Death had now taken away my most beloved. That child who promised so much. It was my joy and my life. But now it had become enough. I had no more strength to resist. I was like the poet of the 77th psalm: 'And my mind searched the reason, Why God sent those adversities in such measure' (v. 4, Psalter of 1773).

"And my spirit found the reason. Like Luther in his cell at Erfurt, I could do nothing but groan, 'My sin, my sin!'

"And what was most remarkable of all: it was not my sins in general, it was not my sinful condition in consequence of which these adversities were my portion. I knew very well *what evil* it was that had cried out for punishment and had been stricken by the judgment of God."

O glorious condition, one which wholly corresponded to that which we discover at Gilead. Now other tears flow than those wept at Bochim; they are now the tears which are the outward sign of the contrition of the heart, without which no atonement is real and no repentance sincere.

Of those tears, a Persian poet once sang:

O, Blessed tears of unfeigned repentance of soul,
By God loosed embalming dew,
Thou makest the penitent heart leap
With the only guiltless salvation filled,
That ever was tasted for guilt.[14]

"They will come with weeping, and by their supplication I will lead them; I will make them walk beside streams of waters, on a level path where they will not stumble," says the Lord in Jer. 31: 9.

We read of Israel's penitence for the first time in Judges 10, and for the first time too we witness its rejection, the *rejection of its prayer*. For the first time we hear an answer of the Lord to the abased people's prayer, that contains no comfort at all. "Go and cry out to the gods you have chosen. Let them save you in your time of trouble" (Judges 10: 14).

The tax collector who dares not lift up his eyes when he prays to God, so severely offended by him; the prodigal son who will have reached the height of his expectation if he is permitted to take a place among his father's servants; everyone who is truly penitent, will, far from marveling at such an answer, find it quite understandable.

It is no small matter to sin against the Lord. It is not for man to take away the separation that willful abandonment of the Lord has brought about, by means of a word of confession of guilt, a tear of penitence. Not

[14] Source unknown.

only ten, but hundreds of years have passed since the deliverance from the house of servitude, and still Israel has not forgone putting appearances before the essence, idols before the true God. If Israel's repentance is now sincere, it can, so to speak, endure refusal and expect nothing better.

It is then in the mood that J. P. Lange attributes to the prodigal son when he envisions him in spirit transported near the father's dwelling, and has him say:

Here wish I to wait, all my life,
With sad complaints and songs of penitence,
Here I will hope.
Then in the end
The dwelling will open
So long misunderstood.[15]

To be sure, the prodigal son experiences the father's seeing him "while he was still far away" and already forgiving him before he even stammers a single word of repentance. So the poet describes the returnee's sensation and puts the words on his lips:

How! it is unlocked.
There, calls the Lord.
How! not rejected,
No more a stranger.
Away, earthly cares,
And fearful sorrow –
I lie secure
On the Father's heart![16]

But God sometimes also takes a different way with His own, often making them experience the wickedness of their existence and the severity of the judgment while doubling the blows and aggravating the pun-

[15] "Terugkeer," in *Nieuwe Christen Harptonen* [New Christian Harpnotes], pp. 11–12.

[16] "Terugkeer," p. 12.

ishment, just when – in our eyes – a word of comfort, of forgiveness and reconciliation would be appropriate. "O my God!" then laments the soul, "I cry by day, but You do not answer; And by night, but I have no rest" (Ps. 22: 2). Yet of these punishments, this smiting, this silence of the Lord, what David says of the smiting of the righteous is true: "That smiting shall not break my head" (Ps. 141, v. 6, Psalter of 1773).

Our gospel work and preaching are in great danger if this element of deep earnestness that leaves room for the waiting and rejection of God, of which we have a striking example here in His answer to Israel, is missed in it. There is a time to be gracious to the Lord's people, and the Lord has determined that time with sovereign omnipotence.

It is erroneous to think that only the proclamation of God's love renders the heart contrite. It can serve just as well to harden it. To this proclamation, which is commonplace among many, one of our poets, also a theologian, alluded when he said, "It is our misfortune that nowadays people are fed before they are hungry." For various reasons, the Lord sometimes keeps Himself at a distance or answers with a refusal when one calls to Him. But more than anything, this happens so that faith may have an opportunity to reveal itself and be confirmed.

Faith trusts God even when He is silent and refuses, and persists even when crying out seems utterly vain. It says, "Though He smite me, yet will I hope in Him." Faith is like the flame that kindles the fuel by which it seemed to be quenched, and finds new food in it. "Woman, what have I to do with thee?" (John 2: 2, KJV) the Savior said when Mary signaled to Him that a miracle would not be unwelcome. That is a rejection. "Whatsoever he saith unto you, do it!" she commanded the servants when she left His presence. Surely the harsh word did not discourage! Such was also the case with the Canaanite woman, and with the disciples at Emmaus when Jesus "seemed to be going farther." Even the children of Israel who are here directed to idols show that their conversion is sincere and that their faith is strong enough to endure this refusal. "Deal with us as You see fit; but please deliver us today!" (Judges 10: 15).

Before they called, God – we see this in retrospect – was already forming the man He intended to be their rescuer, and this is where we would least have sought him – deeper it is surely not possible to descend – *among those who did not come from a lawful marriage and were therefore excluded from Israel's inheritance.* In Jephthah is to be fulfilled what the Lord spoke through the mouth of Isaiah concerning the stranger and the eunuch. "Let no foreigner who has joined himself to the LORD say, 'The LORD will utterly exclude me from His people.' And let the eunuch not say, 'I am but a dry tree.' For this is what the LORD says: 'To the eunuchs who keep My Sabbaths, who choose what pleases Me and hold fast to My covenant—I will give them, in My house and within My walls, a memorial and a name better than that of sons and daughters. I will give them an everlasting name that will not be cut off'" (Jer. 56: 3–5). "No one of illegitimate birth may enter the assembly of the LORD, nor may any of his descendants, even to the tenth generation," says the law, Deut. 23: 2. In this respect Jephthah was equal to the Ammonite and the Moabite, v. 3.

And even though of the lineage of Manasseh, Jephthah, descended from the chief of Gilead, was an illegitimate son. Hence, his brothers would have been entirely in their right if they had only disputed the inheritance with him. They did more: they drove him out and treated him with unnecessary severity, Judges 11: 7. But God, whose ways are higher than our ways, chose the stone which the builders rejected for the cornerstone. What seemed to be the greatest misfortune became a blessing both for him and for Israel. We find him, like David in later times, at the head of a band with which he turned his sword, not against his people, but against their enemies. Through "His humbling him, the Lord made him great" (2 Samuel 22: 36, Dutch translation).

Among the tales which in our childhood we loved to read and hear, is that of the sister who, reduced to the humblest services, met up with a magic goddess, and was later loved by the prince, who sent for the hand of the unknown beauty after she hastily left the ball at midnight. Folklore, let us say, the experience of the centuries, expressed in this way the same truth that Jephthah also found confirmed in his own life, namely, that the way to the heights often leads through the depths.

The land of Tob, where he wanders about living by his sword, became a training school for the future ruler of Israel. That Gilead, when it had fitted itself out for battle and needed a leader, unanimously chose the man whom it had treated so harshly and probably so unjustly, proves both the sincerity of its conversion and the suitability of the man who was, as it were, suited for the place.

The former, because one bows much more easily to those who have wronged us than to those whom we have wronged. This is inherent in human nature. Whoever has been wronged or insulted by us is regarded and treated as an enemy from the outset, as if the injustice could thereby be justified. On the other hand, as soon as we have humbled ourselves before God, we thereby also receive the ability to humble ourselves before men.

The latter, because an idolater, one who out of vindictiveness had turned his sword against his brethren, could not have been considered for the place to which he was called with universal consent. But this naturally leads us to take a closer look at Jephthah. Was he a rough and domineering man who was won to the cause of Israel by the promise that he would be recognized as chief? (Judges 11: 8). Nothing of the sort. In Heb. 11: 32 he is mentioned among the heroes of faith. The promise that he would be a chief was to him a guarantee of the new spirit that animated Gilead. The covenant made with the elders is ratified before the Lord at Mizpah, ch. 11: 9–11.

In His name he accepts the office. He proceeds according to the precept of the law (Deut. 20: 10ff.) when, before going to war against the oppressors of his people, he opens a negotiation and states the question of law. Above all things: he trusts not in the ability, the prowess, the talent by which he had gained the confidence of his tribesmen, but in the Lord, Israel's God, and acts in the spirit of the poet of the 20th psalm when he sings:

Of chariots, horses and heroes
Our enemy is stout;
We shall rest on the honor and greatness
Of God, who preserves us.

Ps. 20: 4a (Psalter of 1773)

Of this, the vow he makes bears witness. The vow is a sacrifice that will be made in the future, and therefore is an imperfect sacrifice by which the need of the pious mind is satisfied to give God already now the tribute of that which one desires and hopes and expects to receive, to bring Him already now the thanks which one feels and to which one is obliged. Jacob made a vow at Bethel where his father's God had appeared to him, saying: "If God will be with me and watch over me on this journey, and if He will provide me with food to eat and clothes to wear, so that I may return safely to my father's house, then the LORD will be my God" (Gen. 28: 20–21).

Taken in this sense, we have to consider the vow as a permanent component of the religious life. It becomes reprehensible only when one forgets that since all things are due to Him, one can only give God what is already His, not ours. Further, that one cannot commit oneself to anything to which God's holy law had not already committed, since the law requires the dedication of ourselves and of all that is ours, in other words, since there are no superfluous good works. And finally, since the Lord is more ready to give us good gifts than we are to receive them, we need not or ought not to talk God into blessing us on account of what we ourselves do and are.

Yet in view of the law that excludes the illegitimate son from the congregation of the Lord, Jephthah's vow had special significance. Would this barrier remain or fall? He does not venture to decide this, but leaves it to God. "Whatever comes out the door of my house to greet me on my triumphant return from the Ammonites will belong to the LORD, and I will offer it up as a burnt offering," ch. 11: 31. Naturally, this refers to a festive entry, as victor. So there is no question of a chance encounter. What is more likely than that *his own child* would meet him at the head of her procession of virgins? Surely he did not come home by night, not without consequence, not as a stranger like Ulysses!

From the apparent emotion he displays in meeting his child, it has been thought that one might infer that she had been unexpected, 11:35, and thus that he had by rashness plunged himself and her into misery. But is it really necessary to explain the disappointment and anguish he displays in this way, and is this explanation plausible?

What or to whom, to begin with the last statement, did he think of when making his vow? Of an unclean animal? Neither in the eye of the pagan nor in that of the Israelite did this constitute a suitable sacrifice. The donkey which opened the womb had to be redeemed with a lamb, according to Ex. 34: 20. If one was not willing to do this, then its neck was to be broken. Of a sacrificial animal? Leaving aside the question as to whether an ox or sheep could come out of the door of his house, Judges 11: 31, it is utterly inconceivable that he could have intended such a gift at the beginning of a venture which, if it failed, would have had the most disastrous consequences for his people but especially for himself and his own. Something else would have been obvious if he, for his part, had prepared to sacrifice everything, even the most precious thing he possessed, to the Lord, had left Him, as it were, the free disposal of everything he possessed and in the meantime cherished the quiet hope that an animal would be designated as a sacrifice by God's own providence.

Of a man, a housemate, one of his subjects? This premise is squelched by the already mentioned objections, and even greater ones. In the eyes of the Israelite such a sacrifice was an abomination. Had there been such a thing in Jephthah's case, he must have sunk to the depths of idolatry, completely alienated from the true knowledge of God. But assuming that this was so: among the servants of Baal, human sacrifice represented the dearest thing one possessed and took the place of the sacrificer himself. "Shall I present my firstborn for my transgression," asked the prophet with an eye to the religious usages of the Canaanites as well as the surrounding peoples, "the fruit of my body for the sin of my soul?" (Micah 6: 7). The king of the Moabites slaughtered his eldest son, as we read in 2 Kings 3: 27, on the walls of his capital in front of the besiegers, after he had made an all-out attempt to break out of the besieged fortress with seven hundred men.

Therefore in this case Jephthah did not make a "careless" promise, but specifically had his daughter in mind.

And yet it is inconceivable that Jephthah, who "judged" Israel, that is, brought it back to God and therefore to itself, to freedom, would have been guilty of the abomination of the Canaanites, as the wicked Ahab later, 2 Kings 16: 3. Not only is he mentioned among the heroes of faith in Heb. 11 but we read in Judges 11: 29 that when he made his vow "the Spirit of the LORD came upon Jephthah." It was contrary to God's express command to allow a son or a daughter to pass through the fire. What's more, this act was among the crimes that had brought judgment of extermination upon the original inhabitants of the land, Lev. 18: 21; Deut. 18: 10; 2 Kings 16: 3, 17: 17. Now add to this that Jephthah, in view of his negotiation with the king of the Ammonites, Judges 11: 12ff., in which he uses almost verbatim the prescriptions in Num. 20–22 and Deut. 2, was too familiar with the history of the desert journey and the details of the entry into Canaan not to know that Jehovah did not require human sacrifice, and we may draw the conclusion from this both that he had his daughter in mind when he made his vow and that he did not intend to slaughter her.

But do we not expressly read in verse 31, that "whatever comes out the door of my house to greet me on my triumphant return from the Ammonites will belong to the LORD, and I will offer it up as a burnt offering"? And in verse 39 that "After two months, she returned to her father, and he did to her as he had vowed"? Certainly. Many interpreters are also convinced that a human sacrifice is indeed to be thought of in this case. Luther even considers it unnecessary to examine the grounds for the contrary opinion. He was as positive on this point as on that of the bodily presence of Christ in, at, with, and under the bread of the Lord's Supper when, likewise on the basis of the literal statement of Holy Scripture, on the occasion of the religious conversation with Zwingli, he pointed out the ground of his opinion with a piece of chalk on the tablecloth: "This *is* my body."

No doubt there is a reference to "a burnt offering," but there is another expression preceding it which is never used in the Mosaic law for the burnt offering in the proper sense, i.e., of animal sacrifice, but only of *the perfect devotion of men to the service of the Lord,* Num. 3: 12–13. The word translated by "burnt offering" originally denotes a "whole sacrifice." Although by this is often meant the sacrifice that is *completely* consumed on the altar, the basic conception has a meaning that is broad enough to encompass all that was wholly consecrated to the Lord, *even should it not end up on the altar.*

> One will say, 'I belong to the LORD,'
> Another will call himself by the name of Jacob,
> And still another will write on his hand, 'The LORD's,'
> And will take the name of Israel.
>
> Isaiah 44: 5

Now when the word is used, as in this case, of something that was not to be on the altar, and moreover could not serve as a "burnt offering" in the ordinary and more restricted sense because only that which was "male" was employed for this purpose, Lev. 1: 3, 10, then the thought is obvious that Jephthah, when he used the expression: "will belong to the LORD," intended to *cover all possible cases* and to this end he coupled two expressions which, although basically meaning the same thing, refer, at least in Israelite parlance, to two distinct kinds of sacrifices, that is, this one to human, the other to animal. Only when this is established are we in a position to explain Jephthah's vow, his emotion, the behavior of his daughter and her companions, in a word, the sacrifice.

Contrary to custom, contrary also to the law of the Lord, he had been called to take a place that was not his. Compelled by necessity, the elders of Gilead had asked him, a bastard, not only to place his sword at their disposal, but even to act as their chief. This agreement had been sealed in the presence of the Lord at Mizpah, Judges 11: 10–11.

Would God, who according to His omnipotence had so far glorified His grace to him, grant him still greater beneficence, and also look favorably upon *his line?* There was some reason, if not to expect this, at least to hope so. The daughters of Zelafead, the son of Hefer, the *son of Gilead,* the son of Machir, the son of Manasseh, had coveted and obtained an inheritance in Israel. "Our father," they spoke at the door of the tent of meeting in the wilderness, "died in the wilderness, but he was not among the followers of Korah who gathered together against the LORD. Instead, he died because of his own sin, and he had no sons. Why should the name of our father disappear from his clan because he had no sons? Give us property among our father's brothers" (Num. 27: 3–4; cf. Num. 36: 1–12).

Why shouldn't this decision also benefit his daughter? It was so terrible to be cut off from the people of God, to be a stranger to the covenants of promise! Yet he had *not dared to make this a condition.* A chief he wanted to be. Israel's interest dictated that he would become one. But it was something else to be "incorporated into Israel" with his line. It was not for him to dictate this, however fervently he might desire it.

This is a personal interest; and Jephthah is willing to leave this to the Lord. That was the reason for his vow. That was the reason he left the sacrifice entirely undetermined. God will Himself provide the sacrifice. The law allowed him to pay a ransom for that which he dedicated to the Lord. Yet he is willing not to avail himself of this privilege, not to make any exceptions, but to stand like a barren tree within the enclosure of the life of the Israelite people, to be extinguished along with his name and his line. And yet, once again, there remains a quiet expectation that the Lord, in the way of His providence, will manifestly intervene, that the riddle of his life will find a more satisfactory solution for him.

Among the German folk tales that most captivate the traveler in the Rhineland is that of the unknown master builder of Cologne Cathedral. For months on end he had tried to put on paper the lofty idea of the building that was always before his eyes and yet always escaped his mind's eye. Already the day was approaching which the bishop had designated as the day on which the plans of the house which he himself intended to found for God were to be handed in, and still the master builder sought to hold onto the majestic lines and dimensions which presented themselves to him for a moment, only to be swept away again as if by an evil power.

With despair in his heart, so the story goes, he set out to carry with him his disgrace and his disappointment to other lands, when, just outside the city gate, he met a strange master builder who was apparently on his way with plans for the requested main church. He inspected them, recognized his own conception therein, and accepted the stranger's offer to exchange his soul for the beautiful plan, together with riches and, what he desired above all, an immortal name, and that henceforth he might be regarded as the soul of a work so great, so artful, as to be unparalleled in Christendom.

Already the outlines, so the story continues, of the gigantic temple were seen, already the pillars had been raised to half their height which were to support the roof, itself which by its height and its vaults was destined to depict the firmament of heaven, when an incomprehensible gloom came over the artist's soul, which found expression in his words and in his looks. Everyone praised him, and praised him joyfully, but he himself withdrew more and more from dealings with people. One always saw him seated at the foot of one of the pillars that stood in the center before the place, where the high altar was to come, the eye fixed on a marble table on which would be engraved his name whose creation and the memorial of whose fame this cathedral would be.

In the midst of all this he finally became too frightened, confessed, was referred to a holy man near Heisterbach, and received from him the promise of complete absolution if he was prepared to smash with a heavy sledgehammer the table which would immortalize his name, and to consent to what had been imposed on him as penance, namely, that his name should never be known and his church never be completed.

And so it came to pass! But, only after long hesitation and fearful soul-searching, only after all light and all warmth had been expelled from the unfortunate's gaze, from his heart and life, only when he was ready to submit to that which was more bitter to him than death, a life without a name, a future without glory.

Who is so dead to all honor and glory as to understand nothing of the suffering, nothing of the struggle that the unfortunate master builder went through before his poor soul was put to rest?

Now then, it is well known that everything that the ambition of our contemporaries and forefathers desires for themselves as *individuals,* to wit, praise in their lifetime and a continuance in the memory of others after their death, is desired by the son of the East for *his line*. For this he seeks "an everlasting name that will not be cut off" (Isaiah 56: 5).

But in yet another and much higher sense is this true of the children of Jacob. Spiritual blessings, the salvation of the world, the promises of the future were attached to the covenant with Abraham and his seed forever. To be cut off from Israel was to be exiled from Jehovah.

Well then, this sacrifice Jephthah offers to the Lord, and, oh wonderful contradiction, while his line is blotted out he himself belongs to the true seed of the faithful, and his daughter becomes wholly the property of the Lord.

Too little is known to us of the religious life, that is, of the customs of those times insofar as they were not founded directly in the precepts of the Mosaic law, to be able to say anything with certainty about the further history of Jephthah's daughter. Everything that has been said by earlier and later interpreters of Scripture about certain institutions of so-called "holy women" that are said to have existed in Israel rests on mere conjecture. Whether these women, like the prophetess Anna, "never left the temple," or whether they lived in seclusion "upon the mountains," who can say?

However, if we look at the report about Jephthah and his vow from the appropriate point of view, we find in the statement, "he did to her as he had vowed. *And she had never had relations with a man,"* Judges 11: 39, not an unnecessary repetition of the indication that she was a virgin, but a further indication of the fate that awaited her.

Without asking whether the expression "address"[17] would have been better translated by another word, we can very well imagine that "the daughters of Israel went forth from year to year to address" or lament the daughter of Jephthah the Gileadite while she was alive, but not so well that year in, year out they set aside no less than four days to keep alive the memory of a sorrowful fact that was in complete conflict not only with the precepts of the Mosaic law but also with everything known to us from earlier and later times about the Israelite way of life.

Her father did not live long after the abasing of the Ammonites. He held the office assigned to him for only six years, ch. 12: 7, and part of that time was embittered not only by the absence of his daughter but also by the struggle against Ephraim. This struggle is very remarkable for us not only because of what it teaches about the claims of the aforementioned tribe but especially because of the insight it gives into some of the political relations of the time.

As to the first thing, Ephraim suffered from the malady with which, alas, so many people and nations are afflicted: it wanted to be first in everything. It is not for the first time in history that we notice the Diotrephes character in Ephraim. Gideon already suffered from the lord-it-over temperament by which Ephraim refused to rejoice in a redemption that its own hands had not wrought. In his days, however, the unsteadiness could still be appeased by "a gentle answer" which "turns away wrath" (Proverbs 15: 1) and the tribe still participated in the pursuit of the enemies, ch. 8: 1ff. Now, after a lapse of some twenty-some years, we find the malady so aggravated that in the time of need they refused help and now wish to revenge themselves on him through whom the Lord has evidently granted a surprise outcome! Judges 12: 2.

---

[17] "aanspreken," the word used in the Dutch States Translation.

There is truly no more unhappy existence imaginable than that of those who insist on their rights and forget their duties, who dare to demand everything and will give nothing. In life we have met with people who have reminded us of Ephraim. One finds them in the world of children and also in the society of adults. They are always on the lookout to see if they are respected and appreciated enough. They crave love and trust as a tribute naturally due to them, are extremely sensitive to any assault on their highness, suffer constantly from injured majesty and never learn to forget and lose themselves. How gladly would one communicate to them the wisdom that a little girl showed in her answer to the question, "How is it that everyone loves you so much?" showed. "I really don't know," she said, "unless it is because I love them so much!"[18]

How sinful, how deeply immoral, yes, how ungodly the existence is which we here have in mind is only revealed when it is seen that it prevents people, even where it would cost them no sacrifice and they can derive no excuse for their shameful selfishness from their own self-interest, from rejoicing with the joyful. We note this in the parable of the elder son who leaves the banquet and is painfully affected by the recurring final verse of the festive song that rings in his ears outside: "Be of good cheer, for this my son was dead and is alive again; he was lost and is found!"

Even more shameful, more heinous, more terrible is the behavior of Ephraim, who for the redeemer of Gilead has only the evil threat: "We will burn your house down with you inside!" (ch. 12: 1).

As has been said, we can deduce from this sad history something about the political relations in the days of Jephthah of which we would otherwise have known nothing, and which are not lacking in importance for us.

---

[18] "It is told of a certain good man's child, whose lineage still is cherished, that when she was asked by her father (half–bantering, half in earnest) to tell him the reason why everybody loved her so, she cast down her eyes with a puzzled air, then opened them wide, as a child does to the sunrise of some great truth—'Father, perhaps it is because I love everybody so'. Lucan has it in a neater form: 'amorem quæris amando'". R. D. Blackmore, *Cradock Nowell: A Tale of the New Forest* (1866), vol. I, ch. 8.

Hence, not all those of whom the Scriptures say that they "judged Israel" were, like Jephthah, heads of a few or many tribes – did not, in other words, stand in the same relationship to the people.

Of some of them there is no evidence that they redeemed Israel with the sword. Of some it is not likely that they themselves acted as head and judge. Barak, for example, conquered the enemies on the battlefield, but Deborah stood by him as a prophetess and found her employment in the field of religious and moral life. Gideon certainly did not, like Samuel later, travel the land, now here now there, to administer justice and uphold the law of the Lord. Samson held no public office. Jephthah, on the other hand, who was elected head, possessed virtually royal power within the narrower boundaries of Gilead, without the royal title. He was prince of Gilead. Apart from the blemish on his birth, there was nothing remarkable in this. He was from the house of the tribal chief.

"Now Jephthah the Gileadite," we read in 11: 1, "was a mighty man of valor; he was the son of a prostitute, and Gilead was his father." Hereby did neither he nor his people presume to exercise any rights over the other tribes. From time immemorial, however, the tribes of Joseph, Manasseh and Ephraim, had formed a *league*. They had waged war together against the Canaanites. "The house of Joseph also attacked Bethel, and the LORD was with them" (Judges 1: 22). As a contiguous unit, they had already acted under Joshua. After all, we read in Josh. 17: 14: "Then the sons of Joseph said to Joshua, 'Why have you given us only one portion as an inheritance? We have many people, because the LORD has blessed us abundantly.'"

Now this closer union was very natural, just as it was natural for it to benefit Ephraim, which would have had priority over its brother tribe Manasseh, if only because the latter was split in two. However, a great danger threatened from this side for the essential unity willed by God among all twelve tribes, the same danger that arises in the church when a group of believers join together as a faction.

It was Ephraim's sin to want to be something else and something more than what God had made him, one of the tribes of Israel, one of the sons of Jacob. He atoned for that sin in appalling fashion; forty-two thousand Ephraimites did not return to their hearths but fell in fratricidal warfare or were killed by the embittered Gileadites at the springs of the Jordan (12: 6).

In the body of the Israelitish people nothing disparate can be taken up without causing, like a splinter that has entered the hand or foot, or like a piece of steel that has penetrated the breast, an aggravation and thereby a fermentation in the blood by which health and, in persistent cases, life is threatened.

The fratricidal war that Jephthah was forced to wage was a judgment on Ephraim. If only it had led to repentance, there would have been no mention later of "a kingdom of ten tribes" that might likewise be called "the kingdom of Ephraim." Ephraim's pride prevented the complete merging of the tribes into the unity of national life.

8. SAMSON

The Nazirite of God, the Avenger of Israel

Judges 13–16

Though I see even an army surrounding me,
Still I fear not; I trust in the Lord
Though they want to force me into war;
I rest easy, trusting in this.

Psalm 27: 2a (Psalter of 1773)

In the days when the star of his greatness seemed to have set for good, King Arthur (according to one of the best-known and most beloved folk tales of England) found refuge in the hut of a swineherd, where he performed the lowest services, while also once coming into contact with the coarse hands of his hostess, the baked good of whom he had not taken sufficient care of. Still greater humiliation was undergone by one of the last Roman emperors, who was insulted in all sorts of ways by his conqueror, the Persian king Sapor, and among other things was forced to arch his back to serve as a footstool when the Persian mounted his horse during his court procession. The state they were in, the work they were given to do, however despicable, nonetheless did not prevent – not Arthur at least – from remaining as Macbeth said of himself, "Every inch a king"!

Of a king and of every man, if we understand this correctly, no one is in a position to enslave him, to humble him, if he does not do it himself. We admire the greatness of soul displayed by a member of the English Parliament when he calmly and with dignity replied to the word which a proud patrician once addressed to him in full session, namely, "Your father polished my father's shoes!" by asking, "Well, sir! did he not do it well?"

More to be despised, if no more to be lamented, were a Heliogabalus, a Louis XI and a Henry the Troubadour when they did what was unworthy of the royal title they held. And saddest of all, not to dwell any longer on such cases from secular history, is a royal position without royal pride or royal heroism, is a slave, a foot-wipe, a characterless creature, clothed with regal purple.

We have in view Judah, the tribe of the king. If ever a prophecy was stymied, a position denied, a blessing rejected, all this can be said of Judah in the days of Manoah and Samson. "Judah, it is you!" exclaimed Father Jacob on his deathbed. "Your brothers shall praise you. Your hand shall be on the necks of your enemies; your father's sons shall bow down to you. Judah is a young lion—my son, you return from the prey. Like a lion, like an old lion he crouches and lies down; who dares to rouse him?" Gen. 49: 8, 9.

When this tribe went out at the forefront of Israel's hosts, Num. 2: 3, cf. 7: 12 – when, at the Lord's command, it first went up to fight against the Canaanites, Judges 1: 2 – and later went to war against the Benjamites, 20: 18 – indeed, even when its chief Othniel delivered it out of the hands of Cushan-rishathaim, it seemed indeed as if this promise stood to be fulfilled.

But since then Judah had been silent. The history of the Age of the Judges after Ehud moves entirely among the northern and eastern tribes. And now, as we once again catch sight of the king's tribe, it has completely degenerated and in its midst reveals a slavishness that is almost unparalleled in history.

Yet in what respect did the time in which Samson acted differ from that in which Ehud, Barak, Gideon, and Jephthah lived? In this, that it did not produce a savior, and when God in His grace created him, did not know what use to make of him. In this, that there was no weeping as with Bochim; no repentance as that which preceded the appearance of Jephthah; not even a cry from misery to the God of the fathers as with the contemporaries of Ehud and of Gideon, who, when the sound of the trumpet announcing the hour of deliverance was heard, were immediately ready to gather around the deliverer.

Even the skittish deer when brought to a halt seeks to defend itself against the dogs that attack it from all sides. But Judah resigns itself to its humiliation and has made peace with its persecutors. In this people all resilience is gone. There is neither the ability to resist nor the desire to. Reviled and dishonored, there it lies, kissing the shackles that its enemy has laid upon it.

The possessions of the Philistines are scattered here and there in its land. The mount of Jebus grants the enemy a foothold. There is no blacksmith in Israel. But with all this we hear no cry of sorrow, see no tear of repentance, discover no sign that Judah is aware of its calling and destiny. Along with its faith, Israel loses its courage and strength. As soon as it ceases to believe in God, its self-confidence also perishes. Let the enemy spare its life, not deprive it of the opportunity to acquire for itself the necessary sustenance – as, apparently, the Philistines did – and it submits to the inevitable. An independent national existence and that which is inseparable from it, the honor of its God, are not worth surrendering its peace, its security, and its welfare.

But then it is hereby also decided that Judah must be oppressed still longer and more severely until it too will be ready to say, "Blessed is He who comes in the name of the Lord!" Or would the redemption of a people, of a tribe be different from that of a man? By no means. The people and the tribe experience that which David does, God's hand pressing heavily upon them day and night, their sap changed into summer drought as long as they remain silent, that is, persist in their unrepentance, Ps. 32: 4.

The very first condition to be saved is the knowledge of our misery and the desire to be saved. The "poor," those who "mourn," those who "hunger and thirst for righteousness," are spoken of as "blessed." It would be a curious gospel that knew salvation for the unwilling. God who redeems also prompts the willingness to accept redemption.

When the people of Paris forced open the dungeons of the Bastille, one of the prisoners refused to leave the only place in the wide world where he felt at home. In any case, they did him no favors when they forced upon him a freedom he had not desired and was not now ready to accept.

Even more striking is the example – even more lamentable is the condition – of the man who in a moment of madness refused to leave a sinking wreck. The ship he was on was loaded with gold dust and gold pieces, when it struck a reef in view of the South American coast. In haste the boats were put out. There was no prospect of saving anything more than the crew. The doomed vessel was already sinking, and people were rushing to abandon it.

Already the lifeboats had been cast off when the carpenter was missed. One of them then returned and, heedless of the danger, sent a few sailors aboard to search for their mate. They found him on deck, in the midst of the tons of gold he had broken open, so that the precious metal surrounded him on all sides; they called out to him to hurry for his life's sake if he wished to escape a certain death, but received in reply a peal of laughter. They called again. In vain. They tried to force him to leave the place. He resisted and furiously swung his axe. A few moments later they could see from the boats that they had escaped just in time. With dismay the same frenzied laughter was heard above the whirlpool into which the wreck was sinking – and all was silent! In the midst of his treasures, the poor man had disappeared into the depths.

It is undoubtedly true that no man can be redeemed unless he desires salvation. But this is only one side of the truth. The other side is revealed to us in what we see happening in unrepentant Judah.

Man's unfaithfulness does not destroy the Lord's faithfulness. God continues to do His work, and even the unwillingness of man will not be able to halt the majestic course of His work of redemption. This tribe must be sustained, must not be lost, and will be lifted up from its deep decay lest it be completely alienated from the rest. Jair and Ibzan, Elon and Jephthah are at work in the north and east. To Judah the Lord gives Samson, who will "begin the deliverance of Israel" (Judges 13: 5). Redemption itself comes about only through and after severe judgments. How could its fruit be picked before it has ripened in the field of abasement and renewal? Surely a corpse is incapable of accepting a gift!

If the action of Samson revived the courage of an unrepentant people when the ark of the covenant was brought into the army at Ebenezer, help still tarries until the day of great atonement at that same Ebenezer, when Judah is brought to God with all Israel under Samuel, 1 Sam. 7: 4, 12.

To understand Samson's actions, one must get a vivid picture of the great danger that threatened Judah from the side of the Philistines, and in what it consisted. Israel's conquerors dealt with it with much wisdom of state. Samson fights, he alone, against the men of Askelon. They let him go. He drives fire through the enemies' fields. They blame the disaster on his father-in-law, who committed a shameful betrayal of him. He finds in this again reason to avenge himself on them. His own people will not be called to account for what he has done, if only they show themselves willing to hand him over.

All this justifies the supposition that the Philistines intended to break and unnerve the Israelite spirit while deliberately avoiding any provocation to resistance. If even Manoah and his wife, who knew what the child was for whom they had received as a gift of grace from God, did not adequately resist his desire to possess a Philistine, the wall of separation between the two nations must have been far from insurmountable. Yes, what is more telling: if God used Samson's sinful lust to tear them apart violently, the danger of merging and amalgamating them was greater than one would suspect at first glance.

Therefore, Samson's work serves exclusively to make possible future redemption. Samuel's runs parallel to his. Samson is the avenger rather than the redeemer of Judah. He is its guardian, the pioneer of the new age that will see a desired reformation come about. Even in this, however, the Lord reveals His grace; where sin has reigned, grace has been far more abundant. On man's side redemption was cut off, but when the Lord found no reason in Judah to be gracious to him, He found it in Himself.

Was there then no point of contact in this tribe for the Lord's work in Israel? Undoubtedly. Not in the disposition and mood of the people but in the covenant, in the law and institutions of the Lord. This will become clear to us as soon as we understand the meaning and purpose of the Nazirite. Before that, however, a remark of a more general nature.

The history of Samson shows us the value of the norms and forms of religious life. Jehovah joins with, and makes use of, an institution which in these times seemed to have lost all meaning and, had it not fallen into oblivion, would have become a dead and bare form. We see from this how one-sided, at best, is the disparagement of such forms that we observe in others or in ourselves. If those forms – so one reasons – do not come from life, do not correspond to it, they are false and therefore extremely harmful. Better life without form than form without life.

The principle stated here can be expressed in this way, that for the vast majority subjective truth has greater value than objective. It leads in its utmost consequence to the denial of the connection between doctrine and life, and to the greatest follies, for example, to the opinion that error from the mouth of a spiritual or renewed man is better than truth from that of an unspiritual or unconverted man.

The great error both in the principle and in its application lies in seeking a contradiction where none actually exists. It goes without saying that the streambed of a river, taken by itself, does not feed the land on its banks and does not provide a waterway for inland navigation if the stream has dried up. It is just as self-evident that the measurements for wet and dry goods, however orderly drawn up, cannot provide us with what we need as long as their content, indispensable to us, is lacking. But does this give us the right to deny, either to the riverbed or to those measurements, the significance they possess in the order of things? Are we then to forget that as soon as proper drainage is missed, rain and flood turn the land into a swamp? Or should we prefer to receive our goods without indicating amounts, for fear of getting the amounts wrong? Is not the signpost, though completely lifeless – since it lets us know the direction in which we have to go – preferable to the most excellent man who leads us astray?

Practice is necessary, but a good theory is equally indispensable; life is indispensable, but the form is far from worthless even if life is missed in it.

Woe to the man who either in contemplation or in application separates what God has united. As long as the objective, that is, the word, the truth, the theory, the law, or whatever is on this line, persists, we cherish hope, we consider it at least possible, that sooner or later life will answer to it. Writing depends on a good hand; the best example cannot make up for the lack of this. However wrong and illegible the handwriting of those just starting out may be, it is only if the example itself is not worthy of imitation that we would no longer dare hope for improvement.

Applied to church life, this means that a church, however impure, however deeply flawed, however depraved, may be considered a false church only when the truth by which, the standard by which, the law by which the desired reformation is to be brought about, that is, the *objective element,* is utterly lacking. In the circle of the moral religious life, this means: as long as evil is called evil and right is called right, in other words, as long as the eternal orders of God are not violated – as is done by those to whom the word of Isaiah applies: "Woe to those who call evil good and good evil, who turn darkness to light and light to darkness," Isa. 5: 20 –

as long as the traces have not disappeared and the boundary lines have not been erased by which those who have strayed from the paths of right can be brought back to their rightful place.

The institution we now have to discuss shows us how God worked an initial restoration through an institution, the full meaning of which would only be understood once what it portrayed was fulfilled. The *law of the Nazirite vow,* as well as the regulations concerning the redemption on the fiftieth day, kept alive the reminder that the Levitical priesthood was of a temporary nature which, together with the entire shadow service, was "added... until the arrival of the seed to whom the promise referred" (Gal. 3: 19).

Israel was no longer a priestly people. This only meant that it was deprived of priestly privileges, that it was no longer allowed to exercise priestly rights, but not that it was not obligated and called to the priesthood. The *ministry* was taken away from it. This was experienced by Korah, Dathan and Abiram, whom the earth swallowed up, and the two hundred and fifty firstborn whom the fire consumed which "came forth from the Lord" (Num. 16: 35). God Himself taught this to Israel by the enduring sign of Aaron's rod blossoming, Num. 17: 8.

But the indivisibility of the *priestly character* was confessed by the pious Israelite when he brought "the atonement money," paid the ransom, and thereby had his child, not redeemed from the service, but *replaced by the Levite* (Num. 3: 45–51). Israel must remember both the one and the other. Between the two lines of this opposition lies the path by which God wants it to reach its original goal. The awareness that its calling is unchanged makes it feel its humiliation, the abnormality of its condition; but inseparable from this feeling is that of desire for and, more or less, hope of restoration.

The angel with the flaming sword stands before the entrance to Paradise. Woe to the man who denies the fall and defies the judgment of God, the man who treads the way to the tree of life before God has opened it! But Paradise itself did not thereby disappear, which justifies the expectation that man was not excluded forever.

In the Nazirite vow we have the complement of the promise that finds its expression in the ransom payment. The Nazirite did not appropriate the priestly office, and yet he acted in the priestly character. In other words, he *exhibited the Israelite as he had originally been, should be,* and *would be.*

This was naturally possible only in the forms of the Old Covenant. Naziriteship therefore belongs to the shadow service. It is not given to the sinner to declare and make himself holy. The holiness that the Nazirite seeks and the ordination that he receives lie in the fact that he obeys the precepts of the law and participates in the *holiness that the priests possess,* and thereby even comes to stand on a level with the high priest.

This becomes clear when we compare the regulations with which the Nazirites complied to the requirements of the priests. Lev. 10: 10 shows that the priests were not to use wine or strong drink when they entered the sanctuary, "so as to make a distinction between the holy and the profane, and between the unclean and the clean." The Nazirite, on the other hand, according to Num. 6: 3, was not only to abstain from wine and strong drink but was not even to consume any vinegar of wine or strong drink, nor any grape juice, nor even to eat fresh or dried grapes. The cheerfulness caused by the enjoyment of spirituous beverages gave way in him to higher inspiration. He was always in the sanctuary, that is, in the presence of God. The requirement by God set for the Levitical priests, as we see, was heightened for him.

According to Lev. 21: 5, the priests were not allowed to shave the corners of their beards. Of the Nazirite, on the other hand, it is said that "no razor shall pass over his head. He shall be holy until the days are fulfilled for which he separated himself to the LORD; he shall let the locks of hair on his head grow long" (Num. 6: 5).

He is like *the altar* upon which no tool was to be wielded, Ex. 20: 25, because it was given by God for a means of atonement and was not to be distorted by art, as if it were made usable by human hands, as if it served to please the eye of man. It was to be used as it had come forth from God's hand.

He is like *the vine* in the year of jubilee, Lev. 25: 5, which uncut was left to the driving force of its own life.

He is like the high priest whose anointed head bears the priestly crown, "for the consecration of the anointing oil of his God is on him." Lev. 21: 12.

According to Lev. 21: 1ff. the priest was not to not defile himself over a dead person unless very closely related to him. The Nazirite, on the other hand, Num. 6: 6–8, "shall not go near to a dead person." For him the requirement is absolute. He must not come into contact with death, the sign of sin, and in this respect he is equated with the high priest, of whom as well it is expressly said, "nor defile himself even for his father or his mother" (Lev. 21: 11).

Is it accidental, is it in consequence of a confusion of thought in the writer or the copyist of the laws, or perhaps of the shifting of a leaf in the scroll from which the law was originally composed, that the high priestly blessing in Num. 6 came to stand at the conclusion of the law of the Nazirite, even though seemingly without any connection to it, instead of at the place where the office and work of the high priest are described?

It is God's grace that begets Nazirites in Israel; the same grace that bestows the gift of prophecy; the same grace that redeemed Israel from the house of servitude in days gone by. "'Then I raised up some of your sons to be prophets and some of your young men to be Nazirites. Is this not so, O sons of Israel?' declares the LORD" (Amos 2: 11).

Well then, in the time of Judah's deepest decline, this institution remains by which every Israelite, whomsoever he might be, can grasp that for which he is grasped, the prize of God's calling, the *priesthood,* that is, the *right and privilege to approach God.* The law in Num. 6 speaks only of a temporary Naziriteship of which we have an example in the four friends of James, Acts 21: 24. The idea of God embodied in it, however, goes much deeper. It is fulfilled under the Old Testament only in Samson, somewhat also in Samuel, and therefore only in truth under the New, in Christ.

In His revelation to Manoah and his wife, the Lord Himself acts as interpreter of the law of the Nazirite, applying not the letter but the spirit, as no interpreter but only the lawgiver himself can do.

Until now the Lord has found and prepared the men in Israel whom He could use as instruments of salvation. Now the time has come when He does not find or form the redeemer, but begets him, that is, causes him to be born. While God usually works through means, He is independent of them; otherwise, He would not be a Creator. To create is to give birth, to "call into being what does not yet exist" (Rom. 4: 17).

True, Jehovah goes along with what exists even in the hour of Judah's deepest decline. Samson is born of a human father and mother. But we do not read that they were well-off, like Abraham and Sarah, Zechariah and Elizabeth, nor that they could be called believers in a special sense, like Elkanah and Hannah, but only that Manoah's wife was barren. The point of contact of which we have hinted above is the Nazirite vow, under which Samson's mother is laid, Judges 13: 4–5.

The grace of the Lord cannot descend any lower prior to His appearance in the flesh, He who is from but not of man, who is man and yet not a sinner. It arrived here in a descending line. Othniel acted under the inspiration of the Holy Spirit; Ehud, because of enthusiasm for his people, and therefore for Israel's God and religion; Barak, because he was called by a person; Gideon, because he was called by God Himself; Jephthah, because he was called by the people after God had formed him for his task in the school of humiliation. But when the Lord begot Samson, all *cooperation on the part of man* was excluded.

Unsolicited, unexpected, the angel comes to the mother of him "who will begin to redeem Israel." Yet we must not overlook one thing, namely, that God's work on Samson begins not with, but even before his birth. Like Paul, he is "set apart from his mother's womb" (Gal. 1: 15).

A lady at the court of Napoleon I once told him that, now that her child was three years old, she would soon start bringing it up. To which the emperor very pointedly rejoined that if she still had to begin, she was already three years too late. The emperor was right. He could also have said that her glances, indeed her entire intercourse, had served to educate the child for better or for worse before a single thought had transplanted itself into the soul through spoken words. But it is even more in accordance with the truth that the child already was unconsciously being worked on by all the mother's thoughts, sensations and hidden moods even before the child possessed a life of its own, as an unborn fruit.

Of the unfathomable influence we have in mind here, traces and characteristics are often seen in the child's body. Everyone knows the phenomena referred to here. Would the mind be free from such influences; would wrath, lust, in a word, disorders and passions, leave no traces? Overwhelming and humbling thought! Yet this is certain: What Mary, the mother of the Lord, experienced when the Spirit of the Lord came upon her was experienced by Manoah's wife *in the shadows of the law*.

In view of this, that which the rabbis communicate is highly important, namely, that she was of the lineage of Judah and appears in the genealogical register, 1 Chron. 4: 3, under the name of Hazzelelponi. Hazzelelponi or Zelel-poni means, "His shadow rests upon me" and recalls the word of the angel, Luke 1: 35: "The Holy Spirit will come upon you, and the power of the Most High will overshadow you."

Surprising though this communication may be since it comes from the Jewish side, where the similarity to the word from Luke just mentioned would most certainly not be thought of, we dare not assign it any value in this context other than that of a striking interpretation which gives us something to think about.

However, there are two statements in the Holy Scriptures themselves which are directly related to this subject and indicate approximately the same thing expressed by the name Hazzelelponi. When Manoah, to whom fell the same revelation with which the woman had been favored, asked about the angel's name, he was answered, "Why do you ask My name, seeing it is *pili,* wonderful?" Judges 13: 18, New King James Version (NKJV).

Is it not remarkable that the child the birth of whom makes the Old Covenant church rejoice through the mouth of Isaiah – "For unto us a Child is born, Unto us a Son is given; And the government will be upon His shoulder. And His name will be called Wonderful" – has the same name? (Isa. 9:5, NKJV).

Equally remarkable is the word with which the patriarch Jacob, on his deathbed, broke off the flow of his thoughts when he had come to the blessing of Dan, Gen. 49: 17, and suddenly exclaimed, "I await Your salvation, O LORD!" It is one of those words of which modern criticism can give no explanation and of which it has no clue. Did Jacob grow weary and pray for the redemption of the body? He looked on *Christ*. An answer, as it were, to this sigh of Israel's would come in the days of the New Testament, in Simeon's shout of joy: "Sovereign Lord, as You have promised, You now dismiss Your servant in peace. For my eyes have seen Your salvation" (Luke 2: 29–30). But he looked on Christ *through Samson, Samson the Danite, born in Judah's tribal territory; Samson, the Nazirite of God*. If the birth of a human child could be sinless, then Samson would have come into the world without sin.

Furthermore, one should also note this. It is not Samson who is put under a Nazirite vow, but only his *mother*. This is what causes Manoah's surprise. His main concern is the education of the boy (13: 8); and to his question, which betrays embarrassment and haste: "When your words come to pass, what will be the boy's rule of life and mission?" he receives the answer: "Let *the woman* pay attention to all that I said" (Judges 13: 12–14).

Samson is *born* a Nazirite. His ordination does not come about as a result of any legal requirement. Nor is he placed under any obligation. He moves about entirely freely. The only thing that distinguishes him is the sign of his Nazirite status. Yet he is recognizable, not by vestments like the priest, but by his hair, his crown. Through Samson, we too look upon Christ. As a Nazirite he is the type of the Savior, and the similarity between the two lies not only in the character in which Samson is announced, the purpose with which he was given, and the manner of his action, but also in the circumstances under which he acted and the manner in which he accomplished redemption.

Was not Jerusalem struck with terror when the tidings that the King of the Jews was born were brought into the holy city by pagan wise men? Did not Judah also then bring ropes to bind its savior? Did not then also from Judah's mouth come the cry, "We have no king but the emperor"? Was it not a man, *Isch,* from Judah's tribe, that is, *the man of Kerioth,* who betrayed Jesus? Did not the Savior, like Samson, fight alone?

Can it not also be said of Him that He *began to redeem Israel?*

So Samson is the priest, as the letter to the Hebrews expresses it, "not according to a law of a fleshly commandment, but according to the power of an indestructible life" (Heb. 7: 16, Berean Literal Bible); the Israelite as he ought to be, and as such, a type of the Christ.

How is this possible when there is so much that mars his character, so much by which we can rightly be disturbed, in which at any rate we cannot find an example to emulate?

Nowhere in the entire Old Testament will we find an *antitype* of the Savior. The limited and defective nature of what is created means that all shadows and examples of spiritual things are imperfect, reflecting only a single moment or a single side of them and therefore needing supplementation. This is all the more the case with the types that anticipate Christ. They are not to be taken separately but together, and in addition they appear in pairs or groups.

When the covenant was made at Sinai, the blood of the sacrificial animals flowed. "Without the shedding of blood there is no forgiveness!" But that blood is immediately collected and sprinkled on both the *book* and the *people*. Pure life is given in death, but passes through death to be communicated as well. The two acts belong inseparably together. The same is true of the two goats on the Great Day of Atonement and the two birds at the cleansing of the leper.

Similarly, Solomon complements David as a type. The latter is the king of Israel in his sufferings and struggles, the former that same king in his glory. David is Christ at His first coming in the flesh, Solomon Christ at His coming in glory.

When we consider Samson as a type of Christ, we are not looking at what he is in himself but at what he is by God's grace, at the Nazirite in Samson, and at what he accomplishes in this character. Every man in whom God glorifies His grace will have to recognize that he carries this "treasure in earthen vessels," that it is God's power accomplished in his weakness. But this is especially evident in the son of Manoah. In his life, as in the Rhone River, we find two sharply drawn, clearly distinct streams flowing side by side in the same bed without mingling. God has taken care that no one can read his history without noticing that sin brought him nothing but suffering, that sin paralyzed his influence, thwarted his labor insofar as it could have effected the redemption of his people. He who observes him reduced by his enemies to the meanest services in the mill, to a slave, nay to a beast of burden; a pitiful object, deprived of the sign of his dignity, a plaything in which wantonness takes delight, eyes dug out, will surely be willing to acknowledge that sin is not excused by Him who wishes to call a sinner like Samson to a great and glorious work, and also intends to enable him to perform it.

Samson is a *Nazirite;* and his only significance lies in his *Naziriteship*. By this alone is he an example of Him "whom the Father sanctified and sent into the world" (John 10: 36). The Nazirite and the man Samson do not coincide. He does not have grace in his own possession and under his own control. He is not a Hercules on whom extraordinary powers of the body are conferred. His great deeds are performed only through the Spirit, who from time to time "came powerfully" upon him and overpowered him.

We humans do not possess an independent life of the spirit. Only the Son could say, "For as the Father has life in Himself, so also He has granted the Son to have life in Himself" (John 5: 26). Even as a Nazirite – he himself knows this very well – Samson must receive his strength from the God of strength. At Ramath-Lechi where he is about to perish of thirst, we hear him exclaim, "You have accomplished this great deliverance through Your servant. Must I now die of thirst and fall into the hands of the uncircumcised?" (Judges 15: 18).

When his hair has grown back in the prison house, and he again possesses the sign of his consecration, he does not again possess a power that flows back into him but begs the Lord to help and save him *one more time*. "O Lord GOD," he says, "please remember me. Strengthen me, O God, just once more, so that with one vengeful blow I may pay back the Philistines for my two eyes!" (Judges 16: 28).

This contradiction that we discern in him and in his life constitutes the very tragedy in his history. The divine and the human component are both found in him, but unreconciled. Yet we would be wrong to continue to dwell exclusively on Samson as an individual. He is the expression and to that extent also the victim of his time and of his people. His fall demonstrates the decay of the whole to which he belonged. The head was dull because the body was infirm.

Man depends not only on the Creator, but also, mediately, on the creature. Whoever wishes to make a correct judgment about him must not discount his environment, the people with whom he associates, the conditions under which he grows up, public opinion in the narrower or wider circle to which he belongs, the level of religious and moral life in his time.

This is true not only of his natural but also of his spiritual life. Just as a plant needs light and air, healthy soil and the refreshing rain, the spiritual man needs the sunshine of sympathy, the atmosphere of common conviction, and the soil of a domestic, ecclesiastical, social life in which are found the ingredients that he will be able to convert into that which promotes maturity.

A single believer is, admittedly, like the palm tree that grows up out of the barren sands of the desert and by its inveterate green stands out so favorably against all that surrounds it. But the source from which its roots are watered is hidden deep beneath the sand. It demonstrates the truth that God's grace is *sufficient* for us always and in everything, and it is so formed and placed by God that it fulfills its calling precisely in this place and under such circumstances.

In him we are dealing with an exception. Usually, the internal life of the single person in its manifestation is determined, at least to some extent, by what surrounds him. Samson is a child of his time, a son of his people, and is entirely under the influence of that which surrounds him. He is less the *servant* of the Lord than the *instrument* of His grace.

This is already evident in the first breach of peace with the Philistines. Contrary to the precepts of divine law, Josh. 23: 12, Judges 3: 6, sinful love for one of the daughters of the oppressors of his people filled his heart.

This "was from the LORD" (14: 4).

Why?

The healing answers to the ailment. Israel's healer attacks the disease of his people in its *cause*. The people of God make common cause with the enemies of their faith and have to learn that the natural enmity between the two nations is stronger than the love between the persons and lines who intermingle from those nations.

When Samson had posed his riddle and his wife had sought to persuade him to tell her his secret, vanity and fear were most certainly at work in her heart. The wedding guests, her countrymen, did not spare themselves from threatening her. She and her father's house would be burned with fire if she did not allow them to harm her husband, Judges 14: 15. But the lack of confidence she displays and the expression, "You have posed to my people a riddle" (14: 16), clearly show that nationality is involved. From the same principle we also have to explain the riddle and the disproportionality of his stake to that of the wedding guests.

Indeed, when Samson went with his father and his mother to Thimnath for the purpose of asking for the hand of the young daughter on whom he had set his sights, and for which reason he had taken another path for some distance, we read in Judges 14: 5 that "a young lion came roaring at him." Unarmed he stands there, the Nazirite of God, the redeemer of his people, allying by marriage with the enemy of that people! But now he also experiences what the unarmed, what Israel is able to do in the power of his God.

The Spirit of the Lord "came powerfully upon him." He ripped the beast of prey apart and understood the meaning of this incident so well that it did not even become a topic of conversation between him and his entourage. We hear the Israelite speaking in him when he later, having found the desiccated carrion occupied by bees and filled with honey, verse 8, posed the riddle: "Out of the eater came something to eat, and out of the strong came something sweet" (Judges 14: 14). From the advantageous opportunity he offered, one man against thirty and thirty garments against thirty, it appeared that the parties were not to be equal but that he was opposing the Philistines *as one man* (14: 12, 13).

The struggle between faith and unbelief, the enmity between the people of God and the children of the world, the gulf between Israel and the Philistines, Jehovah and Dagon, may be hidden under cozy repartee or innocent jest; the fellowship, the union which seems to be so enduring and intimate amidst the clinking of cups, later proves to be like the thin crust of ice covered with a layer of snow which hides the rocky gorge from the eye of the hiker and, while it seems to offer a sure support for his feet, does not bear his full weight and would, if he were not on his guard, cause him to find a grave in the depths.

Samson had to gain this experience to enable him to act as an *avenger* of his people and thereby "begin the work of redemption." He cannot fight for the honor of God, for the freedom of his people. There is no awakening; there is no inclination to be redeemed. Therefore, the battle against the Philistines has a purely personal cause; but in that *personal cause* Samson serves the *national cause*. It was the Philistines against whom he fought when he struck thirty men of the Askelonites, albeit not those who had insulted and betrayed him, Judges 14: 19. This was repeated when his father-in-law, as faithless as she, gave the faithless one to someone among those with whom she had made common cause against her conjugal mate (15: 2).

Samson stood and fought alone. He found no select band in Judah of three hundred men willing to rally around him. Hence he sought his allies in the foxes and jackals, which he chased through the enemies' fields in one hundred and fifty pairs with one hundred and fifty burning torches attached.

It happened the third time when it pleased the Philistines to avenge themselves in the cruelest manner on his wife and her father, as the actual causes of their calamities, v. 6, and most likely it is the band returning from this reprisal experience whom Samson made experience what Israel is capable of if it stands in the name of the Lord against His and its enemies.

Yet the end is not yet. The struggle continues. Always in the same character. In the end it is about his person. *Samson alone against the Philistines!*

Only when they encamp against Judah for the sake of Samson, and the royal tribe – oh, for shame! – provides ten times three hundred men to bind and deliver up the savior (15: 16), does he surrender to the inevitable and resign himself to the betrayal committed against him, and in him against itself.

Those who are not in favor must be against. If ever a time was propitious to become a free people, then the hour of redemption had struck. But if Judah does not now know the day of its visitation, it will be forced in its unbelief to go one step further and deliver up its redeemer. It desires peace at any price. So be it then! Samson willingly allows himself to be bound. He does not raise his hand against his own and has nothing left to live and fight for. Yes, when the cheers of the enemy were heard and he was already surrendered into their hand, then "the Spirit of the LORD came upon him mightily," he broke his bonds and struck a thousand men with the only weapon that lay to hand, a fresh donkey's jawbone.

Samson against the Philistines! Afterwards when, having entered Gaza, he was in the hands of the enemies, who closed the gates and had the streets guarded. Nine hours from Gaza lies Mount Montor in the vicinity of Hebron. There, according to tradition, stood the doors which Samson lifted out of the gate of Gaza along with both posts and bar and, in spite of the enemy (cf. Gen. 22: 17, 24: 60), carried on his shoulders to the height that overlooks the tomb of the patriarchs. In the early Christian church, this act was always considered a symbol of the resurrection.

He arose the third day,
Whom death could not keep.

Hymn 21, v. 5, *Evangelische Gezangen*[19]

Can any image be more appropriate to express this truth? In Ps. 68: 19 (KJV), a still stronger and truer image is used. "Thou hast," sings the poet, "led captivity captive!"

Samson against the Philistines! For the last time. No, the Philistines against Samson, when the latter, entangled in the snares of sensuality, betrayed the secret of his strength to Delilah, but thereby also betrayed his calling, himself.

The king of Greek poets relates of Achilles that he was immersed in the river by the goddess, his mother, and thereby was rendered invulnerable except in the heel where she held him. In that place, the only place where the weapon of the enemy could strike him, the poisonous arrow penetrated which laid him, the invincible one, in the dust.

There is only one vulnerable place to be found on the Nazirite of God, and it lies in his *Naziriteship*. What took place at the brook Sorek is only a repetition of what Israel lived through in the fields of Moab. Balaam's curse could not afflict him. Neither could Balak's army. It was his own sin, sensual lust, inseparable from idolatry, that made him an easy prey for the enemy. If Samson as a Nazirite is a type of the *Christ*, in this he is an image of and a terrifying example for the *Christian* who sinks into the arms of sin and who from that point has nothing that distinguishes him from others but only this, that he sinks deeper, becomes an object of scorn and ridicule, and that his God is blasphemed in him.

In the vicinity of the same stream Sorek from which David took the stones to fell Goliath to the ground, Samson gradually divulges his secret to Delilah. His answers take the form of riddles containing all the constituents of truth, but a form in which they are only known once the *full truth* is discovered. Seven ropes indicate that the power is derived from the *covenant* which has the number seven as its characteristic, its expres-

---

[19] *Evangelische Gezangen om nevens het Boek der Psalmen bij de Openbaren Godsdienst in de Nederlandsche Hervormde Gemeenten gebruikt te worden*. Amsterdam, Haarlem, Groningen: J. Brandt en Zoon et al., 1851.

sion. The same thoughts are expressed by the bowstrings. That which is new and has not yet been used to any other purpose, has among all nations the meaning of *dedication*. The power, therefore, lies in the *dedication of the covenant*. The seven *locks of hair* are the sign of the *Naziriteship*. In fact, Delilah is already in possession of his secret before Samson has even spoken his last word. But he must sink even deeper. The riddle must not be guessed but betrayed.

O Sensuality, how you bring down the strong! David has defeated his thousands; Delilah her tens of thousands! And yet the history of Samson does not end in the prison house. Samson fulfills his mission to the last. That is worthy of God! That is fitting! Even in his death he avenges Israel.

But to the last it remains: Samson against the Philistines! When his hair has grown back, and he therefore again displays outwardly the image of the Nazirite, but also receives in it the sign of the Lord's grace which initially restores what he has corrupted, the Philistines are gathered to a great sacrificial feast in the temple of their God.

Samson's humiliation brings shame on Israel and reproach on Jehovah. He stands there among the columns supporting the roof, which, like the house itself, is occupied by a dense crowd of people. His life is forfeited, his future destroyed through his own fault. A Nazirite of God, stumbling along at the hand of a lad, the string music of his and God's enemies, forced to sing the praises of Dagon while the living, eternal God in Israel, *his* God, is...! That cannot be, that must not be, that will not be. He has faith, this Samson, faith, despite what he hears and experiences, to cling to that God and encompass again the salvation that was forfeited.

"O Lord GOD," we hear from between the pillars, "please remember me. Strengthen me, O God, just once more, so that with one vengeful blow I may pay back the Philistines for my *two eyes*" (16: 28). There the pillars tremble and shake, bend and break, and an entire people in its chief and noblest representatives is buried under the ruins of its idol temple, and with them a single person who alone fought them, would not make peace with them, and now died with them.

In his life he was the avenger of his people, yet in his death he avenged the most. Avenged himself, yes, with one blow for both his eyes! Verily! But he is Israel, he is Judah. He is the Nazirite of God. In his life it was, in his death it remained, "Samson against the Philistines!"

He could not champion the national cause. There is no redemption for a people who prefer slavery to freedom. But he represents, he embodies that cause; and his labor and his life, and much more his death, benefit Israel.

THE OPPRESSION by the Philistines, according to Judges 13: 1, lasted forty years and seems, cf. 10: 7, to have begun simultaneously with that of the Ammonites. Since the removal of the ark and the defeat at Ebenezer, cf. 1 Sam. 7: 20, twenty years had elapsed. As Samson judged Israel for twenty years, when we compare these indications it becomes more than likely that Samson was a contemporary of Eli, that he was born during the last twenty years of his priesthood.

His first appearance then falls just before the battle of Ebenezer, in which the ark was taken, 1 Sam. 4: 1ff., and gave the impetus to this awakening, which was *unaccompanied by penitence*. He was then the terror of the enemies in the time of Israel's deepest humiliation that preceded redemption. Samuel's activity then dovetailed with his own, but served to effect an inner change in the people; and Samson's death then preceded Israel's conversion.

Samson stands in the history of the Age of the Judges as a wholly singular appearance, a memorial of God to men's misery, a token of the Lord's grace and of the way in which it aims to be glorified.

9. CONVERSION WITHOUT REPENTANCE

1 Samuel 3: 20–4: 11

He is robbed by each, a reproach to his neighbor;
You have raised the right hand of him that hates him;
You made the enemy rejoice in his calamity;
His sword lies down, it is blunt, and useless in battle;
You make him flee from the bloody field of battle.
And, forsaken by You, to sigh under the enemy's yoke.

Ps. 89: 17 (Psalter of 1773)

To cry out and receive no answer from Him whose ear never grows weary that He could not hear; to cry out for help in distress and find no relief, though the Lord's hand is not shortened that it could not save; such was the condition of Saul, of whom we read in 1 Sam. 28: 6 that he "inquired of the LORD" but received no answer, neither by dreams, nor by the Urim, nor by the prophets. In that condition, all that remains of religion is the *oppressive fear of the approaching judgment and the realization that it has already begun.*

That, thank God, was not yet the case with Israel! The Lord intervened with the apostate people. That there was "a remnant according to the election of grace" among that people, we see from Hannah and Elkanah. A man of God was found, a prophet who announced to the people that the judgments of God would come upon him and his house, 1 Sam. 2: 30.

To some extent, however, what was said of its first king and of Israel in that time applied to the people as a whole, the people as such: "Now in those days the word of the LORD was rare and visions were scarce" (1 Sam. 3: 1).

The lamp in the temple at Shiloh, which, as the original indicates, was about to go out, was the image of a people who, originally called to be the bearer of revelation, did not understand or fulfill its mission and almost went astray in darkness. That light yet dances and flickers, but it will soon be extinguished forever!

Israel came to Shiloh but found no rest there; entered the house of God, but the Lord had departed from it. Its offerings were accepted by priests who dishonored their office and their ordination. For weeping Hannahs, no comfort in the house of prayer! For the pagans roundabout, no glimmer in it to whom "the words of God were entrusted." And meanwhile, even after the Lord had given a Samson, a continuation under the yoke with no prospect of redemption.

Something was still lacking for that which the Lord spoke through Hosea to be fulfilled in Israel: "The days of punishment have come; the days of retribution have arrived—let Israel know it. The prophet is called a fool, and the inspired man insane," Hos 9: 7; and through Amos, 8: 12: "People will stagger from sea to sea and roam from north to east, seeking the word of the LORD, but they will not find it."

What was it?

Every man, as long as God has not given him over to a false sense, has the sense that he must get in touch with God. We see this in those peoples who grope around in the house of God's creation to see if they can find the Lord of the house as well, in the Baal priests on Carmel calling out, cutting and prodding themselves in order that Baal might give a single sign of life. We hear it in the cries heard at the foot of Mount Sinai on the fortieth day, after Moses has gone to God as their representative, now that it remains so quiet up there. Likewise in the complaint of Israel as recorded by Isaiah: "If only You would rend the heavens and come down, so that mountains would quake at Your presence" (64: 1).

And yet! One can become so accustomed to the condition of a God who hides and keeps silent that one does not feel all the awfulness of it and is shamed by the searching pagans, the bigoted Baal priests and apostate Israel. The most appalling thing in the state of alienation from God is this, that the awareness of it will soon cease to live.

One then asks:

Does the Father really live up there,
Did ever star fall from the height?[20]

One then complains:

---

[20] "Onvergankelijk" [Incorruptible], in de Génestet, *De Dichtwerken van P. A. de Génestet* [The Poetry of P. A. de Génestet], p. 285.

There is no priest, who declares Him.
In riddles man walks on earth![21]

One then thinks to come to God by way of thought, of feeling. God is then an inference of the mind, a name for what we dream or hope or fear.

The first sign of spiritual life, on the other hand, consists in no longer being satisfied with contemplations about God, no longer being satisfied with religious forms, ceasing to pray without expecting the answer to that prayer, and realizing that, even where He keeps Himself at a distance and makes us experience His wrath, we have come to stand in *a substantial relationship with Him.*

This is what we may notice in Israel when we see Samuel appearing as a prophet. "All Israel," we read in 1 Sam. 3: 20, "from Dan to Beersheba knew that Samuel was confirmed as a prophet of the LORD." We then find *initial awakening*. From whence? From the mercies of God.

Israel did not owe it to itself. The priest had not come to refill the lamp of the Lord with oil – it raised itself up again. The people did not pray for the Word, for the revelation of the Lord, for their misery consisted precisely in not feeling it as such. Samson had come and it had not understood what God had given in him; it had the courage to bind him, but not to be unbound by him.

Nevertheless, God was on His way to complete the work He had begun when Samson had begun to redeem Israel. And so Hannah pours out her prayer in the court, from which we understand that her desire, like Manoah's wife's, is aroused to receive a seed of God. Hence the nightly revelation to the youthful Nazirite who, himself of priestly lineage, grows up under the eye of Eli in the house of the Lord. Hence also the Word of God was heard at Shiloh, informing them that the Lord proceeded to reveal himself to Samuel (3: 20). As a first consequence of this, all Israel knew that a prophet had risen among them. The people became one, united not by the forms of the temple service, but by the living Word.

---

[21] "Peinzensmoede" [Contemplation fatigue], in de Génestet, *De Dichtwerken*, p. 367.

When the church – and the same is true of each person in particular – awakens, then "the name of the Lord is near"; His revelation is not regarded as a thing of the past, as something that comes to us only by way of tradition, something in which we find no benefit in our times of burden and of need, but as the Word of the living God Who Himself speaks to us, seeks us out and makes His ways known to us. How fresh, suitable, and rich that Bible then becomes! How much power then lies in those words, to make us, like Samuel, cry out, "Speak, Lord, your servant hears!" But that same Word which brought awakening also *unites*.

A wonderful people are Israel, both of the Old and New Covenant! One by virtue of descent and destiny, it is divided like no other. Not history, not tradition, but the living Word brings and keeps it together. However long separated, however divided, when God appears again in its midst all Israel "from Dan to Beersheba" becomes one.

If God appears again in its midst? Most assuredly! We are at the entrance of a new era. Prophetic voices were heard before the time of Samuel. "From the day your fathers came out of the land of Egypt until this day," says the Lord (Jer. 7: 25), "I have sent you all My servants the prophets again and again." But from Samuel onward we find a coherent history of *prophetism in Israel,* to the degree that in Acts 3: 24 the apostle Peter ventures to speak of "all the prophets from Samuel on."

The Angel of the Covenant does not return to the sanctuary. But in place of the immediate revelation of Israel's King comes the revelation, mediately, through the intervention of human organs.

When, as we have seen in an earlier chapter, Israel was unable to draw near to Jehovah, hear His voice and commune with Him, God accepted the intervention of Moses by virtue of His own intention to send a prophet *like* Moses, Deut. 18: 15. It is this revelation that is prepared by prophecy. After all, "a mediator is not a mediator of one" (Gal. 3: 20, KJV). Moses was an imperfect mediator. He represented the people to God but could not represent God to the people.

The Lord descended when He made His glory to dwell in the midst of Israel and His name to dwell "in Him" who led the people through the desert (Ex. 23: 21, NKJV). But He will have to descend even deeper to come to man. His visible presence has been taken away, and now He comes through the *Word of prophecy*. The ordinary explanation of Deut.

18: 15, as if the promise concerning the prophet whom God would raise up were referring to prophecy, prophetism, is incorrect and does not take the slightest account either of the historical context in which it occurs, the occasion for which it was given, or the circumstances under which it was given. The great prophet is also the true mediator, and the true mediator is also the only one who fully explains to us the hidden counsel and will of God concerning our salvation, who speaks the words of God; and the Word of God is, in other words, the true prophet.

Yet it is prophecy that prepares his way. The sinful people, who could not endure the presence of God, in whose midst the Kingdom of God could not be established and the King of that Kingdom could not appear, was unable to learn to understand God and itself, the past and the future, law and grace by other means than through the living Word of God, the word of prophecy, through which the purpose and content of all the shadows and precepts are perfectly unfolded.

Therefore, we can say that in the word of the prophets, God Himself descends to the people. It is the spirit of Christ that is in the prophets, 1 Pet. 1: 11. It is that spirit by which what in itself is a bare and dead form becomes alive. The words that Christ speaks through the prophets of the Old Covenant are spirit and life, John 6: 63.

Because the gift of prophecy is poured out, it is both impermissible and unnecessary that one "practices divination or conjury, interprets omens, practices sorcery, casts spells, consults a medium or spiritist, or inquires of the dead" (Deut. 18: 10–11). As long as there is a "God in Israel" who will speak through human organs, one need not go with his questions to Baal-Zebub at Ekron (2 Kings 1: 6).

From Samuel onward Jehovah dwells again among Israel, in the word of prophecy.

This, indeed, is the fact which we have assumed, to which we are returning, and which in this connection especially deserves our attention.

The distinction between Samuel and the prophets who had been before him is determined by this. We read of Miriam, for example, that she was a prophetess. Likewise of Deborah. From time to time we have also encountered prophets who reminded the people of their sins or announced the punishment, as was the case before the appearance of Gideon and after the birth of Samuel, Judges 6: 8, 1 Sam. 2: 27. They were prophets in the same sense in which also Abraham is thus called, Gen. 20: 7, and in which this can be said of every one at all times with whom God desires to commune and who receives a revelation from the Lord. "Hear now My words," God said to Aaron and Miriam. "If there is a prophet among you, I, the LORD, will reveal Myself to him in a vision; I will speak to him in a dream" (Num. 12: 6).

Prophecy starting from the time of Samuel is a phenomenon of an entirely different nature and has an entirely different meaning. It is a new form of revelation. In the shadow service of the Old Covenant, as we have seen, everything was given that Israel, that the sinner needs for salvation. Both law and gospel, promise and initial fulfillment. But even though it is all there, it cannot be used by man and only insufficiently for him, because he is a sinner.

This determines the need for a new revelation. We find the law of its development in the Savior's word, occasioned by the coming of the Greeks, John 12:24: "unless a kernel of wheat falls to the ground and dies, it remains only a seed." Jesus cannot communicate Himself to the pagan, nor at bottom to Israel, except through death. Not only must He appear in the flesh, He must humble Himself even more deeply. The sinner can take Him in only as the Crucified, Risen and Glorified One.

In the same way, the law is also transformed into prophecy. Paul had known and kept the law from childhood, and yet he speaks of a time when the commandment came, sin became alive and he died, Rom. 7: 9. The letter was resolved for him in the spirit. He learned to understand that "the law was spiritual," i.e., he received a prophetic understanding of that law. So it was with the Emmaus travelers. Indeed, also with the confessors from the circumcision to whom the letter to the Hebrews was addressed. They knew history, had read the books of the Old Covenant, had been raised in the shadow of the temple. And yet, they did not "understand the Scriptures." The interpreter had to come. Light had to be shed by prophecy on all those events, those sayings, those institutions and ceremonies before they had and found in all this what they needed for their external life.

Prophecy aligns itself with the law, explains it, applies it and provides the true understanding of its inner meaning. That is why it arises at the end of the age that we now consider to be the fruit of the entire preceding development. Prophecy does not bring a completely new revelation. If that were the case, the law would in actuality be superfluous.

The newer criticism, misled by the apparent anomaly in Israel's relationship to the law and in its history, has seen fit to reverse the order and let the law emerge from prophecy. For it, prophecy is the record of life in Israel, the result of the unfolding thereof under the influence of all kinds of social and political events; prophecy betrays the driving force of Israelite thought, that is, of the prophetic spirit that keeps its eye on the ideal and seeks to realize it.

It is not possible to invent a theory that is more contrary both to reality and to the idea than this one. It uproots the tree in order to plunge it with its crown of leaves into the earth; it assigns paternity to the child; it makes, in a word, cause into effect and effect into cause.

Prophecy, precisely the other way around, has the law as its premise, joins up with what is once given, is bound to the Word, and comes not to abolish, but to fulfill. Only now that the law has asserted its dominion over Israel, and the people, though not yet inwardly, have been converted to it, now that it has entered into its life, and this tabernacle, the service, the priesthood have become the center of the whole, only now can prophecy fulfill its mission. From this point of view it is significant that God had Israel's prophet, who as such is the most perfect example of Christ, *brought up in the tabernacle at Shiloh.* Of all the judges, he is the only one who takes a central position.

Prophecy honors the law, points to it, seeks to uphold it, and stands to it in the same relationship as John the Baptist stood to Christ. In revelation, the new is old and the old becomes new, for it is from God and, like God Himself, unchanging and eternal.

When the apostle Paul in the Epistle to the Romans preaches justification by faith, he begins by proving that Abraham was justified by the *same* faith by which we hope to be saved. The prophets before Samuel sang of salvation, like Miriam; they were preachers of righteousness, like the unnamed prophets of whom we spoke above, or received revelations in connection with their own calling, like Deborah, or with the redemptive acts of the Lord, of which we later find an example especially in Elisha. But with Samuel we are taken one step further on the road to the incarnation of the Word.

Yet a people brought to God in this way also comes to itself, feels its deep humiliation and seeks to shatter its chains. The battle is joined. One begins to distinguish enemy from friend. No more marrying a Philistine woman from Timnath! No more defeating the Askelonites, destroying the cornfields of Gaza one moment, and whoring after the woman in the city of Gaza and by the brook Sorek the next! There comes movement, fervor, zeal. People have understood the preaching of Samson's life, guessed the secret of his power, of Israel's power.

"Thus the word of Samuel came to all Israel. Now the Israelites went out to meet the Philistines in battle and camped at Ebenezer" (1 Sam. 4: 1). The two sentences are linked to each other, like the two facts mentioned here; the one is a direct consequence of the other.

Israel beaten while on the path of obedience! How is it possible! Does this people then stand and struggle alone? Has God not begun to redeem it? Has His Word not returned? Yet if God is with it, why has this happened to it?

Israel is upright. Its defeat it attributes not to the power of their enemies, not to Dagon, but to Jehovah. "Why has the LORD brought defeat on us before the Philistines today?" (4: 3). It also knows what is written in the law, "When you go out to war against your enemies and see horses, chariots, and an army larger than yours, do not be afraid of them; for the LORD your God, who brought you out of the land of Egypt, is with you.... The LORD your God goes with you to fight for you against your enemies, to give you the victory" (Deut. 20: 1, 4).

Well then, "Let us bring the ark of the covenant of the LORD from Shiloh, so that it may go with us to save us from the hand of our enemies" (1 Sam. 4:3b). They think they know. There was a defect in the form. They should have laid it out differently. The sign of the covenant was missing.

So they ask, but already have the answer. No falling before the ark with Joshua after the defeat at Ai! No fasting and crying, "We have sinned!" as in the day of Mizpah, when they drew and poured out water before the Lord, 1 Sam. 7: 6. No, God must come to them to serve them! They are in possession of the sign of the covenant, and thereby the means to partake of the blessing of the covenant.

The priests in Anglo-India call themselves Brahmins, "Lords of prayer"! By very simple and formally correct reasoning, they attribute to themselves greater power than the Godhead itself possesses. Brahma is moved by prayer. The Brahmins are in possession of prayer. Therefore the Brahmins move the world. The closing argument is very compelling. But woe to the faith that lives by suchlike reasoning. We have sometimes heard tell of stolen faith. Who will argue that it does not exist?

Israel choked with thirst at Raphidim and exclaimed: "Is the LORD among us or not?" (Ex. 17: 7). It refused to go to Canaan. It received orders to return to the desert, but later came on its own to lay claim to the promise. "'We have indeed sinned,' they said, 'but we will go to the place the LORD has promised!'" (Num. 14: 40).

"Throw Yourself down," says Satan to the Savior on the pinnacle of the temple, "For it is written: 'He will command His angels concerning You, and they will lift You up in their hands, so that You will not strike Your foot against a stone'" (Matth. 4: 6).

These are all examples that show how lightly one can tempt God when one selfishly and self-willingly disposes over what God wants to do in His time, along His path, according to His sovereign good pleasure. Israel here commits the same error as the false prophets when, contrary to the Word of the Lord, they announced, through Jeremiah, "peace" and not danger!

The Lord's temple was with them. God could not deny Himself. The Lord's inheritance was not to be handed over to the pagans. But that is not faith, that is hubris, the hubris of an unrepentant heart, which – instead of being completely amazed when it experiences God looking down on sinful men and remaining faithful to the covenant they have a thousand times violated – is amazed that God does not hear and help, and so takes the liberty to dispose over Him.

The faith in Jehovah that Israel demonstrated when it had the ark brought into the camp at Ebenezer on the shoulders of the wicked priests Hophni and Phinehas – as if that were no cause for concern! – causes it to sink back into paganism. The ark has become an idol instead of what it should be, the throne of Jehovah, the sign of the covenant, inseparable from the obedience to which that covenant commits.

How often has the church, even the child of the Lord, seized the ark that, carried around the fortress of Jericho at the command of the Lord, made its walls fall! How often have those means of grace ordained by God been used, those promises of God appropriated, but in such a way that the very first thing that God demands of us is overlooked and passed over, namely, obedience, attentiveness, submission, self-knowledge, a seeking not of the blessing of God-service and God's fellowship but of God Himself, God alone!

Let us then pay closer attention to the enigmatic guidance by which Jehovah caused Israel to come to Him and to itself! Half-conversion, the mere form of godliness are being judged. "So the Philistines fought, and Israel was defeated, and each man fled to his tent. The slaughter was very great—thirty thousand foot soldiers of Israel fell. The ark of God was captured, and Eli's two sons, Hophni and Phinehas, died" (1 Sam. 4: 10–11).

A great cheer had gone up when the ark appeared in the Israelite army. The victors had reason to marvel at the exuberant and boisterous joy, so incongruous given what the Israelites had so recently experienced. The more so because they had reason to fear, for the memory of the Lord's great deeds had been revived. "The Philistines were afraid. 'The gods have entered their camp!' they said. 'Woe to us, for nothing like this has happened before. Woe to us! Who will deliver us from the hand of these mighty gods? These are the gods who struck the Egyptians with all kinds of plagues, by the wilderness'" (1 Sam. 4: 7–8).

And yet the time had come for Jehovah to give up His honor, His name, the grace-benefits of the church, to the enemy, and humble Himself in order to humble Israel. Israel had shown a great faith, clinging to the external sign and pledge of God's grace, but it needed God Himself, God, who had withdrawn the visible sign of His presence from the ark, and whose covenant was inseparable from all that belonged to it, promises, laws, institutions, in a word, His entire revelation.

We can certainly characterize God's guidance as mysterious. God cares for His glory even when the ark is captured. But He does not want anything to stand between Him and His confederate, not even the *sign* He left of His presence among Israel. He bestowed Isaac, but Isaac had to be laid upon the altar of dedication. The water bottle must be emptied to the last drop; only then is the spring at Beersheba revealed.

Rest assured: at this very same Ebenezer, He will one day thunder over His enemies and grant salvation to His people. But before that, the word must come through His prophets such as Samuel; before that, a work must be accomplished in man; before that, pride must be bruised and self-will must be disciplined; before that, the enemy must be allowed to trespass upon the sacred things of the Lord.

They will find that Jehovah does not let the unbelief of the Philistines go unpunished, any more than He does Israel's superstition!

10. JUDGMENT OVER ELI AND HIS HOUSE

1 Samuel 2: 12–36, 4: 11–18

They turned aside by faithless dealing
And so followed the evil ways of their fathers.
This God heard, and in most fierce anger,
Avenged this evil on Israel;
He forsook tent and tabernacle,
Which He had established there as a dwelling
And erected to His honor at Shiloh.

Psalm 78: 29–30 (Psalter of 1773)

The emigrant who settles in the far West of the United States and starts clearing land, not only cuts down the trees of the forest – by its very nature a difficult job that progresses slowly – but over a large area takes care to "girdle" them, as this operation is called, i.e. strip them of their bark in the round, to the extent necessary to prevent the upper part of the trunk from getting a fresh supply of sap from the root.

For a time, the forest seems to undergo no change. The canopy remains as dense as before. But this does not prevent the settler from breaking the soil between the tree trunks. He opens, sows, and plants in the assurance that he is not wasting his time. For a while the leaves may remain green, but soon they will wither; at least when spring comes, the "girdled" trees will not sprout. This, then, is that on which he has counted. Now he can proceed calmly and regularly to clear away the timber. Having settled in the dark forest, the time for sowing would otherwise come too soon for him to clear a big enough field over a large enough area.

Many an establishment and institution bears some resemblance to such a forest when the conditions of flowering and growth, and herewith of a sustainable existence, are removed, while to the naked eye everything remains as it was. Even a corpse is not immediately, at least visibly, in a state of decomposition. Under certain circumstances, the dead body can retain for years, even centuries, the form which was once animate; and the moral bodies, the spiritual organisms which we have in mind here, like the trees which we have chosen for an image, are not so much dead as devoted to death.

For example, in God's ordinary way of doing things, He does not immediately eradicate that which He instituted but which is no longer animated by its original life and no longer conforms to its original purpose, which in a word is corrupted and alienated from its proper disposition; rather, He allows it to exist temporarily until it decays of its own accord or is struck down by His judgment.

We mortals have reverence for the dead. We do not regard the corpse of a dear departed person as an assembly of certain substances the components of which can be expressed in certain chemical formulas, but as the body of him or her whom we loved, as the dwelling in which the soul has so long resided. In the same way the Lord God honors, as it were, the body of the institution He had chosen. It remains an object of His divine care. It is not given over to the demolitionist but must pass away; it is replaced by something else in God's time.

Adam is driven out of Paradise, but Eden's garden does not disappear before his eyes. It still stands. Only after the Flood do we discover no trace of it.

Christ instituted the New Covenant in His blood, Matth. 26: 28. The first covenant is thereby "made ... obsolete; and what is obsolete and aging will soon disappear" (Heb. 8: 13). But for a generation the temple is still found at Jerusalem. Sacrifices are offered there as before. The Apostle of the Gentiles goes up to Jerusalem to celebrate Pentecost. Although in Christ neither circumcision nor uncircumcision means anything, Gal. 6: 15, Paul still allows Timothy to be circumcised. He does not condemn in all circumstances those who keep the Sabbath. The threat of the Lord: "Look, your house is left to you desolate!" (Matth. 23: 38) is not yet fulfilled. The time is coming when not one stone will be left upon another. But that will happen in the time of tribulation.

So it was with the rule of God under Israel, under the law of shadows and with the tabernacle. The wife of Phinehas, when the sad news reaches her that Israel had been smitten, her husband fallen, her father-in-law dead and the ark taken, calls the child she delivered Ichabod, saying: "The glory is departed from Israel!" If we went by this exclamation alone, we would get the impression, despite all the abnormalities we have found in the history of Israel, that the covenant, the rule of God, the tabernacle and worship – taken as divine institutions – had remained pristine, like tools only waiting for use, like rigged vessels ready to sail at any moment, as soon as the wind were to fill their sails.

If, on the other hand, we take into account all the other data, we get a completely different picture. The ark was the visible pledge of the covenant, the throne of Jehovah and more than His throne in a certain sense, namely Jehovah Himself in the shadows of the Old Covenant, that is, the sign of His presence. But the glorious indwelling of God, the visible revelation upon which the entire covenant was built, had gone missing since the days of Bochim. With that, both the tabernacle and the rule of God had lost their proper meaning. Not as if the covenant had perished, as if the ideal and rule of God had been abandoned, as if Jehovah had forsaken His people, but such that the entire shadow service had fallen into decay. The ark had not come to rest, 1 Chron. 6: 31; 28: 2; 2 Chron. 6: 41. But it meant that judgment was to come upon the entire provisional condition. The tree of the theocracy had been "girdled"; life had departed from the body of the ceremonial law. Both remain in existence and to some extent in force; but only if the Old Testament Sabbath is maintained as the shadow of rest, not of the first, but of the second creation, the rest, not of God, but of Christ when He shall have overcome death.

The old remains, though "near disappearance," for the new is born in the womb of that old, but it remains as does the whole law, not as a means of justification, not as the way by which Israel reaches its destiny, but solely as a punitive witness concerning man's sin, as a prophetic witness concerning his redemption.

The people have failed to fulfill the condition of the covenant; the goal of redemption has not been achieved. It follows that revelation must enter a new stage, and equally that judgment will have to pave the way for this.

God does not do the same thing twice. His glory does not suffer that. There will be new life, but it comes through death. The restoration His grace works is not a repetition of the old, not a bare revival of what died, but renewal, resurrection, glorification.

The Egyptians embalmed the corpses of their great men. After three thousand years, they believed, the souls of the dead would return and therefore need a home. The body that had served this end would soon be reanimated.

This is not the way things are in the Kingdom of God. Death is not followed by revivification, but by resurrection.

We notice this, for example, at the first violation of the covenant on the occasion of the golden calf. Moses shatters the tablets of the law. The history of the first covenant has thus ended, it has passed irrevocably. To what purpose would the stone charter of that covenant still serve? God does not allow Himself to be played with and mocked. He shows mercy, but not at the expense of His justice.

Yet the covenant is renewed, the *same* covenant. God also commands Moses to hew himself two stone tablets like the first, and writes on them the *same words,* Deut. 10: 1–4, all seemingly in direct conflict with what we have just elaborated.

Seemingly, but not in reality. After all, the renewed covenant has substantially changed in character. It no longer has the promise of obedience made by Israel, Ex. 19: 8, as its foundation, guarantee, and supposition, but the gift of God, foreshadowed by the ark.

"Chisel out two stone tablets," we read in Deut. 10: 1–2, "like the originals, come up to Me on the mountain, and *make an ark of wood.* And I will write on the tablets the words that were on the first tablets, which you broke; and you are to *place them in the ark.*"

The meaning is not puzzling to him who has seen in this "ark" the Christ of God, the Mediator of God and of men, the Angel of the Covenant, in whom is God's name, Ex. 23: 21; and in the requirement to manufacture this ark a coming of that Redeemer who introduces Himself in Ps. 40: 7–8: "Then I said, 'Here I am, I have come—it is written about me in the scroll: I delight to do Your will, O my God; Your law is within my heart.'"

Equally striking and even clearer for our purposes in this connection is the depiction given us by the prophet Hosea of the renewal of the covenant. Israel is the adulterous woman who forsakes the covenant of her God and runs after her lovers, to whom she considers herself indebted for the prosperity that comes to her in the widest measure. We hear her speak, Hos. 2:5: "I will go after my lovers, who give me bread and water, wool and linen, oil and drink."

In vain. She does not find them. God has closed with thorny hedges the path that leads to the temple of the Baals and erected a fence in front of her. Her feast days have been turned into days of fasting, her dancing into mourning. To what end? "Then she will say, 'I will return to my first husband, for then I was better off than now'" (v. 7). And that husband would accept her, now that she, impelled by need, returns to give him the poor remnant of her unclean love. He, the Holy One, who does not tolerate evil; she who even now would not care for Him if her lovers had not left her!

Can the sad past then be undone and the stain of sin erased? No, but something different and better than this. God has said of her: "Lo-Ammi," she is no longer My people, and "Lo-Ruhamah," I will not have mercy on her again, Hos. 1: 8, 9; and "God is not a man, that He should lie, or a son of man, that He should change His mind. Does He speak and not act? Does He promise and not fulfill?" (Num. 23: 19).

But a *miracle* happens to her. She is young again. With a pure, divine love, her God wants to woo her. He lures her and leads her to the desert, that is, the place where it pleased Him to reveal Himself to her, to join herself to Him, Hos. 2: 13; "I will betroth you in righteousness and justice, in loving devotion and compassion," says Jehovah, v. 18. It is a repetition of what happened when He bought her out of Egypt; and the splashing waves of the Red Sea, when its swirls swallowed Pharaoh, were they not her wedding song? Nay, the old has passed away; for it is not bunches of grapes, cut off in the valley of Eskol, that are brought to her; "There," i.e., from Sinai, "I will give back her vineyards, and make the Valley of Achor," the valley in which Achan was stoned and the curse of Israel was averted, "into a gateway of hope. There she will respond as she did in the days of her youth, as in the day she came up out of Egypt," v. 14.

From the days of Bochim, to return to our subject, the tabernacle stands as a memorial of a state that has passed away. In that dwelling from which the sin of Israel has displaced Him, God does not return in His glory. But days of visitation are coming, a day of judgment is coming when it will become visible to all eyes that God has despised Joseph's tent. The people erected the tabernacle at Shiloh. Shiloh – rest – was the name of this place. But that was not the place of which Jehovah had spoken: "When you cross the Jordan and live in the land that the LORD your God is giving you as an inheritance, and He gives you rest from all the enemies around you and you dwell securely, then the LORD your God will *choose a dwelling for His Name*" (Deut. 12: 10–11).

Had Israel entered into rest? Had Jehovah said of Shiloh, "This is My resting place forever and ever; here I will dwell, for I have desired this home"? (Ps. 132: 14). No, the Lord chose Zion. He desired Zion to be His dwelling place, v. 13. Did He speak a word to one of the judges of Israel, whom He commanded to watch over His people, saying: "Why haven't you built Me a house of cedar?" (1 Chron. 17: 6). Only when He gave David rest from his enemies all around did the time come when it would be said to Jehovah, "Arise, O LORD, to Your resting place, You and the ark of Your strength!" (Ps. 132: 8).

Permit us here a digression concerning the fact that men of God like Gideon, Samuel, David and Solomon, as well as the people, erected altars and offered sacrifices to Jehovah not only in but also outside the tabernacle. To those who overlook the abnormality of the state of Israel in Canaan, who do not understand that the Sinaitic covenant was actually suspended and why, this conduct of Israel's judges and kings is inexplicable. For us, on the other hand, this is the proof that they took a deep, a prophetic look at the meaning of the ceremonial law. The patriarchs were in possession of the pure knowledge of God. They were in the position of John 4: 21. For them whose God is bound to neither time nor place, this was the only conceivable position. The restriction of the freedom with which they permitted themselves to erect altars wherever Jehovah revealed himself to them, nay, wherever they pitched their tents, Gen. 12: 7, 8; 13: 18; 33: 20, etc., is exclusively of an *administrative* nature. It lies in the ceremonial law, which, according to Gal. 3: 19, was "added ... until the arrival of the seed," and is partly of a pedagogical character, partly of typical significance.

Now as soon as Jehovah ceased to reveal Himself in the tabernacle, Israel to a certain extent arrived at the same condition in which it had been in the wilderness after the refusal to go into Canaan and the announcement of the judgment on the entire generation that had gone out of Egypt. Now as then, it passed under God's judgment. At that time, this resulted in the people not getting circumcised, Joshua 5: 4–7. As a rule it did not bring its sacrifices into the court, which may be inferred from the precepts given by Moses in the fields of Moab with a view to dwelling in

Canaan. One was to "seek the place the LORD your God will choose from among all your tribes to establish as a dwelling for His Name, and there you must go." "You are not to do," says Moses, Deut. 12: 8–9, "as we are doing here today, where everyone does what seems right in his own eyes. For you *have not yet come to the resting place*." Yes, what was worse, they carried about – this is true at least of a part of the people, who had separated themselves from the camp – "Sakkuth your king and Kaiwan your star god, the idols you made for yourselves" (Amos 5: 26).

It now resulted that the service in the tabernacle, although as little entirely suspended as it was in the desert, albeit sometimes less, sometimes more faithfully attended by a part of the people, did not possess the exclusive character that it should have had according to the law, that is, in normal conditions. The tabernacle would have been completely taken away if God did not maintain the existing in order to bring forth the new from it. God goes from tent to tent, until rest shall have come.

It is the attempt, in disregard of the actual state of affairs, to put the ark at the forefront of the battle against the Philistines that brought the judgment on the whole shadow service, a judgment coinciding with and prepared by the fulfillment of what had been threatened against Eli and his house.

In the first chapters of the first book of Samuel, we are transported to Shiloh and brought into contact with the priesthood in its decline. In several places in the book of Judges, the existence of the tabernacle and Levitical worship is assumed. The exceptions here confirm the rule. The occasion of the founding of the temple in the house of Micah and its transfer to Dan would not have been described in such detail if this case had not stood alone. There is no false currency where there is no real currency in circulation.

But, as has been said, the tabernacle does not occupy a central place. This is due not only to the abnormal nature of Israel's condition but, inseparably from this, to the low standard of religious life at the time of the Judges.

In the first of Zechariah's night visions, we are presented with the church under the image of a grove of myrtles in the valley. A band of horsemen under the Angel of the Lord as captain – a symbol of the powers that rule history under the direction of Israel's ruler – comes together here to bring tidings. Which is to say, the church is the center from which the movements emanate and upon which they converge. In everything history shows us, it is ultimately about the good of that church.

From this we learn the church's significance. The decay of popular life emanates from her, is seen in her, and later also, if it comes to a reformation, halted in her. In line with our forefathers but in opposition to the parlance of the modern age, we speak of "the church in Israel" because religious life, under the Old Covenant as much as under the New, found its own expression distinct from the social institutions and the institution of the state. Now this church is at all times the light, the salt, the leaven through which workings for good are exercised in a wider circle. If little or nothing of these workings is to be seen, as was apparently the case in the time of the Judges, we are entitled to draw the inference that the salt has lost its savor, that the light has been placed under the bushel, that the leaven has lost its power.

If priest and prophet are "muddled in their visions and stumbling in their judgments," Isa. 28:7, if the leaders of the people have become its seducers, Isa. 9: 15, then the situation is hopeless indeed. Hence Satan directs his first attack at the teachers and ministers, at those who are the bearers of the Word of God, at the institutions of religion, just as the enemy tends to cut off or defile the springs and wells watering the armies facing him or the cities he besieges. Hence also, no *conclusive* restoration is possible unless this church is lifted out of her degradation.

It is necessary to remember this because we discern in ourselves and in others the tendency to leave the fallen church to herself, and to accomplish by other means the task assigned to her.

Not only do the Micahs establish their own houses of God opposite her, but likewise the Gideons deem it necessary to fabricate an ephod. One repulsively turns away from the priests who serve the holy with unholy hands. One asks oneself, "To what purpose must these institutions be maintained that have become meaningless forms." One has, in a word, no "pity on her dust." After all, as soon as the Lord's servants delight in her stones and pity her dust, it is time to be merciful to Zion, for the appointed time has come, Ps. 102: 14, 15.

But the same history that teaches us how little influence for good the church exercised after the days of Joshua proves most clearly that the spiritual prosperity of the people depends on her. Not Micah and not Gideon but Jehovah Himself seems to leave the church to herself. He interferes with His people, stopping the destruction by which they would have been ruined, and to this end makes use of the *Judges,* men charged with an extraordinary mission. But the divine purpose is not to bring about the restoration, the renewal of Israel in this way. Nor does it come to this. The infirmity of His people is terminal, the heart is stricken. Relief may come, life may be prolonged, but there is no change in the overall condition until the *cause of the ailment* is removed.

We discover something similar in the history of the ten northern tribes. Jehovah sends His prophets again and again (Jer. 26: 5). Most of His powers were effected there. Men like Elijah and Elisha labored there. Even in the days of Ahab and Jezebel, when the servant of God in his deep despondency thought he was the only one left, seven thousand were found who had not bowed the knee to Baal. But none of this prevented Ephraim from being lost. The judgment was only postponed. A few were saved but the nation as a whole was left in its degradation.

But things have not yet reached that point. The Age of the Judges constitutes only a transitional era in history. The Lord is in the process of preparing a thorough reformation that will only be completed under Solomon, the beginning of which is seen in the judgments brought upon the house of Eli.

When Samson, the Nazirite of God, committed treason against himself, and God's righteousness was glorified in him, we read in Judges 16: 22 that "the hair on his head," the sign of his Naziriteship, "began to grow back" in the prison house. Before the eyes of men he stood among the pillars in the house of Dagon as the same as he had been before his deep fall, and although the past could not be revoked, although the damage caused by his sin could not be repaired, God heard his prayer, restored his strength and still allowed him to perform in his death an act by which he fulfilled his destiny.

This event is repeated in the history of Israel. The Nazirite of God has become unfaithful to the covenant, has lost his strength, has not come to rest but through his own fault has had to share his inheritance with the enemies of God and his kingdom. However, this state of affairs visibly changes over the centuries. Under David, even the surrounding nations were initially conquered. The kingdom in its outward form corresponds to what it was originally destined to be and would have been if Israel had fulfilled the condition of the covenant. But now that "the king had settled into his palace and the Lord had given him rest from all his enemies around him," he also receives the promise: "I will raise up your descendant after you, who will come from your own body, and I will establish his kingdom. He will build a house for My Name, and I will establish the throne of his kingdom forever" (2 Sam. 7: 1, 12, 13).

This, then, indicates the end point of the provisional state that entered a new stage when the tabernacle was struck by God's judgment. The death of the old precedes the coming of the new. The dilapidated hut must be torn down if a new and more beautiful building is to be erected in the same place.

Nevertheless, this refers only to the form in which the Lord shows Himself active. In this connection we have only to point out the remarkable fact that this activity of His is transferred from the outer circumferences to the center of the people's life. Judgment begins at the house of God, and there we also find the beginning of the reformation.

If it has been a mystery to us that the priests during the Judges, with the exception of the last two, Eli and Samuel, made so little of themselves, that their influence for good was so imperceptible, the history of Eli and his sons provides us with the key to the explanation.

The fall of the tree or of the boulder takes only a few moments, but the causes of that fall date from much earlier. The tree first slowly decayed; and before the rock crashed, the cracks that foretold its fall were already noticeable.

For centuries Shiloh remained shrouded in an almost impenetrable mist. At the distance we stand from what took place there during the centuries that constitute the Age of the Judges, we have only been able to discern the bare outlines of things. But now, in the first chapters of the books of Samuel, this haze lifts as it were, and we can see the sanctuary in the full light of history. We are witness to a decay, a destruction that had to be the outcome of the many things that preceded it.

The sins of Eli's sons are the full fruit of a mechanistic formalism, an estrangement from God, over which the judgment of God was *bound* to pass. That precisely a man like Eli should be stricken by this judgment, namely a man who is not an idolater, who has personally kept himself within the bounds of the law, who – far from being on a par with his sons – in the way he acquiesces in the judgment of him and his house, in his trembling before "the ark of God" when it was carried into battle, and in the emotion with which he learned that the ark fell into the hands of the uncircumcised, shows the characteristics of piety, all this tells us that it was not only his own sins for which he suffered, but also those of his family. The justice of God is aptly expressed in this.

We notice something similar in the history of the last kings of Israel and Judah, indeed even in that of the pious Josiah. Neither Hoshea nor Zedekiah personally brought about the fulfillment to them and theirs of the threats that the prophets of the Lord had been making for years and centuries. The former is even one of the best kings who sat on the throne of Ephraim. But it goes with them according to the law the Savior pronounced when He announced that "upon you will come all the righteous blood shed on earth, from the blood of righteous Abel to the blood of Zechariah son of Berechiah, whom you murdered between the temple and the altar" (Matth. 23: 35).

We must not dwell on Eli, on Hophni and Phinehas, as if they had been greater sinners than all who came before them. The judgment is over them, but in them over their generation and in that generation over the *institutions of the ceremonial law*.

To Eleazar was promised an eternal priesthood (Num. 25: 13). Eli was from the line of Ithamar (1 Chron. 24: 3ff.). Thus, during the time when the house at Shiloh was hidden from our view, a change of priesthood must have taken place. This indicates a judgment by which the descendants of Eleazar were deprived of the hereditary blessing. Details are not communicated to us in this regard. But the fact itself is sufficiently guaranteed under these circumstances because it is entirely consistent with what could be deduced from the silence of history regarding the tabernacle and worship.

So that judgment was personal. It applied to one of the two priestly families. But it is different with the judgment on Eli and his house. Now that the priesthood as a whole has proven negligent in fulfilling the exalted calling assigned to it, God not only abandons it, but in it also "treats

Joseph's tent contemptuously" (Ps. 78: 34, Psalter of 1773). They are living in the time of visitation.

This is one side of the truth. But let us also look at the other side. God reveals His forbearance as well as His justice. And this forbearance ultimately serves to glorify righteousness, because the virtues of the Lord do not stand alongside, much less in opposition to one another, but blend together as it were. Indeed, if God had acted rightly, He would have taken back not only His glory but also the ark which was the bearer of that glory, and with that ark the entire shadow service. After all, the tabernacle is a body from which the soul is missing! Yet God for centuries bears this form, which must be broken, until the servants of the sanctuary caused this judgment to ripen by their sins.

This is how the Lord acts at all times. We have seen this before in Saul, whose kingship could not be upheld, but nevertheless was maintained until it was lost through his own fault. We therefore turn our attention to the behavior of Eli and his sons, which must be considered more directly as the reason God rejected Shiloh.

"THE SIN OF THESE YOUNG MEN was severe in the sight of the LORD" (1 Sam. 2: 17). Were they hypocrites? Worse than this. They sin "defiantly," Num. 15: 30, "flaunt their sin," Isa. 3:9, and "refuse to be ashamed," Jer. 3: 3.

We have an abhorrence of the hypocrite, of the sin presented in the name of virtue, of the smirk behind the mock face of devotion, of the pretense presented as if it were the reality. But even more heinous and God-denying than feignedness, which at least still pays its homage to godliness and shows that it knows the distinction between good and evil, is the wickedness that casts off its mask and does not refrain from acting in its own name, defying the wrath of God.

Although every sin makes us damnable before God and carries within it the germ of all others, so that Scripture, when it declares that whoever transgresses one commandment is guilty of all, unfolds to us its real essence, yet there are degrees and stages in evil. But that evil reaches its highest stage if the sinner no longer benefits from the prayer, "Father! forgive them, for they know not what they do!"

Evil and darkness suit each other. Whoever commits sin is under the power of the Prince of Darkness. How terrible then must be the iniquity *committed in the full light!*

Sacrilege and perjury are on a par in this respect. And this sin is not least found in the circle of those who have become acquainted with the holy. "The closer to Rome, the worse the Christians!" people used to say in the days of the Reformation. Not only Luther, but many a person who visited "the holy city," hoping to see there attained and embodied the ideal of a religious life that he knew only approximately, was disillusioned and discovered the truth contained in the proverb.

While this did not argue in favor of Rome, in itself it would not have been a conclusive proof against Roman religion (i.e., if her error by which great value was attached to religious operations as such – ex opere operato, i.e., separated from the principle from which they originated and the purpose for which they were carried out – had not fostered mechanism and Pharisaism). After all, every religion exercises a double effect. It constantly makes one either better or worse. One cannot engage with the truth without granting it dominion over life, for if one fails to do so, it avenges itself by working a blindness and hardening unparalleled elsewhere. Judas matured in the proximity of the Son of God, in the circle of his disciples. Caiaphas grew up in the shadow of the temple. Achaz and Manasseh were children of pious parents. Hophni and Phinehas had religion as their profession.

The servants of the Lord served themselves. Contrary to the provisions of the law, Lev. 3, they took what was the Lord's before it came on the altar, 1 Sam. 2:15 ff. – probably, although this is not expressly communicated, not only because it tasted better but also because they regarded it as an article of commerce, as was the case in the pagan temples.

And what is worse, they did not refrain from using violence, v. 16, so that the people despised the Lord's meat offering, v. 17. Moreover, the house of God had become a school of fornication, v. 22. In a word, Israel's pastors led the way on the path to destruction.

And now it is perfectly true that the value of the office is not diminished by the unworthiness of the ministers, that the law of God is not rendered powerless by its transgression, that the truth remains *true* no matter who pronounces it, that the sacred in itself is not profaned by the unholy hands that minister to it. But it is also true that "I will be sanctified in them that come nigh me" (Lev. 10: 3, KJV), that the truth will be judged according to its professors, and that the spotless purity of the holy should be reflected in the holiness of those who serve and represent it.

God must stand up for His honor and uphold His right against those who act in His name and take His covenant on their lips, Ps. 50: 16. The history of Israel is one continuous revelation of the holiness of the Lord, demanding much from those to whom much has been given.

Nadab and Abihu, sons of Aaron, when they brought strange fire on the altar, were not spared because their father was the minister of the sanctuary. Miriam had no license to sin because she was the sister of the mediator of the Old Covenant. Moses and Aaron themselves fell with those who had sinned in the wilderness. David, the servant of God, suffered bitterly because he had "given great occasion to the enemies of the Lord to blaspheme" (2 Sam. 12: 14, KJV).

The sin of Hophni and Phinehas was grave also because they "caused Israel to sin." The place they held enabled them to cause a people to be lost by their word and example. Levity and carelessness are always culpable, but in the man by whose rashness human lives are lost, they are punishable by the courts, and, if he held a post of trust and the kind of omission he committed brought this about, equal to wanton manslaughter.

But though the sons of Eli were punishable, Eli himself was no less so, though for a different reason. They were "wicked men," worthless, and "had no regard for the Lord," 1 Sam. 2: 12. Although they entered the veil of the sanctuary, ate the bread of the Presence, i.e., the bread through which the face of the Lord was beheld, had walked in the light of the lampstand, i.e., were irradiated by the Holy Spirit, and were enveloped in the cloud of incense which was kindled on the golden altar, i.e., were surrounded by the revelation, the name of God, they did not come into contact with God and had "never heard His voice nor seen His form, nor does His word abide in you" (John 5: 37–38).

But Eli knew the Lord and knew the justice of his God. No excuse for him! Something different and something more is demanded of a child than of a servant. If his children were practical atheists, he knew what it meant "to despise God," 1 Sam. 2: 30.

In what, then, did Eli's sin consist? In weakness, but in the weakness of a *father,* a *ruler,* a *high priest;* in the weakness that presupposes a life of dereliction of duty, betrays lack of the true fear of God, and in its consequences drags him, his house, yes all Israel, down to ruin.

Let us dwell on this point by point for a moment. Eli was weak. However, weakness is not innocuous. In fact, it is not to be considered in isolation, but is the result of all kinds of causes. If the cast iron pillars of a bridge are weak, there is a defect in the casting, the form in which they were cast was not evenly filled with iron, was not solid. If the foundations of a building are weak, it is due to the unsoundness of the materials or of the masonry, or also to the fact that they have been undermined by subsidence in the ground or by water. In other words, we do not content ourselves with stating the fact, but are not satisfied until we have discovered the cause.

Whence, we ask, comes this weakness? This also applies to a human being, including Eli. But hardly have we asked the question before we discover the sinful cause of this weakness. In the moral world, it is always something relative. Weakness with respect to this or that impelling force indicates strength with respect to its opposite. Here it is impossible to serve two lords; I hate the one just in the proportion in which I love the other. For example, if Eli is weak toward his sons, he is strong enough to overcome the sense of duty, the requirement of God's holy law, the fear of His judgment. His earthly, sinful love, his laziness, his superficiality brought about this weakness. Eli was weak as a father, as a judge, as a high priest.

According to a quite equitable rule of the civil code, we are responsible for the actions in society of our minor children and of our household members and subjects. Those in whom the power to command is assumed are not to be held blameless because they have not exercised this power in a given case. Aaron may say, "You yourself know that the people are intent on evil.... I said to them, 'Whoever has gold, let him take it off,' and they gave it to me. And when I threw it into the fire, out came this calf!" (Ex. 32: 22, 24), but he makes a mockery of himself. For the temporary head of Israel, it is in vain to want to cast the blame on those whom he should have restrained, the actions of whom he should have to give account.

Eli gave enough notice to his sons of their wrongdoings, 1 Sam. 2: 24. But in his case, giving notice is not enough. He should have, in the various relations in which he stood to them, maintained discipline, and is shamed by the behavior of a Brutus.[22]

When Sultan Mahmood II learned that the chiefs of his people not unjustly feared for him and his empire, viz. for the future of Mohammedanism, feared danger from the love he bore his consort Irene, a Christian, he led her into the assembly of Dragomans and pointed to her, blossoming in feminine beauty, hair flowing in long braids over her white neck and shoulders, while he spoke in a voice trembling with emotion, "Now feast your eyes, Muslims! Tell me: is she not a lovely sight? Would she not be worth a crown? Well! I sacrifice her, and in her my own heart, to the cause of our holy religion!" And at the very instant he uttered those words, he wound her wavy hair about one hand and with the other grasped the scimitar with which with one stroke he separated her head from the torso. There was a sacrifice to be made. He was willing to make it; in so doing he showed his supremacy in a way that won him the attachment of his underlings, which had already begun to falter.

Nothing of the spirit and character of a Mahmood was found in Eli, even though this was about the honor of his God and the future of his people. The weakness of Eli presupposed a life of dereliction of duty. By now he was quite old, 1 Sam. 2: 22. There is something mitigating in this communication. But he was not so old when his sons were children. The old trees could not be bent; they had to be felled. In the days when they were young and pliable, why had paternal discipline slept?

Most certainly, grace is not inherited. The godliness of parents does not guarantee that of sons. Many a Hezekiah gives birth to a Manasseh, many a Josiah to a Jehoiakim. It is likewise said of Samuel that "his sons did not walk in his ways," 1 Sam. 8: 3. From Adam came forth not only an Abel but also a Cain, from Isaac not only a Jacob-Israel but also an Esau-Edom.

---

[22] A reference to Marcus Junius Brutus (85–42 BC), the assassin of Julius Caesar, who is viewed either as a traitor or a selfless champion of the greater good – for Hoedemaker, apparently the latter.

But of Eli it is expressly said, "his sons blasphemed God and he did not restrain them" (1 Sam. 3: 13). He failed to arrest the evil in its inception and thereby deprived himself of the power to intervene later with force. He was unable to take the reins he had previously let slip.

Yes, there was a means to that end, namely true confession of sin. Had he had the courage to say to his children, "I have been to you an indulgent but not a good father; I have treated you with gentleness but not out of true love; I have loved you but not with that love which aims at nothing but your temporal and eternal welfare!" he could have regained something of the lost authority.

He who does not have himself under discipline cannot exercise discipline over his dependents. But the way to recovery lies in the depths, and leads via voluntary humiliation and sincere confession of guilt to true conversion.

Eli's weakness betrays the absence of the fear of God. If he had lived under the constant and vivid awareness of the harmful and shameful nature of sin, it would have been impossible for him to tolerate what he was now turning a blind eye to or chastising with words that had no force.

Eli admonished, punished, called sin by its name. At times he could be very severe, as witness his words to Hannah. But how? It was the same Eli who spoke. "When two say the same thing," as a well-known proverb teaches, "it is not yet the same thing." The truth of this word cannot be contradicted and is confirmed daily by experience. In explaining and valuing a word, we have to take into account the man who uttered it, his inner existence, his character. Grammar, logic and rhetoric cannot make up for what is lacking in character. Character is to the speaker what muscular strength is to him who swings the axe or to him who draws the bow. With the same instrument, the one swings the steel much deeper and sends the arrow much farther than the other.

What was still missing from Eli's words? The fear of God, the abhorrence of sin, the passion with regard to its consequences, by which they could have exercised moral dominion.

Peter speaks with authority and makes the evil spirits hear. Simon the magician wants to renounce the artifice and learn the art; but to possess the miracle power, he would first have to become Peter. The same is true of counsel, of exhortations, in a word, of everything we say and do.

Alas! Eli's own earthiness and unbelief made him like somebody in suspended animation, who dreaming wishes to escape the imagined danger. What he saw, felt, feared and desired did not leave him unconscious, but powerless. He could not ward off this mysterious influence by which he was kept back from the work that befitted the father and spiritual head of the people. But the cause of this lay within himself.

We now bring only this one element into account because we have no right to say or think of Eli that his own personal and domestic life was wanting. But when we speak of upbringing more generally, we have yet to mention the unintentional contradiction often found between word and life. There are parents who know how to properly point out to their children what is wrong in their actions, but who, without knowing it or wanting it, offer them a completely different standard by which to judge their actions. According to the theory of their exhortation, sin is the most harmful and piety the most desirable thing imaginable. But let the child break a cup, or tear a garment, and at the same time invent a lie. In the outburst of wrath that now follows, the little one immediately senses in his father or his mother what weighs most heavily with them and deserves the most punishment in their eyes. Let the youth be opened to a circle or offered a position where social position and advantage are weighed in the balance against what would promote his spiritual well-being. By the advice now given, by the desire now made known, the child of pious instruction actually comes to know what he has to adhere to in order to please his parents.

In its consequences, Eli's weakness dragged down himself, his house and the Lord's people. If the evil may or must also be judged according to its effects, Eli's guilt is no little thing. The man of God announcing to him the judgment, 1 Sam. 2: 27ff., and the nocturnal revelation of the Lord received by Samuel, 3: 11, point to the judge and high priest as the protagonist in the appalling drama to which we shall shortly bear witness.

Eli's weakness caused death to come to his sons and judgment to come upon Israel. He does not get off, even though, like Lot, he torments his "righteous soul" over what he hears and sees in his and the Lord's house.

Nature teaches us that the crimes of those who belong to us do not leave us unaffected. A member of our family or of our lineage sins severely, and we dare not lift our eyes out of shame. It is our sin, our shame, that there became public knowledge, even if we did not a little to prevent it. When toxins in the body form a growth that ripens and so eliminates them, even though it is a particular part of the body that is concerned, the toxins affect not only that part but the whole body.[23]

The father is complicit in what his sons do. How terrible it must have been for him to carry this awareness within himself! His weakness opened a fountain of misery that would not soon stop flowing.

The death of his sons, his own untimely end, the defeat of the people, the degradation of the ark, the murder of the priests at Nob, the rivalry between Abiathar and Zadok, in a word, all the suffering that came from the curse by which Eli was afflicted, is the harvest of what he sowed in his sinful abstinence. So he bows before the judgment. "He is the Lord .... Let Him do what is good in His eyes," we hear him say in 1 Sam. 3: 18. But although we do not overlook the fact that piety gave him these words, we are at the same time obliged to note that the grace of repentance was withheld from him.

He no longer prays for his own; he does not humble himself under the threat of the Lord and does not approach God in a priestly manner with a "Who knows, the Lord may well avert the fierceness of His wrath!" or a "Punish me, I have sinned; but what have these poor sheep done?" That too goes along with, nay more than that, forms part of the judgment!

---

[23] This example reflects the medical understanding of that time.

11. THE DAWN OF THE NEW DAY

1 Samuel 1:1–2, 3: 1ff.

O afflicted city, lashed by storms, without solace,
Surely I will set your stones in antimony
And lay your foundations with sapphires.
I will make your pinnacles of rubies,
Your gates of sparkling jewels,
And all your walls of precious stones.
Then all your sons will be taught by the LORD,
And great will be their prosperity.

Isaiah 54: 11–13

History is like a precious carpet hanging down in broad folds from the ceiling to which it is attached. It takes little observation to discover that it is woven in one piece, artfully, according to a certain plan. One detects at first glance that those threads do not lie tangled together, that those colors have not been brought together in variegated shades by mere chance. But little can be said of the pattern itself. One sees mere fragments that are best viewed from a distance in order to form an idea of the whole. Only when the entire fabric is pulled up evenly, when it shows itself to the eye without folds in its full dimensions, are we able to grasp the great idea of God of the whole.

Then the soul honors with praise,
God's arrangement in its coherence.

Hymn 192: 7, *Evangelische Gezangen* [Gospel Hymns]

After all, it is because of our shortsightedness that we notice so little down here of the Lord's manifold wisdom in history. We live in the passing moments. If we continue to stare at what is immediately before us, of which we see neither the beginning nor the end, everything looks piecemeal. This is why it is so necessary to have history as our teacher, that is, to supplement our limited experience with that of our ancestors. Our life is thereby prolonged, as it were. This widens our field of vision.

But we who find in Scripture the revelation of God's counsel and will for our redemption, which is the centerpiece of His world plan, have in our examination of that history something above all else. We find in Scripture the basic forms of things, the expression of God's idea of redemption, the indication of the fundamental principles according to which He governs.

With all this in mind, we already in this life are better able to get a correct, albeit very incomplete, representation of the whole. We also have another advantage: there is a place in Holy Scripture for the small as well as the great, for the life of the family, for the experience of the person as well as the history of the people, for the internal, spiritual life as well as the external, natural life; here they are presented in connection with each other and with the whole.

In the annals of secular history we usually find only what stands out, what makes a noise, what can be considered of general interest. The hidden motive forces and reasons are usually lost, though one tries in many ways to fill in the gap. In Scripture, on the other hand, the Lord brings us, as it were, into His workshop; He explains to us the purpose of the work of His wisdom, in which it pleases Him to glorify Himself. "A servant does not understand what his master is doing" (John 15: 15). This knowledge is the privilege of friends, of the children of God.

These thoughts were prompted by an attentive reading of the first chapters of the first book of Samuel. A family history is supplied to us here. We find outlined the experience, the state of mind of a woman, of Hannah. But the final goal of those reports lies in the reformation in later times brought about by the son of this woman, Samuel. How the great and the small, the external and the internal, the private and the public are intertwined here!

Famous travelers the tales of whose travels captivated our interest even in our childhood, sought, one after another, to penetrate to the heart of Africa and achieve the goal of their endeavor, the discovery of the sources of the Nile River. One wished to see the proud river in its first beginnings, a very natural desire; and the difficult, mysterious nature of the undertaking always provided, after each failure, a new impetus to this exploration which only in recent years has been crowned with a favorable result.

The origins of things, the first beginnings of great events, the profound changes in the field of popular life, likewise in the history of church and state, usually evade sight. But before Scripture moves us into the circle of events preceding the foundation of the kingship, it shows us where the new era began, namely in the *inner life of Samuel's mother*. Now we again see what we already noticed at Samson's birth: how God's grace is glorified in that insignificant *beginning*.

While the Philistine oppression continues, and even though Israel has not yet been converted, and notwithstanding the insusceptibility of the people, God is already, in the heart of a woman, quietly preparing the future redemption. She is aggrieved by the delayed hope and mortified by the humiliation inflicted on her by one she could not escape; but precisely because of that, she is prepared for the grace that stands to be glorified to her.

How very slight are the beginnings of the great work of God of which the Lord Himself says, "the ears of all who hear it will tingle!" (1 Sam. 3: 11)! When great changes in church or state are imminent, attention is focused and expectation is set on the men of renown who come to the fore, and on the events that are rumored. One watches the Boulangers and the Bismarcks with the greatest interest. One watches "the divisions of Reuben," in which "there were great thoughts of heart" (Judges 5: 15, KJV). At the least, one expects it from Samson, who is furnished with such marvelous powers.

And God begins His work with the strife in the household of Elkanah, and the desire He put in the heart of Hannah!

Who would have suspected, in the days of Israel's heaviest tribulation in Egypt, that the Lord was on His way to redeem His people, and that the labor that was to lead to this end had begun when Jochebed had woven her casket of rushes in which the newborn of her house was soon to be laid? Who was there among the many who, like Staupitz with his older contemporaries and kindred spirits, eagerly awaited the "reformation of the church in head and members," who did not expect great things from the reformatory councils that succeeded each other, and had at their disposal the learning, piety and power of all Europe? And whose courage did not fail when the last of these assemblies was dissolved? Who did not know that in the same remarkable year, 1484, in which the hope of better conditions was thwarted, Luther was born in the hut of a charcoal burner?

Wonderful are the ways of God! Such facts humble man, for they make him see how little he is to be esteemed; yet they exalt him again, for they furnish a clear proof of how God has "chosen the things that are not to nullify the things that are"; how the base and vile of this world are used to something great and glorious, lest man should boast before the Lord, saying: "My hand has redeemed me!" God has His Hazzelelponis laboring in the field and His Hannahs laboring in the home; and while the later historians labor to place the course of events in the right light and to search out the motive forces of history from their origin, they may overlook just him or her or that by which it especially pleased the Lord to work.

The opening words of the first book of Samuel transport us to the mountain range of Ephraim, where once Deborah dwelt, and to the lineage from which Israel's first guide and savior emerged. After all, we may safely assume, notwithstanding the disagreement of many scholars, that Samuel was of priestly descent. That Elkanah, his father, is "from Ramathaim-zophim," 1 Sam. 1: 1, does not argue against this view. The Levites, who, as is well known, lived scattered throughout the land, were named after their dwelling places, not after their lineages. "And there was a young man," we read in Judges 17: 7 (KJV), "out of Bethlehem-Judah of the family of Judah, who was a Levite" (cf. Judges 19: 1).

The genealogy of Samuel is given in 1 Chr. 6: 16, 22–28. From this it appears that he was of the Kohathites, who, according to Josh. 21: 20ff., dwelt on the mountains of Ephraim. "The remaining Kohathite clans of the Levites were allotted these cities: From the tribe of Ephraim they were given Shechem in the hill country of Ephraim (a city of refuge for the manslayer)," etc. For the sake of completeness, it may be mentioned that Heman, the head of one of the Levite singer families, was of the lineage of Samuel; his father was Samuel's son Joel, 1 Chron. 25: 4, cf. 6: 28, 33.

Even in the days when the house of Aaron was an affront to Israel, Elkanah annually visited Shiloh with his entire family. The feast mentioned once and again in the story was, as we may assume on this ground, the Feast of Passover, 1 Sam. 1: 3, 21. Then, although the law did not require it, the women were usually present. "Men," we read in 1 Sam. 2: 17, "abhorred the offering of the LORD." This man, on the other hand, "would go up from his city to worship and sacrifice to the LORD of Hosts at Shiloh," 1: 3. Indeed, it is not without significance that this is immediately followed by: "where Eli's two sons, Hophni and Phinehas, were priests to the LORD."

Toward the end of the Age of the Judges, the institution of the Lord, the objective aspect in religion, comes to the fore. Judgment will come over this, although the closer the judgment approaches, the more we are reminded of the value of legitimate worship. It was the intention of the Lord to make the sanctuary, the priesthood, the faithful observance of the precepts of the law subservient to the restoration of Israel. The youthful stem emerges from the decay of the old trunk. The concern now is not the removal of the Baal service but the renewal of the people's entire existence from out of the center of their religious life.

Hannah, the childless wife of Elkanah, desired a child, a very natural desire in Israel. The fact that Peninnah, a woman less beloved by her husband, took such pride in the fact that she was the mother of his children, constantly reproached poor Hannah for her infertility, and found reason in this to mock her, proves, as is evident from all kinds of data, that the blessing of children was highly valued among this people. There was a moral, religious reason for this.

When the highest goal of life is the possession and enjoyment of the earthly and transient, life loses so much of its meaning that the bearing of children who will spend their years in the same circle of laboring, acquiring, retaining, and enjoying as the parents is no longer considered the highest privilege. The life of pleasure engenders the pessimism that makes Nero say, "Oh, that Rome had only one neck, to be killed with one blow!" and makes Schopenhauer indulge in the thought of how desirable it would be to put an end to the survival of our race, if necessary by force or by abstinence. This tendency to consider living on in the children who constitute the emerging generation to be a disaster, modified or limited according to circumstances, is found among pagans, among all those who do not appreciate the ideal things. In China and India, and among the

Indians of North America, for example, the life of a woman has no value and only the birth of a male seed is greeted with joy.

Israel had a different and higher purpose of life, namely the honor of God and the future of His kingdom, and thus had reason to regard children, both male and female, as an inheritance of the Lord. Hannah desires not only a child, but a child for the glory of God.

The song of Hannah, 1 Sam. 2: 1–10, gives us a glimpse into her heart, into the activity of her inner life, and points out the source from which her desire springs. She does not desire a child only for herself, to serve as a shield off of which the poisonous arrows of "her adversary," ch. 1: 6, would bounce, or to be a plaything, but for the Lord, to whom it is devoted from childhood. The history of Samson is known to her. She knows what great deeds the Nazirite performed. It is not hidden from her where Israel's strength lies. She lives in expectation of the institution of kingship, and already in her vow she relinquishes that which will be born of her. While the priests do not enter into the service until they are twenty-five years old and participate in the sacrificial service until they are thirty, she pledges Samuel to Jehovah from the time when he will be able to dispense with maternal care. He will be a servant of the sanctuary and grow up under the eye of Eli, in the courts of her God.

So her prayer and her vow are related to what she desires and expects for Israel.

Let us consider both more closely. Her prayer was by faith. Why? Because she was assured that the answer would not fail her? We see nothing of this assurance when she stands in the court, "a woman oppressed in spirit" who has "poured out my soul before the LORD," ch. 1: 15. It is Eli who informs her that her prayer has been answered, v. 17. Rather, because she sought the right means to redeem Israel, in the right way, to the right purpose! Her faith rested not on a vow that she unbosomed for herself, which would entitle her to expect an answer, but on her confidence in Israel's future and in the power of Israel's God.

We do need to distinguish these two things. Our Christian people speak of a "given" and a "stolen" faith. Rightly so! One can, misled by the urgent desire to receive something that appears to us to be necessary or desirable, seize a promise that does not belong to us, that we do not understand properly or that we misapply, and hold God to it. To some extent, we cannot deny this act the name of "faith." Nor is it always put to shame. We human beings do not ourselves eagerly shame the faith placed in us, even if it is misplaced, even if it demands too much of us. Do we not get up in the dead of night to lend the three loaves that one was impertinent enough to ask of us? That confidence itself, mixed with however much wrong, honors us and gives us enjoyment.

A father once told how, playing with his children in the hallway of his house, he tested their faith by having them jump from several steps high into his arms. It amused him to notice that the younger ones dared to go much higher, i.e., so much further away from him than the older ones. But to his dismay, the next day, while he was busy in the cellar, he heard his littlest daughter call downstairs just when his hands were full and he was not thinking of it: "Daddy, here I come!" whereupon she came plunging through the dark basement hatch. Fortunately, he had time enough to grab her, for otherwise she might have ended up dead or crippled for life.

Here was confidence that was not betrayed by the father. The child acted in all simplicity; and now that the matter had this outcome, what she did was reported as an endearing proof of trust. But in an older child what this little girl did with impunity would surely have been severely punished. One must not only be capable of such great faith, but also *entitled* to it. Faith must have a command or promise to which it appeals.

Though Hannah hoped, or knew, that the time to be gracious to Israel had come, she could not know what was in the Lord's counsel. Her faith revealed itself in her *submission*. It is necessary to point this out because very often, even from the pulpit and in religious works that deal with answers to prayer and healing by faith, a false conception of faith is given that can be highly pernicious in its consequences and which has led many into Satan's sifter.

Even where, like Daniel, one thinks one has a certain indication of the Lord's will, one is not yet entitled *arbitrarily* to dispose over what should be God's to grant. Daniel "understood from the sacred books, according to the word of the LORD to Jeremiah the prophet, that the desolation of Jerusalem would last seventy years" (9: 2). But there is nothing in the entire prayer, recorded verbatim in this chapter, that resembles encroachment on the rights of the Lord. Daniel makes *confession* and begs God, for His sake, to lift up His countenance over His sanctuary which had been destroyed, Dan. 9: 17.

For all that, one would not dare to say that Daniel did not exercise faith.

And yet, should we ask if Hannah would have prayed like this if God had not wanted to hear her, we would have to deny it. God promises in Ezek. 36: 36, 37 not only that He will cultivate the disturbed places, but *also* that He will be *requested* by the house of Israel to do so for its sake. He gives both the promise and the prayer that pleads upon this, or through which one flees to Him, and therein a sign of His good pleasure.

It is no coincidence that the congregation in Jerusalem meets in the house of Mary to lift up a continual prayer to God for the brother who is sighing in prison and will be arraigned the next day. It does not know what surprise has been prepared for it that very night. When the answer to its prayer comes, it appears from everything that this was not expected. But with hindsight they will have remembered that a hidden urge was felt in them, something that did not leave them alone but drove them to prayer and kept them from delaying, notwithstanding the seemingly utter hopelessness of the situation.

Here we have the solution to an objection that unbelievers often raise to prayer. Our interests, it is said, are often in conflict with those of others. This same conflict also comes forth in our prayers. One prays for rain, another for a dry spell. One for a blessing on the arms of one kingdom, another for a blessing for those who are considered enemies by the believers in that kingdom.

Neither prayer nor faith are in our power. And the child of the Lord often feels it with sorrow that he has been denied free access to God with his desires. Sometimes God says, as He did to Moses, "Speak no more to Me about this matter!" Sometimes, as in the case of Jeremiah, "Pray no more for this people!" Sometimes the sky is as it were made of copper and the earth of iron, that no prayer can pass through it. Sometimes, too, one feels the need to leave the outcome of prayer to the Lord. After all, we are admonished to make our desires *known to God* in everything, by prayer and supplication, with thanksgiving, Phil. 4: 6.

No prayer is without meaning. Not one prayer goes unanswered. God deals with His children as our fathers dealt with us. If we did not receive what we desired in the manner and at the time we desired it, we received something else or something better, and even the refusal benefited us. How much more is this true with respect to the Lord! To pray is to have fellowship with God, and this is *salvation*.

In times of pressure and distress, for example, it is not in vain to complain to the Lord of our needs. If the pressure is not relieved, the burden not lifted, God grants strength to bear it, and this amounts to the same thing. Asaph's circumstances remain the same whether his "heart was grieved" with wrath, he was "pierced within" with envy because of the prosperity of the wicked, or whether he exclaims, "My flesh and my heart may fail, but God is the strength of my heart and my portion forever!" (Ps. 73: 21, 26). Yet everything has changed. The song that begins with a bitter complaint turns into praise.

Who will say that prayer is not answered if God gives no change in the external condition but only in the inner state of mind? Faith, in short, reveals itself in very different ways and is crowned in different ways. It does not consist in a logical conclusion of the mind but in fleeing to, holding onto, relying on God, without condition and without reservation.

Yet when God makes us prayerful, when He grants us the activity of faith, it often pleases Him to give us the grace of perseverance. Jesus is silent, but the Canaanite woman calls after Him. The angel commands, "Let me go, for the sun has risen!" and Jacob replies, "I will not let you go unless you bless me!"

Already the *prayer* of Hannah is the beginning of an answer. In that and in every true prayer, what is written in Isa. 65: 24 is fulfilled: "Even before they call, I will answer, and while they are still speaking, I will hear."

Of course, we do not know what went on in the mind of the wizened Eli when Hannah poured out her heart to him, but this is certain, God spoke at that moment through the mouth of him who was the head of His visible church on earth: "may the God of Israel grant the petition you have asked of Him." That word was faithfully accepted by both Elkanah and Hannah.

That the "barren becomes a joyful mother of children" is God's work, of which He alone deserves the credit. But in Heb. 11: 11, Scripture points to faith as the *power* by which this miracle is brought about. "By faith," we read there, "Sarah, even though she was barren and beyond the proper age, was enabled to conceive a child, because she considered Him faithful who had promised." From this point of view, the notice that before leaving for Ramah not only Hannah but also Elkanah "worshipped before the Lord," is very remarkable.

"And Elkanah," we read further, "had relations with his wife Hannah, and the LORD remembered her," 1 Sam. 1: 19. "Her face was no longer downcast," v. 18, i.e., she believed the word of Eli. May we not assume that this faith was also wrought in her husband? Of Isaac we are told that he prayed to God for a son "on behalf of his wife," Gen. 25: 21. We also know of Sarah that, though unbidden, she witnessed the negotiation between the Angel of the Lord and Abraham in the oak groves of Mamre, Gen. 18: 9ff. Further, it was not enough that the angel had appeared to Manoah's wife. He came again to repeat in the presence of Manoah what he had told the woman; certainly not solely for the purpose of satisfying an undue curiosity, but because it was necessary for the achievement of the goal.

Samuel was a child of "many prayers," a child of faith. His name was a "miraculous sign" in Israel, just as were the children of Isaiah with their meaningful names, Isa. 8: 18. Everyone who heard and called out this name was thereby reminded how "God hears."

Israel's last judge is on a par with Samson in this, that, like him, he was not only called, and not only formed, but even *conceived and given* by God. In distinction to Samson, he was not born of a mother who was put under a Nazirite vow, that is, received a purely external or legal ordination, but of a mother who herself showed that she possessed the life of faith and sanctified him from childhood, yes, before his birth. In this respect, he is on a par with John the Baptist, Timothy and so many others in whom the seed of regeneration was laid before the natural birth, who therefore did not need conversion, that is, never knew a time when they served sin, or rather never walked the broad path of sin, so that they never experienced that great, visible, conscious reversal which is usually denoted by the word "conversion."

We preach that the greatest of sinners can be saved. It is the glory of God's grace that even those who are lost in the eyes of the world can be rescued. In a finely worded essay published in *De Gids*, A. Pierson, in response to the activity of the well-known evangelists Moody and Sankey in London, gave "orthodoxy" praise for doing much more for the salvation, the uplifting of the most profoundly sunken of our generation, than modernism did. "We moderns," he wrote more or less, "do not understand the art of reattaching severed flowers to their stems. Regardless of how far we have progressed in hygiene – the science of health," he continued, "we know very little of therapy – the science of medicine."

Thank God that in our gospel preaching we need not make a distinction between those who can still be saved and those who cannot. Whitefield once preached under the gallows at Tyburn that mercy could be shown to the greatest of sinners, and the fruit of that preaching was seen also in the hardened criminal whose life, as he confessed, had been forfeited tenfold, but who, at the very moment when he was undergoing the sentence of earthly justice, could testify that he had been acquitted in the righteous judgment of his God, that God would not be angry with him or curse him.

But this glorious, soul-comforting truth, inseparable from the gospel, need not prevent us from placing all emphasis on what is also a truth, that the reformation of a life spent largely in the service of sin can never be so complete as to erase the traces of the sorrowful past; it must not lead us to the homage of the erroneous conception that a soul brought back to God only in later life can be as much to the glory of God as if it had been devoted to God from childhood.

The murderer on the cross entered Paradise. Manasseh in prison became another man. But neither the one nor the other gave their Savior the service and honor due Him during their lifetime. Wounds can be healed but scars will never be effaced. Pieces of firewood can be snatched from the fire, but they could have become ornamental columns in the temple of God if their lives had not been charred in the fire of passion. Wrong habits, evil dispositions remain with man until the last days of his life, even if by God's grace he is delivered from their dominion. There are few believers whose character is evenly developed, who are paragons of what grace is able to do.

In the growth, that is, in the revelation, of spiritual life as well as in the life of nature, as in the plant kingdom, two factors come into play, namely, the seed from which the plant sprouts and what we might call the condition for flowering. This is because it requires not only seed but also soil in which that seed germinates. Great care must be taken of that soil. The plant presents itself differently in the far north or on a barren sandy soil than in a lush natural area.

So it is also with the seed of new life. If the soil of the moral life in which it is deposited has been ruined by a life in sin, then its consequences will always be visible, not to mention the impression others receive as a result, and the influence it has on others.

When God wished to bring about a general, decisive change in the life of Israel, He began this work in a prophet who had been sanctified in and by his mother before he was born, and who from childhood had lived under the eye and in the fear of the Lord. The significance of this fact is explained by Hannah in her song.

We would certainly judge the pious ones of the Old Covenant differently and wrongly if we did not have their psalms and hymns. What a rich treasure of spiritual experience is found in those songs! How deeply did Hannah, for example, look into history, that is, into the meaning of Israel and into the order of salvation! She expected a new order of things. Earthly kingship was before her. Jehovah, Israel's King, will be represented by a man anointed by the Holy Spirit, and assisted by the prophet who makes the Word of God heard. Moses, at God's command, had set a man over the assembly who took the place of the mediator. But Joshua was not replaced. As a result of Israel's abnormal condition, there was not even a question of transferring his office to others. But this will change. Hannah beholds the dawn of the new day, and in that light, certainly part of the way that leads to the incarnation of the Word.

The true poet is a prophet, a seer. He sees deeper and differently than ordinary people. He shows the spiritual, the ideal side of things, the meaning of the mundane. This is already true of natural life. Cowper's masterpiece is the poem entitled "The Table" because its subject is this piece of household furniture. One of Burns' most beautiful poems describes and sings of a cottager's Saturday night. We feel rightly the glory of the ordinary, the mundane, only when the artist who molds the forms of language, who knows how to paint it with words, shows it to us as it appears under his treatment.

But the Psalmist, who sings the praises of the Lord, who has an eye for the works of God's hand, the acts of His redeeming love, is more than an artist. He brings nothing of himself to the substance of his representations. He is like one who holds up the dull rock crystal in the light, where its full beauty comes out in a multitude of colors.

And what Hannah sang was realized in Samuel's life. As a child he is brought to the temple of the Lord. His mother asks nothing for herself, but only that she may show her motherly care for the little one in the annual gift of the garment which she has crafted, and that her mother's heart may delight in the lad whom she has surrendered to the sanctuary and who with her annual visit she sees grow up and increase "in wisdom and stature, and in favor with God and man" (Luke 2: 52).

IT WAS DEEP in the night. An unbroken silence reigned in the room adjacent to the holy place where the boy had laid himself to rest. The seven-branched candlestick was still burning, but not brightly. It was already near morning. The lights flickered as if they had to depart; they were about to go out when the mysterious, wonderful voice was heard that came to awaken the boy from his rest. Those lights were the symbol of the religious life in Israel; it was dying away, like the glow that illuminated the holy things.

If the light of the Holy Spirit is quenched, the night is much more impenetrable within the place of revelation than out there in the open air of the court, where even in the midst of the greatest darkness there is still light enough to discern objects close by.

"Now in those days the word of the LORD was rare and visions were scarce" (1 Sam. 3: 1). If God had not taken care of His people, they would have become like Sodom and Gomorrah (cf. Isaiah 1: 9). "Samuel! Samuel!" was the cry. It was repeated three times, and three times it awakened the lad, who had heard the voice of the Lord but had not yet recognized it.

Not from him, not from Eli came this sound. It was not a product of his imagination; God had spoken! God also does speak, as 1 Sam. 16: 7 shows, in the hidden parts of the mind, but here in the sanctuary He did so with an audible voice, for Samuel did not yet know the Lord, ch. 3: 7.

God speaks, that is, emerges from the hiddenness of His Being to make Himself known to man, to come into contact with him. He speaks not only to those who, like Samuel, are called to a particular office, but to everyone who enters into fellowship with Him.

It was in the night when we first heard that voice, while we were immersed in deep sleep, when we neither knew the Lord nor ourselves. After all, the life we led was a kind of dream life, a life of passing impressions, from which God's Word roused us, made us reflect and come to ourselves. We knew that this voice was calling us, for we were called by name; we did not yet know that God was calling us; and sleepily we slumbered on and on, until the dream was disturbed a second and third time. No, it was not the work of imagination, but the work of God!

Rarely is that calling repeated so soon as here with Samuel. Sometimes there are years between the time when the voice of the call is first heard and the time when we answer with full awareness, "Speak, Lord, your servant hears!" Nevertheless, Samuel's calling, the direct working of the Lord, was preceded by a *preparatory activity*. He had been brought up at the feet of Eli, had learned to understand the law, and had certainly heard many of God's earlier sayings. This preparation must not be disregarded. While not sufficient, it was far from unnecessary, nor was it without influence. We see this in the childlike simplicity and obedience which he displays.

Without hesitation he rises from the fast sleep of youth to ask the second and third time as cheerfully as the first, if he can be of help to Eli. Had he less deference and a less childlike disposition, he would not have so willingly done the unpleasant work of leaving his bed. The obedience that made Samuel willing to listen to Eli also enabled him to hear the voice of the Lord. Without it, he might have laid himself down in a deeper sleep or thought he was hearing a weak and aged man who himself did not know or mean what he was saying.

Moses was entrusted to the care of Jochebed and learned about the God of the fathers by her side, before he received the further revelation of the Lord at the burning bush. Ruth, out of love for Naomi, followed her mother-in-law to Bethlehem, not only to be incorporated into Israel but also to become the mother of Israel's kings and of the Christ of God.

With the calling and preparation, however, also came the *indirect working of grace*. Samuel might have laid himself down so as not to get up again when the event was repeated, if God had not provided a means by which he could be instructed in the meaning of the voice. "Eli realized that it was the LORD who was calling the boy," ch. 3: 8.

This is God's ordinary way of doing things. Even though Paul is gripped in his heart on the road to Damascus, it is a humble disciple of the Lord, an Ananias, who must come to teach him. Even though an angel appeared to Cornelius, he was pointed – which was, in fact, the purpose of this revelation – to Peter, who would give him the necessary instruction. The Ethiopian courtier possessed the Word of God but needed the interpreter.

God honors the offices He has instituted. Happy is everyone who obtains an experienced guide on the way of life, who, like Eli through his own experience, understands the voice of the Lord and knows how to interpret its meaning. The speech of God to the soul is then followed by a speaking of the soul to God. It is not enough for Paul to be cast into the dust on the road to Damascus; he must also be brought to his knees in the inner chamber.

God spoke to Samuel, but His further revelation comes in answer to his childlike prayer. Speak, Lord, in that voice which brought light out of darkness, which caused Adam to come out from behind the thicket, which sustained Saul at the head of his band of horsemen. Speak to me, personally, by name, now, what it is You wish and how it is You wish. Your servant hears! He was sunk in deep sleep but now he is awakened; he did not know You, but now he has started to come to know You, only that You might teach him to understand Your will and lead him to the work that You have given him to do.

For Samuel that work was to stand between God and Israel, to be the bearer of the word, of the revelation of the Lord to his people. "And the LORD continued to appear at Shiloh, because there He revealed Himself to Samuel by His word," 1 Sam. 3: 21. God returned in compassion to His people. He does not dwell in His palace in the way He would have in normal circumstances; but He descends in the word, the word of prophecy. It is the beginning of a new line of revelation.

Later, when all these lines come together in the center from which they actually emanate, the Mediator of God and man, we will also recognize that they come together. He who makes the apostles rejoice: "We have seen His *glory!*" is also the *Word* through which God speaks and in which He comes to us, is also the *King of Israel,* Prophet, Priest and King together. With Samuel we are one step closer to this glorious, perfect revelation.

The old must pass away, the new draws near. But what will later be said of the Jerusalem below – "For the law will go forth from Zion, and the word of the LORD from Jerusalem!" (Isaiah 2: 3) – is now true of Shiloh.

At Shiloh, the revelation of the Lord is received "by His word."

12. THE ARK IN THE LAND OF THE PHILISTINES

1 Samuel 5 and 6

The Lord is at the forefront
Of those who help me.

Ps. 118: 4a (Psalter of 1773)

In Sinai's desert, a fire burns. It keeps burning. A bush stands in flames and is not consumed. Let us go and behold this grand sight!

"God is within her; she will not be moved" (Ps. 46: 5).

It was He who, in the wondrous glow which attracted Moses' attention, made His presence visible, and in this "sight" gave the solution to the riddle of the ages.

"Had not the LORD been with us, when people rose against us, then they would have swallowed us alive, for their fury blazed against us" (Ps. 124: 2–3, New American Bible Revised Edition).

Israel is the people of God. For centuries its enemies have sought its destruction. But neither this enmity, nor its own weakness and unworthiness, have been able to erase its name "from the scroll on which God writes the nations." The water does not destroy it and the fire does not consume it. It is Moses, raised out of that water, and Daniel, preserved in that fire.

The history of the Age of the Judges clearly demonstrates this, as does its history before and after. But nowhere is this more evident than toward the end of the first period, that is, during the *domination of the Philistines.*

Under its previous oppressors, as before in Egypt and later in Babylon, Israel maintained an independent nationhood. Even tyranny had the effect of alienating it from its oppressors. But under the Philistines it was in great danger of merging completely with those who dominated it. If, as is highly probable, the purpose was to bring this about, then this purpose was fully accomplished when the Ark of the Covenant was placed in the temple of Dagon at Ashdod. According to the superstition of those times, this meant nothing more or less than the subjection of Israel's God.

They had trembled for the ark and exclaimed, "Woe to us! Who will deliver us from the hand of these mighty gods?" (1 Sam. 4: 8). But now, drunk as they were in consequence of the unexpected victory, they did not refrain from taunting Jehovah in the sign of His presence, committing sacrilege even by their own standpoint, committing the same sin that God had so severely punished in Pharaoh, depriving Israel of its God and thereby its religion and its existence.

A people without God was effectively no longer a people! When we consider what here happened in the light of this thought, it will become clear to us that we have reached the extreme limit of Israel's humiliation and the high point of God's revelation. The ark in the house of Dagon! Viewed superficially, this fact indicates the deepest humiliation Jehovah could undergo. God in the temple of idols! It is almost unthinkable. In reality, however, it is man who is here humbled most deeply, and God who is glorified most highly.

Until now, Jehovah always used men to bring about the redemption of His people. Now what we read in Isa. 63: 5 is coming true: "I looked, but there was no one to help; I was appalled that no one assisted. So My arm brought Me salvation, and My own wrath upheld Me." Israel was redeemed, that is, its national existence was maintained, when the ark, after being in exile for seven months, was returned. It does not become accustomed to captivity, but its continued existence is guaranteed.

This is the first and, in connection with the whole thrust of the history of this era, the primary point of view from which we have to consider this fact. Inseparable from this, however, is the revelation of God's power in the pagan world. *Jehovah is glorified to the gods of the nations.*

It is too often overlooked in the study of Israel's history that this nation was given "for a light to the nations." Had it fulfilled the purpose of its election, it would have fulfilled its destiny in this regard already in the days of the Old Covenant. Abraham was blessed "that he might become a blessing." In everything he does, he has the honor of God's name in mind. Israel's deliverance from Egypt was a triumph of true religion over paganism. "I will execute judgment," God spoke to Moses, "against all the gods of Egypt. I am the LORD" (Ex. 12: 12).

Prophetic preaching comes with the exaltation of the "Anointed of the Lord" before the kings of the earth. "Therefore be wise, O kings; be admonished, O judges of the earth. Serve the LORD with fear!" (Ps. 2: 10). Israel's later prophets had a message to the nations, as can be seen not only from Jonah's mission to Nineveh but also in their surviving writings. All the Lord's acts to Israel have the purpose of making his name known among the pagans.

When God seems to disown His people, Moses pleads the shame this would bring on Israel's God. "What would that do to Your holy name?" is his question. "The nations will say, You have not been able to bring Your people into the land of promise!" he assures Him. Even under the idolatrous Ahab, Israel is saved because the Syrians said, "Their gods are gods of mountains and not of valleys." The Philistines know very well what Jehovah did to the Egyptians.

The fact is, Israel not only does not fulfill its destiny, but by its sin brings a curse, not only on itself, but also on other nations. Therefore God goes to work in a different way and Himself acts in the pagan world. The sin of His people will become subservient to this purpose. The Egyptians will know "that God is the Lord."

At the same time, this is a judgment brought upon them. They fell into the snare that their own superstition laid for them. They were like Pharaoh when he heard that Israel had not gone into the wilderness between Pitom and Ramses but had wandered south to Baal-Zephon and Pi-hahiroth. The fact that the temple there established was dedicated to the god who sent back the runaway slaves suddenly made him forget everything he had learned and suffered in the battle against Jehovah. The idolater was able to give only one explanation of Moses' strange movements, and to act accordingly. He thought Israel's God was unable to keep them on the right path. They were aimless and lost! Fool that he was. Israel's God would now be sanctified before him. He has only himself to blame for his and his army's downfall.

The Philistines, among whom the memory of these events has not yet been lost after so many centuries, are also prone to forgetting when the honor of their gods is involved. They too know only one explanation of what happened, namely, that Israel's defeat betrays the weakness of Jehovah. But this superstition will also cost them dearly.

The ways of God are often obscure, but they lead to the most glorious goal. God saves His honor and maintains His glory. This was evident when, the day after the ark was brought into the sanctuary at Ashdod, the priests of Dagon found their god stretched out on the floor, face down, before what they regarded to be Israel's God, that is, as the visible sign of His presence.

Remarkable! God very severely punished superstitious reliance on the ark, outside the covenant and its conditions. And now from that same object, which in itself is nothing but wood overlaid with gold, emanates a mysterious power reminiscent of magic!

Most certainly. And the men of Beth-shemesh are killed because they took the cover from the ark, though the Philistines may have done the same with impunity, 1 Sam. 6: 19. God speaks in words borrowed from human language. To each in his own language. He speaks to be understood. Even to the pagans. What takes place in the temple of Dagon cannot be said in any other way. Dagon lies on the ground before Jehovah like a conquered man before his conqueror, like a slave before his lord. That they could understand! But since they did not want to understand, they brought new misery upon themselves and theirs. It only made the judgment heavier.

What explanation did they give for what happened? They thought of every cause except the true one. Man is resourceful when it comes to upholding himself before the Lord. At any rate, "they took Dagon and returned him to his place," 1 Sam. 5: 3, so that God had to speak differently, more clearly than before. A day later Dagon lay again at the threshold, head broken off, both his hands cut off. This was the greatest affront that could be done to the idol, the memory of which is perpetuated in the custom of his priests. Only the form of the animal remains. For Dagon is the god who displayed the head of a man on the body of a fish, as also seen in the depiction of the deity which Layard found at Khorsabad, on the memorials of the campaigns to Syria.

Is this still not enough? God smites the Ashdodites with "an outbreak of tumors," 1 Sam. 5: 9, cf. Deut. 28: 27; hemorrhoids which, according to some, were considered a punishment for the sacrilege; and their land, as later shown by the guilt offering, with mice which damage the field crops, 1 Sam. 6: 5.

Are they now unwilling to bow down before Jehovah? Gath, where the last descendants of Enak's children live, is given the not very desirable honor of rendering Jehovah powerless. They carry the ark around the fortress as was once done at Jericho. It only served to make them suffer the fate of the people of Ashdod.

Will they now continue to harden their hearts? Ekron, the holy city of Baal-Zebub, likewise suffers the same judgment, which is not only severe but also deeply humiliating, because the second main deity of the league of the Philistines is exhibited in its nullity, 1 Sam. 5: 11. Those who did not die were smitten with tumors.

It was hard for this people to kick against the pricks. If God withholds the grace of repentance, then the creature continues to sin, hardens its heart against the Lord and increases its torment. This is evident in the history of Pharaoh and all the enemies of God. In their blindness they walk headlong into their destruction.

We find a striking example of this in the negotiations between Balaam and the king of the Moabites. The seer blesses Israel even though he had resolved to curse it. That should have been enough to convince Balak that his aim would not be achieved. Not so, for there was a chance that in some other place from which Israel's army could not be surveyed in its entirety, where the prophet was therefore in no danger of being awestruck by the order in which the tribes lay around the sanctuary, the incantation would succeed. "You will only see the outskirts of their camp—not all of them," speaks the king, Num. 23: 13, and thereby accomplishes what he had wished to prevent, that Israel should again receive another and higher blessing, vv. 18ff. Yes, more telling, the same thing is repeated a third time. vv. 27ff.

God must also be glorified by His enemies, and His hand presses heavily upon them until they are willing to acknowledge that He has been righteous. Yet the message concerning the capture of the ark after the defeat at Ebenezer has a much broader scope. The meaning of this fact is only rightly understood if we confine ourselves not to the Israel or the pagan world of those days, but also turn our eye to the revelation as a whole and, in connection with it, to the basic forms of God's redemptive activity. It presents us with one of the greatest riddles of God's government, but a riddle that hides a glorious revelation of His being and way of going about things.

If anyone were called upon to answer in the abstract the question, "Can it be thought conceivable that God, faithful as He remains to Himself and jealous as He is of His glory, would deliver up the place where His glory is enthroned, the sign of His covenant, the surety of His grace, into the hands of unbelievers?" he would undoubtedly say that this is impossible. Our common sense would just as surely agree with him and come up with all manner of sound arguments to support this judgment.

Experience, however, shows the polar opposite. Jerusalem will be destroyed, the temple will go up in flames even though false prophets by the dozen argue and prove that this could not possibly happen. The Savior will suffer and die, be delivered into the hands of the unrighteous, by the elders of the people, even though Peter cries out with emotion, "Lord, that shall never happen to you," though the people read in the law, "the Christ will remain forever" (John 12: 34).

Injustice triumphs; innocence is condemned; the grace-benefits and sacred ordinances of the church fall into the hands of her enemies; those who stand up for the truth remain the losing party, though they invoke God's judgment which proceeds according to the purest law. But in the end, the wisdom of God is vindicated by her children.

They sooner or later confirm the word of Holy Scripture, "The words of the LORD are flawless, like silver refined in a furnace, like gold purified sevenfold" (Ps. 12: 7).

God speaks the *last* word of history. For "the fool [who] mocks You all day long" (Ps. 74: 22), He repays tenfold. The world disposes over the appearance of a moment; the Lord God disposes over the future. "Even the wrath of man shall praise You; with the survivors of wrath You will clothe Yourself" (Ps. 76: 10). The defeats of God pave the way to His victories.

Among the folk tales of the Middle Ages, there are several that refer to the "dumb devil." Satan – this is the thrust of all these stories – finds himself deceived in the agreements he makes against God and souls. While they are maintained to the letter, the goal is missed. He builds a proud castle on an inaccessible height on the condition that the soul of the first one to enjoy the beautiful view from the windows of the building, will belong to him ... and is outsmarted by the cunning lord of the castle who causes a donkey, covered with a monk's hood, to appear before the opened window. He exchanges the right he acquired after the fall to the souls of all the children of Adam for the surrender of the one and only, the Son of God, who is treated, judged and rejected as a sinner ... but apparently did not count on a life that could not undergo death and be held down by death. All such stories, in terms of their tenor, simplicity, and sensorial, often very unscriptural representations of those times, are at any rate an expression of the truth that the wisdom of the world is folly with God and that "the foolishness of God is wiser than men."

The evil one pursues his goal. The moment of his victory is also that of his humiliation. "And having disarmed the powers and authorities, He made a public spectacle of them, triumphing over them by the cross" (Col. 2: 15). The Lord, reverently speaking, cannot often exhibit evil in its weakness, cannot expose the false pretense, cannot let full judgment come, cannot glorify Himself in the redemption He wrought, unless He seems to relinquish for a time the ark of truth, of right, of His holy cause, and allows His enemies to raise their songs of triumph.

Peter is then taken to the dungeon; the Philistines then rejoice when Samson appears in the temple of Dagon; St. Bartholomew's Day then occurs; the unbelief that undermines the authority of Scripture and snatches Christ's crown from His head then seems to have the last word. But such victories are dearly bought and paid for by the enemy. The ark makes its appearance at Ashdod, at Gath and at Ekron, to show in enemy territory that Jehovah is "God above all gods," that "His Kingdom rules over all."

Yet when we consider what was already expressed before, that Israel's sin necessitates this revelation of God's power and justice in the realm of the pagan world, we find here an intimation of the times of the New Testament in which the judgment over God's chosen people coincides with the mission to the heathen.

The word of God is brought to the pagan world in the way in which Paul went to Rome, in which he was brought into the dungeon at Philippi, a prisoner. Not to judge, but to save. The Old Testament dispensation is not yet over. At present the captivity of the ark is not yet made subservient to the welfare of Israel as a people. Soon it will be called, "I will make you jealous by those who are not a nation" (Rom. 10: 19). "Their voice has gone out into all the earth, their words to the ends of the world," v. 18. But then the reality will also have come that was foreshadowed in the ark: Jesus Christ, the Word of God, in whom God dwells and on whom His glory rests. Even more, the Christ according to the flesh is then rejected by "His own," John 1: 11; rejected by "the lost sheep of the house of Israel" to whom he was sent, Matth. 15: 24; the covenant with all the people broken, Zech. 11: 10; the sign of God's grace delivered into the hands of the heathen, Luke 18: 32, and the word fulfilled, spoken to the Greeks in the courts of Jerusalem's temple when they "desired to see Jesus," namely, "I, when I am lifted up from the earth, will draw everyone to Myself," John 12: 32.

That same word which now becomes a judgment in the land of the Philistines, though it causes the idol to fall, then becomes a blessing. Indeed, now Dagon is again set up, now the broken image is again restored; but paganism then lies felled to the earth never to rise again, then the homage one pays to the living God does not consist in making Him depart from the country gates, in merely seeking to avert His judgments but without coveting Him as God; no, then God is revealed to those who did not ask after Him, Rom. 10: 20. The oak at Geismar bends its proud crown in the dust, the books of magic are burned in the marketplace at Ephesus in front of the crowd, the temple of Serapis, with which, according to popular belief, the world will collapse, is reduced to rubble and in its place is put, not the visible and in itself lifeless sign, but the *living Word of the living God.*

Presently the ark will be returned to Israel. It is to be kept until the days of kingship. No, it is no longer brought up to Shiloh. Since the days of Joshua it had been as though interred in its grave. After the fall of Jericho, no forces connected with that ark issued forth *before it was brought into the pagan world.* But now, with God's judgment being accomplished at the sanctuary, it has become apparent to all eyes that this condition was not normal, had to come to an end, and would be replaced by something else.

God will dwell again among Israel with the ark of His glory and His strength; not after twenty years, when the people have been brought to repentance; not even when they receive a king in the Lord's wrath; but when David, God's servant, His Son, is joined to Him and the kingdom with holy anointing, and thereby the revelation enters into another and higher stage.

And even this stage is not the last and highest. What happened at Shiloh, what was seen at Ebenezer, is only a foreshadowing of what will happen when the temple goes up in flames and the judgment of God also passes over the ark of the covenant.

In the second temple, as in the tent at Shiloh, the holy of holies is empty. The ark goes missing. But then as well, the word of Jeremiah is fulfilled: "they will no longer discuss the ark of the covenant of the LORD. It will never come to mind, and no one will remember it or miss it, nor will another one be made," Jer. 3: 16.

INDEX OF SCRIPTURE REFERENCES

GENERAL INDEX

www.ingramcontent.com/pod-product-compliance
Ingram Content Group UK Ltd.
Pitfield, Milton Keynes, MK11 3LW, UK
UKHW021905190726
13853UKWH00002B/527